Advanced Exercises in Microeconomics

Advanced Exercises in Microeconomics

Paul Champsaur and Jean-Claude Milleron

Translated by John P. Bonin and Hélène Bonin

Harvard University Press

Cambridge, Massachusetts, and London, England   1983

Publication of this book has been aided by a grant from the
Republic of France.

This book is a translation of *Exercices de Microéconomie,*
© Dunod 1971, and is published by arrangement with
Editions Bordas.

Library of Congress Cataloging in Publication Data

Champsaur, Paul.
  Advanced exercises in microeconomics.

  Translation of: Exercices de microéconomie,
niveau avancé.
    Bibliography: p.
    Includes index.
    1. Microeconomics—Problems, exercises, etc.
I. Milleron, Jean-Claude. II. Title.
HB172.c4713 1983   338.5'076   82-9214
ISBN 0-674-00525-2   AACR2

12

9

Preface

The exercises in this book, by taking the modern general equilibrium approach to economics, cover a broad range of topics appropriate for graduate and advanced undergraduate courses in both mathematical economics and economic theory. A background in linear algebra and multivariate calculus is sufficient for the reader to work through all but a small number of the exercises. This volume may be used as a companion to a modern text in mathematical economics, or as the primary text in a course combining references from classic sources, modern texts, and journal articles. To aid in its use as a primary text, suggested references are provided at the end of each exercise.

The first two parts of the eight in this book develop the foundations of modern equilibrium theory. The exercises in consumer theory look at an example of a boundary solution to consumer choice, aggregation problems (both over goods as indexes and over agents to characterize social welfare), and the relationship between utility maximization and demand functions. In production theory, the basic notion of efficiency is developed in an activity analysis model; the envelope property of enterprise cost curves is highlighted; and a full treatment of price decentralization properties and the construction of aggregate production sets from enterprise technologies is given.

The remaining six parts consider issues of equilibrium and optimality in competitive and noncompetitive environments. Part Three contains an example of a private-property production economy exhibiting multiple equilibria, followed by a general treatment of the existence and stability of competitive equilibrium in an exchange economy. Part Four contains an interesting proof of the substitution theorem using dual prices, an example both developing marginal cost pricing for a public enterprise and highlighting the importance of convexity in the competitive equilibrium, and a derivation of the surplus criterion for evaluating Pareto improvements based on the equilibrium prices of an optimal benchmark. The next part develops the notion of the core, with a discussion of the limit theorem in an exchange economy for a nonconvex example, and treats imperfect competition in product markets using modern game theory analysis. Part Six contains an exercise characterizing an economy with a public good, discussing both the free rider problem and the Lindahl solution, and also an exercise considering policy solutions for production externalities. Temporal aspects are introduced in the next part, first by treating imperfect capital markets both from the consumer's perspective in a problem involving the storage of commodities and from the producer's perspective by linking investment projects to financial considerations, and second by analyzing golden rule growth in an activity analysis framework. The final section considers risk aversion and uncertainty by developing the notion of a contingent commodity in an exchange situation and the notion of contingent prices in a resource allocation problem under production uncertainty.

The exercises are cumulative in nature; techniques and results developed early in the book are applied in later exercises. To grasp the basic content of the book, the reader should work sequentially through exercises 1, 2, 5, 6, 7, 9, 10, 12, 13, 15, 17, 18, 19, 20, 22, and 23. Only slightly more complicated are exercises 3, 8, 14, and 21; a reader with the minimum mathematical prerequisites may wish to skim these. The mathematics in the above exercises involves computational techniques using Lagrangian multipliers and Kuhn-Tucker conditions and a conceptual framework based on convex geometry, set theory, and linear analysis. Finally, exercises 4, 11, and 16 are more advanced and require some familiarity with topology, real analysis and differential equations. Although the reader with the appropriate mathematical background will find these exercises insightful, other readers may safely ignore them, with little loss in comprehension.

WE ACKNOWLEDGE the invaluable assistance of Christopher Maxwell in revising and updating the reference sections, and we thank him for his helpful comments on the exercises.

J.P.B.

Contents

PART ONE

Consumer Behavior and Demand Functions

The Construction
of Demand Functions

A consumer must divide his income r $(r > 0)$ among three goods only, indexed by $i = 1, 2, 3$. Here the set of feasible consumption bundles X is the set of all x with nonnegative coordinates $(x_i \geq 0, i = 1, 2, 3)$. The consumer's preferences can be represented by a utility function,

$$V = (x_1 + \bar{x}_1)x_2^m x_3^n,$$

where $\bar{x}_1$, m, and n are positive constants. Given prices p_1, p_2, p_3 (assumed to be strictly positive), determine the consumer's demand function for each of the goods.

PROPOSED SOLUTION

Before making any calculations, we shall find it useful to consider a geometric representation to help understand this problem. By the definition of the consumption set the utility function V is nonnegative on this set X. The lowest indifference surface $(V = 0)$ is made up of the union of the two quadrant planes $\{x_1 0 x_2\}$ and $\{x_1 0 x_3\}$ (see Fig. 1.1). If we are interested in an indifference surface corresponding to a strictly positive level of utility $V = V^*$, we notice that this surface cuts the face $\{x_2 0 x_3\}$ of the positive orthant following a curve $\mathscr{C}$ expressed by the following equation:

$$\bar{x}_1 x_2^m x_3^n = V^*.$$

On the other hand, the surface $V = V^*$ does not intersect the faces $\{x_1 0 x_2\}$ and $\{x_1 0 x_3\}$ of the positive orthant. A representative point M^* of the chosen set for a system of prices p may very likely be found, as it is in the present case, on the boundary of the consumption set. In Fig. 1.1 the

3

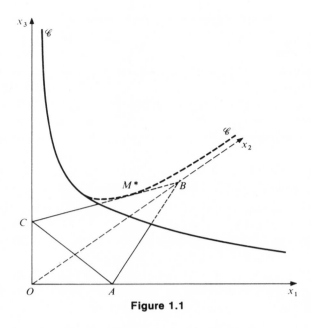

Figure 1.1

intersection of the consumption set and the budget set $X \cap \{x|px \leqslant r\}$ is represented by the tetrahedron $OABC$. Here the optimal point M^* belongs to the face $\{x_2 0 x_3\}$ of the orthant and corresponds to a tangency between the curve $\mathscr{C}$ and the segment CB. However, in a case like this there is no tangency between the budget constraint *plane* and the indifference surface passing through M^*. Nonetheless, it is obvious that if we modify the budget plane by moving point A away from the origin (which is equivalent to lowering the price of good 1), we reach a critical value where a tangency between the surface passing through M^* and the budget plane is assured. Beyond this critical value M^* leaves the plane $\{x_2 0 x_3\}$, so that x_1 becomes positive, which brings us to the classical case where the point M^* is interior to the consumption set. We then have a tangency between the indifference surface and the budget plane. This tangency is characterized by the Lagrangian conditions that express the proportionality between the price vector and the gradient of V in M^*. The following analytical calculations will make these geometric notions more explicit.

The problem that we have to solve is written:

$$\max V = (x_1 + \bar{x}_1)x_2^m x_3^n,$$

subject to the constraints

$$r - p_1 x_1 - p_2 x_2 - p_3 x_3 \geq 0 \quad \text{and} \quad x \geq 0. \tag{1}$$

If we follow the convention that $\log 0 = -\infty$, we are allowed to transform the utility function V by using the monotonically increasing function $U = \log V$, which is defined over the same set as V. Under these conditions we maximize the concave function $U = \log(x_1 + \bar{x}_1) + m \log x_2 + n \log x_3$ subject to the constraints given by (1). This is a standard optimization problem and the Kuhn-Tucker conditions are then necessary and sufficient.

Before we write the conditions that characterize the maximum, two remarks are in order. In the first instance, because r is positive, we will necessarily have $V^* > 0$ at the optimum and consequently $x_2^* > 0$ and $x_3^* > 0$. On the other hand, since the objective function is monotonically increasing with respect to each of its arguments, the budget constraint will necessarily be binding ($px = r$) at the optimum.

When we take these considerations into account and designate the Lagrangian as $\mathscr{L}$, the optimal solutions are characterized by the following:

$$\frac{\partial \mathscr{L}}{\partial x_1} = \frac{1}{x_1^* + \bar{x}_1} - \lambda^* p_1 \leq 0, \quad \text{with} \quad x_1^* > 0 \Rightarrow \frac{\partial \mathscr{L}}{\partial x_1} = 0; \tag{2}$$

$$\frac{\partial \mathscr{L}}{\partial x_2} = \frac{m}{x_2^*} - \lambda^* p_2 = 0, \quad \text{since} \quad x_2^* > 0; \tag{3}$$

$$\frac{\partial \mathscr{L}}{\partial x_3} = \frac{n}{x_3^*} - \lambda^* p_3 = 0, \quad \text{since} \quad x_3^* > 0; \tag{4}$$

and $\quad r - p_1 x_1^* - p_2 x_2^* - p_3 x_3^* = 0. \tag{5}$

Then two cases can be distinguished.

- Case 1: $x_1^* = 0$.

Eliminating λ^* from Eqs. (3) and (4) and taking (5) into account, we have

$$\lambda^* = \frac{m}{p_2 x_2^*} = \frac{n}{p_3 x_3^*} = \frac{m + n}{r}, \tag{6}$$

from which we can calculate

$$x_2^* = \frac{mr}{p_2(m + n)} \quad \text{and} \quad x_3^* = \frac{nr}{p_3(m + n)}.$$

This solution is valid as long as the following inequality is satisfied:

$$\frac{\partial \mathscr{L}}{\partial x_1} = \frac{1}{\bar{x}_1} - \lambda^* p_1 = \frac{1}{\bar{x}_1} - \frac{m+n}{r} p_1 \leq 0,$$

or
$$p_1 \geq \frac{r}{(m + n)\bar{x}_1}. \tag{7}$$

Our calculations corroborate the geometric notions in Fig. 1.1. The second equality in (6) expresses analytically the tangency between curve $\mathscr{C}$ and segment BC. The solution obtained is applicable only for sufficiently large values of p_1, that is if point A is sufficiently close to the origin—see inequality (7).

- Case 2: $x_1^* > 0$.

   Conditions (2) through (5) are all satisfied with equality, so they are the same conditions that we would have if we used the technique of Lagrangian multipliers. From these we derive

$$\lambda^* = \frac{1}{p_1(x_1^* + \bar{x}_1)} = \frac{m}{p_2 x_2^*} = \frac{n}{p_3 x_3^*} = \frac{m + n + 1}{r + p_1 \bar{x}_1}.$$

It then follows immediately that

$$x_1^* = \frac{r}{p_1(m + n + 1)} - \frac{\bar{x}_1(m + n)}{(m + n + 1)},$$

$$x_2^* = \frac{m(r + p_1 \bar{x}_1)}{p_2(m + n + 1)},$$

and
$$x_3^* = \frac{n(r + p_1 \bar{x}_1)}{p_3(m + n + 1)}.$$

This solution is valid for $x_1^* > 0$, from which it follows immediately that

$$p_1 < \frac{r}{(m + n)\bar{x}_1}. \tag{8}$$

The different solutions we have obtained depend on the values of the ratio p_1/r and require the following remarks:

(a) We can show that, for each of the cases, the demand functions are homogeneous of degree 0 with respect to prices and income.

(b) We can show also that for $p > 0$ and $r > 0$, the demand functions are continuous. It is obvious that each component is continuous in each of the cases. We prove directly that there is continuity between the two cases when

$$p_1 = r/(m + n)\bar{x}_1.$$

Indeed, if we consider the second case, it is obvious that when p_1 tends toward $r/(m + n)\bar{x}_1$ from above, the components of x^* have as their respective limits 0, $mr/(m + n)p_2$, $nr/(m + n)p_3$. These are precisely the solutions found in case 1.

(c) We note finally that even though they are continuous, the demand functions are not everywhere differentiable (nonetheless both a right-hand and a left-hand derivative exist at the critical point).

In the interest of economic realism we should point out that the solution studied here is a rather general one. Surely a consumer does not always demand every good. Good x_1 might be considered a luxury good. Since the price p_1 is fixed, this good is demanded only if the consumer's income has reached a sufficiently high level. Figure 1.2 represents the Engel's curve corresponding to good 1 taking prices as given.

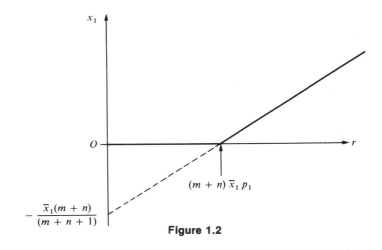

Figure 1.2

The demand functions derived from the utility function chosen here belong to a category known in the literature as Stone functions. These have the property that the expenditure on each good is linear with respect to prices and income. Conversely, one could attempt to characterize the class of utility functions that would yield demand functions exhibiting this property. This will be the purpose of exercise 5.

Suggested Readings

Dixit, Avinash K. 1976. *Optimization in Economic Theory*. Oxford: Oxford University Press.

Intriligator, Michael D. 1971. *Mathematical Optimization and Economic Theory*, chap. 4. Englewood Cliffs, N.J.: Prentice-Hall.

Malinvaud, Edmond. 1972. *Lectures on Microeconomic Theory*, trans. A. Silvey, chap. 2. Amsterdam: North-Holland.

Milleron, Jean-Claude. 1972. "The Extrema of Functions of Several Variables with or without Constraint on the Variables." In Malinvaud, 1972.

Phlips, Louis. 1974. *Applied Consumption Analysis*. Amsterdam: North-Holland.

Stone, Richard. 1954. "Linear Expenditure Systems and Demand Analysis: An Application to the Pattern of British Demand." *Economic Journal* 64: 511–527.

Varaiya, Pravin Pratap. 1972. *Notes on Optimization*. New York: Van Nostrand Reinhold.

Aggregation of Goods

Let us consider an economy in which there are ℓ goods indexed by $i = 1, \ldots, \ell$. Assume that the prices of some of these goods (the first k, for example) are proportional to each other; that is,

$$p_i = \lambda p_i^0 \qquad (i = 1, \ldots, k).$$

If we are interested only in the total value $\Sigma_{i=1}^k \, p_i q_i$ of an individual's consumption of the goods belonging to the group $i = 1, \ldots, k$, show that in the framework of consumer theory we may as well consider this group of goods as a single fictitious good, defined in a way that we shall clarify below (a proposition called the Hicks-Leontief theorem). This proposition can be demonstrated by assuming that we always find ourselves in the interior of the consumption set (so that we can use the technique of Lagrangian multipliers). Show that the proposition remains true when the chosen consumption bundle is on the boundary of the consumption set for the following particular case:

$$U = x_1 x_2 x_3 + x_2 x_3, \quad \text{with} \quad p_1 = p_2/2.$$

PROPOSED SOLUTION

In econometric analysis the issue is not to represent totally and in their diversity the demand functions for all goods to which the consumer may have claim. It is necessary to form groups—to construct aggregates—by substituting for the notion of physical quantity that of quantity index and for the notion of price that of price index. The composition of such aggregates amounts to replacing a complicated model (of ℓ goods and ℓ

prices) with a simpler model consisting of a smaller number of quantity indexes and price indexes.

Assuming that the elementary demand functions satisfy the axioms of consumer theory (that is, that they are derived from utility functions), can we express the aggregate demands (for the groups of products) as a function of price indexes and income only? In general, this problem does not have a satisfactory answer. Nevertheless, there exists a particular case where the aggregation can be done in a simple way and the aggregate demand functions preserve the classical properties of demand functions. This case is the one where the prices of a group of elementary products vary (or are constrained to vary) equiproportionately. To this particular case correspond the properties described by the Hicks-Leontief theorem.

We first demonstrate this theorem making the usual assumptions found in the literature on consumer theory.[1] Consider only points situated in the interior of the consumption set. Later show that the theorem holds for the particular case proposed, if optimal consumption bundles are situated on the boundary of the consumption set.

Solutions in the Interior of the Consumption Set

Consider ℓ goods indexed by $i = 1, \ldots, \ell$. Let X be the consumption set. The consumer maximizes his utility function $U(x)$ on $X \cap \{x|px \leqslant r\}$. Under the assumptions made, the set of consumption bundles maximizing U is defined in a unique way by the following equations (which are necessary and sufficient):

$$\frac{\partial U}{\partial x_i} - \eta p_i = 0 \qquad i = 1, \ldots, \ell \tag{1}$$

---

1. The following assumptions are used extensively in these exercises:

(1) The feasible set X is convex, closed, bounded from below, and contains the origin. If it contains any vector x^1 it also contains every vector x^2 such that $x_h^2 \geqslant x_h^1$ for $h = 1, 2, \ldots, \ell$.

(2) The utility function U defined on X is continuous and increasing; that is, $x_h^1 > x_h^2$ for $h = 1, 2, \ldots, \ell$ implies that $U(x^1) > U(x^2)$.

(3) The utility function U is twice differentiable. Its first derivatives are never all simultaneously zero.

(4) The utility function U is strictly quasi-concave in that if $U(x^2) \geqslant U(x^1)$ for two different vectors x^1 and x^2, then $U(x) > U(x^1)$ for every vector x in the open interval (x^1, x^2); that is, for any vector x such that

$$x_h = \alpha x_h^1 + (1 - \alpha)x_h^2 \qquad (h = 1, 2, \ldots, \ell),$$

where α is a positive number less than one.

and
$$\sum_{i=1}^{\ell} p_i x_i = r. \tag{2}$$

Let $x_i(p_1, \ldots, p_\ell, r)$ be the demand functions derived from these equations. Let I be the group of goods defined by $I = \{1, \ldots, k\}$. If we try to define aggregate demand for this group of goods, for example by the expression $\sum_{i=1}^{k} \alpha_i x_i(p_1, \ldots, p_\ell, r)$, there is no reason why this aggregate, and a fortiori the remaining basic demand functions, will depend on the prices $p_1, \ldots, p_k$ only by means of a single function of these prices (which could be interpreted as a price index).

Suppose from now on that $p_i = \lambda p_i^0$ when i belongs to the group of goods I. We aggregate the consumption bundles of group I by taking $\alpha_i = p_i^0$, which allows us to define the quantity index q by

$$q = \sum_{i=1}^{k} p_i^0 x_i. \tag{3}$$

At this point we show that the consumption value of goods in group I is the product of the quantity index q multiplied by λ, which can therefore be interpreted as a price index:

$$\sum_{i=1}^{k} p_i x_i = \sum_{i=1}^{k} \lambda p_i^0 x_i = \lambda q.$$

Then the functions

$$q(p_1, \ldots, p_\ell, r)$$
and
$$x_i(p_1, \ldots, p_\ell, r) \qquad i = k + 1, \ldots, \ell$$

depend only on the variables $\lambda, p_{k+1}, \ldots, p_\ell, r$.

When we study the properties of the aggregate demand functions defined in this way, it follows immediately that they are homogeneous of degree zero and satisfy the budget constraint with equality: $\lambda q + \sum_{i=k+1}^{\ell} x_i = r$.

Since $\dfrac{\partial x_i}{\partial p_j} (\lambda, p_{k+1}, \ldots, p_\ell, r) = \dfrac{\partial x_i}{\partial p_j} (p_1, \ldots, p_\ell, r)$ for all i and for all j that do not belong to group I, the aggregate demand functions satisfy the Slutsky equations if and only if:

$$\frac{\partial q}{\partial p_j} + x_j \frac{\partial q}{\partial r} = \frac{\partial x_j}{\partial \lambda} + q \frac{\partial x_j}{\partial r} \quad \text{for} \quad j = k + 1, \ldots, \ell. \tag{4}$$

However,

$$\frac{\partial q}{\partial p_j} = \sum_{i=1}^{k} p_i^0 \frac{\partial x_i}{\partial p_j}, \qquad \frac{\partial q}{\partial r} = \sum_{i=1}^{k} p_i^0 \frac{\partial x_i}{\partial r}, \qquad \text{and} \qquad \frac{\partial x_j}{\partial \lambda} = \sum_{i=1}^{k} p_i^0 \frac{\partial x_j}{\partial p_i}.$$

Equation (4) is therefore equivalent to

$$\sum_{i=1}^{k} p_i^0 \left(\frac{\partial x_i}{\partial p_j} + x_j \frac{\partial x_i}{r} - \frac{\partial x_j}{\partial p_i} - x_i \frac{\partial x_j}{\partial r} \right) = 0,$$

an equation that is always satisfied, since the basic demand functions satisfy the Slutsky equations. Thus the aggregate demand functions could be derived in principle from a utility function (a point that will be clarified in exercise 4).

How would one characterize this utility function defined on the space $[q, x_{k+1}, \ldots, x_\ell]$? We shall define a function directly on this space and show that it is indeed the utility function from which the aggregate demand functions are derived.

If we fix the amount q of total consumption of goods in group I and the level of each of the amounts consumed of the other goods $x_{k+1}, \ldots, x_\ell$, the consumer knows how best to allocate his consumption among the various goods belonging to group I by maximizing his utility under the constraints imposed. In other words, for each good of group I he will make sure that his marginal utility is proportional to the corresponding price, all the while keeping in mind the total constraint represented by the amount q. (Remember that we have assumed that the optimal bundle of goods belongs to the interior of the consumption set.) Thus we can associate the basic quantities $x_1, \ldots, x_k$ with the aggregate consumption bundles $x_{k+1}, \ldots, x_\ell, q$ so that the following hold:

$$\frac{\partial U}{\partial x_i} (x_1, \ldots, x_\ell) - \mu p_i^0 = 0 \quad \text{for} \quad i \in I, \tag{5}$$

and

$$\sum_{i=1}^{k} p_i^0 x_i = q. \tag{3}$$

This system defines the quantities $x_1, \ldots, x_k$ as implicit functions of $x_{k+1}, \ldots, x_\ell$ and q, since the Lagrangian conditions are necessary and sufficient and the equations have a unique solution. Then U becomes a function V of $x_{k+1}, \ldots, x_\ell, q$:

$$V(x_{k+1}, \ldots, x_\ell, q) = U[x_1(x_{k+1}, \ldots, x_\ell, q), \ldots,$$
$$x_k(x_{k+1}, \ldots, x_\ell, q), x_{k+1}, \ldots, x_\ell].$$

To prove that the function V obtained in this way is really the utility function from which the aggregate demand functions are derived, it is sufficient to show that maximizing V subject to the budget constraint generates demand functions identical to those obtained by aggregating the basic demand functions.

The following schema emerges:

$$\text{Max of } U \text{ subject to } \sum_{i=1}^{k} p_i^0 x_i = q, x_{k+1}, \ldots, x_\ell \text{ fixed}$$

$$U \longrightarrow V$$

Max of U subject to

$$\sum_{i=1}^{\ell} p_i x_i = r$$

Max of V subject to

$$\lambda q + \sum_{i=k+1}^{\ell} p_i x_i = r$$

Basic demand functions $\xrightarrow{\text{Aggregation}}$ Aggregate demand functions

Maximizing V subject to the budget constraint yields the following equations, which are necessary and sufficient:

$$\partial V / \partial q = \gamma \lambda, \tag{6}$$

$$\partial V / \partial x_i = \gamma p_i \quad \text{for} \quad i = k + 1, \ldots, \ell, \tag{7}$$

and
$$\lambda q + \sum_{i=k+1}^{\ell} p_i x_i = r. \tag{8}$$

It is now sufficient to show that given V as defined above and p such that $p_i = \lambda p_i^0$ for i belonging to the set I, the systems of equations consisting of (1), (2), (3) on the one hand and (3), (5), (6), (7), (8) on the other hand have the same solutions $x_{k+1}, \ldots, x_\ell, q$.

We begin by making explicit the form of the partial derivatives $\partial V/\partial q$ and $\partial V/\partial x_i$:

$$\frac{\partial V}{\partial q} = \sum_{j=1}^{k} \frac{\partial U}{\partial x_j} \frac{\partial x_j}{\partial q}$$

and

$$\frac{\partial V}{\partial x_i} = \frac{\partial U}{\partial x_i} + \sum_{j=1}^{k} \frac{\partial U}{\partial x_j} \frac{\partial x_j}{\partial x_i}, \qquad i = k+1, \ldots, \ell.$$

Taking Eq. (5) into account, these equations can be written as follows:

$$\frac{\partial V}{\partial q} = \mu \sum_{j=1}^{k} p_j^0 \frac{\partial x_j}{\partial q}$$

and

$$\frac{\partial V}{\partial x_i} = \frac{\partial U}{\partial x_i} + \mu \sum_{j=1}^{k} p_j^0 \frac{\partial x_j}{\partial x_i}, \qquad i = k+1, \ldots, \ell.$$

Since the functions $x_j(q, x_{k+1}, \ldots, x_\ell)$ are defined by Eqs. (3) and (5), we can calculate their partial derivatives. The calculation is especially easy: indeed, by taking the partial derivatives of the two sides of (3), we obtain immediately:

$$\sum_{j=1}^{k} p_j^0 \frac{\partial x_j}{\partial q} = 1, \qquad \sum_{j=1}^{k} p_j^0 \frac{\partial x_j}{\partial x_i} = 0.$$

Given the assumptions made above, we proceed to show the identity of the solutions $x_{k+1}, \ldots, x_\ell, q$ of system (1), (2), (3) on the one hand; and, on the other hand, those solutions of the system made up of Eqs. (3), (5), (8), and

$$\mu = \gamma\lambda, \tag{6'}$$

$$\frac{\partial U}{\partial x_i} = \gamma p_i, \qquad i = k+1, \ldots, \ell. \tag{7'}$$

Taking into account the way in which p_i is defined, when i belongs to I, this last system is then equivalent to the following system when μ is eliminated:

$$\frac{\partial U}{\partial x_i} = \gamma p_i, \qquad i = 1, \ldots, k, \tag{5'}$$

$$\frac{\partial U}{\partial x_i} = \gamma p_i, \qquad i = k + 1, \ldots, \ell, \tag{7'}$$

and Eqs. (3) and (8) are combined. Setting $\eta = \gamma$ gives the identification immediately.

In closing we note that we have not given the precise conditions under which the following partial derivatives exist: $\frac{\partial x_i}{\partial q}(x_{k+1}, \ldots, x_\ell, q)$ or $\frac{\partial x_j}{\partial x_i}(x_{k+1}, \ldots, x_\ell, q)$. We suggest that assumption (3) of note 1 is sufficient for the above, and for the existence of the partial derivatives of the basic demand functions as well.

Solutions on the Boundary of the Consumption Set

Now let us tackle the particular case where $U = x_1 x_2 x_3 + x_2 x_3$.

In exercise 1 a similar utility function was employed. Therefore we are familiar with the basic demand functions obtained by maximizing U directly.

For $r > 2p_1$, the maximum of U is obtained at a point located in the interior of the consumption set and our previous derivation remains valid. On the other hand, for $0 < r \leq 2p_1$, we have seen that

$$x_1 = 0, \qquad x_2 = \frac{r}{2p_2}, \qquad \text{and} \qquad x_3 = \frac{r}{2p_3}.$$

The point that maximizes U is located on the boundary of the consumption set.

Since $p_1 = p_2/2$, using our earlier notation we have:

$$p_1 = \lambda, \quad p_2 = 2\lambda, \quad \text{and} \quad q = x_1 + 2x_2.$$

Therefore, for $0 < r \leq 2p_1 = p_2$, the aggregate demand functions are equal to

$$q = \frac{r}{2\lambda} \qquad \text{and} \qquad x_3 = \frac{r}{2p_3}$$

and satisfy the budget constraint with equality:

$$\lambda q + p_3 x_3 = r.$$

Now we define the function $V(q,x_3)$. To do so it is necessary to maximize U subject to the constraints

$$x_1 + 2x_2 = q \qquad x_1 \geq 0, \qquad x_2 \geq 0,$$

$$x_3 = \text{constant},$$

that is, to maximize $(x_1 + 1)x_2$ subject to

$$x_1 + 2x_2 = q, \qquad x_1 \geq 0, \qquad x_2 \geq 0.$$

Since q is strictly positive, the same applies to x_2 at the maximum of U and there are only two possible cases to consider. The first, when $x_1 > 0$, falls within the framework of our results for the interior of the consumption set. Only the second, where $x_1 = 0$, is of interest to us here. The Kuhn-Tucker conditions yield

$$x_1 + 1 - 2\mu = 0, \qquad x_1 + 2x_2 = q, \qquad x_1 = 0,$$

where $\mu = 1/2$ and $x_2 = q/2$. This case holds for $\partial L/\partial x_1 = x_2 - \mu \leq 0$, that is, for $q \leq 1$. Thus we have $V = qx_3/2$. Maximizing V subject to the constraints $q \geq 0$, $x_3 \geq 0$ and $\lambda q + p_3 x_3 \leq r$, yields

$$x_3 = \frac{r}{2p_3} \quad \text{and} \quad q = \frac{r}{2\lambda}.$$

Taking into account that $q \leq 1$ then implies $r \leq 2\lambda = 2p_1$, we find again (as we should) the same aggregate demand functions with the same domain of applicability.

THE ECONOMETRIC APPLICATION of the property furnished by the Hicks-Leontief theorem could lead us to regroup extremely different goods, as long as the structure of the corresponding prices does not change. In general, though, how can we attach any significance to such aggregates when, for example, we can group diverse goods such as a paperback book, aspirin, a haircut, and wine? We prefer to group goods depending on the type of need they satisfy, by creating categories such as clothing and food. (Within a category such as food, however, it might be interesting to use a detailed list and regroup the goods according to the speed of price changes.)

Suggested Readings

Hicks, John R. 1946. *Value and Capital,* ed. 2, chap. 3. London: Oxford University Press.

Leontief, Wassily. 1936. "Composite Commodities and the Problem of Index Numbers." *Econometrica* 4: 39–59.

Malinvaud, Edmond. 1972. *Lectures on Microeconomic Theory,* trans. A. Silvey, chap. 2. Amsterdam: North-Holland.

Samuelson, Paul A. 1947. *Foundations of Economic Analysis,* chap. 6. Cambridge, Mass.: Harvard University Press.

3 Aggregate Demand and the Social Welfare Function

Problem 1

A. Let $V(x)$ be a real-valued function defined on $\mathbb{R}^{\ell+}$ with values in $\mathbb{R}^+$, and assume that this function exhibits the following properties:

Assumption (1)   It is continuous;

Assumption (2)   It satisfies the condition that when $V(x_1) > V(x_2)$, then $V[\theta x_1 + (1 - \theta)x_2] > V(x_2)$ for $0 < \theta \leqslant 1$;

Assumption (3)   It is homogeneous of degree one, that is, $V(\lambda x) = \lambda V(x)$ for $\lambda \geqslant 0$.

Establish the following properties sequentially:

(1) $x \geqslant 0$ implies $V(x) > 0$;

(2) $V(x)$ is a concave function on the set int $\mathbb{R}^{\ell+} = \{x | x \gg 0\}$;

(3) $V(x)$ is concave on $\mathbb{R}^{\ell+}$.

B. Show that if $V(x)$ (mapping $\mathbb{R}^\ell$ into $\mathbb{R}$) is concave and if $f[V]$ (mapping $\mathbb{R}$ into $\mathbb{R}$) is concave and nondecreasing, then $f[V(x)]$ is concave.

Problem 2

Let a group of m consumers be indexed by $j = 1, \ldots, m$. The choices made by these consumers are concerned with ℓ goods, indexed by $i = 1, \ldots, \ell$. For each of these the set X^j of feasible consumption bundles is the positive orthant of $\mathbb{R}^\ell$. The preferences of each are represented by a nonnegative utility function $V^j(x^j)$, which satisfies assumption (2) above and is both continuous and homogeneous of degree λ^j. Finally, the distribution of income is constant—that is, if total income is r, the jth consumer receives a fraction μ^j of this total income that is fixed once and for all, with $\Sigma\mu^j = 1$. Therefore $r^j = \mu^j r$.

Show that we can represent the preferences of each consumer by $W^j(x^j) = (1/\lambda^j) \log V^j(x^j)$, and that this function is concave.

Problem 3

Using the Kuhn-Tucker conditions, write the equations and inequalities that are necessary and sufficient to characterize the demand functions of the jth consumer. (Designate by p the price vector whose components are $p_1, \ldots, p_\ell$.)

Problem 4

Now consider the social welfare function $W = \sum_{j=1}^{m} \mu^j W^j(x^j)$. Show that if we set $x = \sum x^j$, maximizing W subject to the constraint $px \leqslant r$ leads to the same result as in problem 3.

Problem 5

Show that the procedure considered above is applicable only for homogeneous utility functions. Under these conditions does such a presentation lose much relevance?

PROPOSED SOLUTION

Individual demand functions derived from a utility function exhibit numerous properties that are interesting because of their econometric applications. When we do not take the distribution of income into account, are aggregate demand functions derivable from a social welfare function as well? Naturally, such a social welfare function makes sense only if it is sensitive to individual preferences and reflects the weight given to each individual by his share of the distribution of income.

This problem can be related to exercise 2 (which utilizes the Hicks-Leontief theorem). In fact, here we wish to aggregate individual functions (that is, to achieve an aggregation over the agents), whereas the Hicks-Leontief theorem solves the case of aggregation over goods.

Problem 1

A(1). Suppose that there exists an $\bar{x}$ such that $\bar{x} \gg 0$ and $V(\bar{x}) = 0$. Let $\hat{x}$ be any element (we assume that there exists at least one) such that $V(\hat{x})$ will be strictly positive.

The element $\bar{x}$ belongs to the interior of $\mathbb{R}^{\ell+}$; since $V(x)$ is a continuous function, we can find a real number θ, which is negative, such that the element $x_0 = (1 - \theta)\bar{x} + \theta\hat{x}$ belongs to $\mathbb{R}^{\ell+}$ and such that $V(x_0)$ is inferior to $V(\hat{x})$ at the same time. Therefore we can write:

$$\bar{x} = \frac{1}{1 - \theta} x_0 - \frac{\theta}{1 - \theta} \hat{x}.$$

From assumption (2), we deduce $0 = V(\bar{x}) > V(x_0)$, which contradicts the fact that $V(x)$ is not negative.

A(2). Let x_1 and x_2 be any two elements of $\mathbb{R}^{\ell+}$. We wish to show that, for $\lambda \in [0, 1]$:

$$V[\lambda x_1 + (1 - \lambda)x_2] \geqslant \lambda V(x_1) + (1 - \lambda)V(x_2).$$

When $x_1 = \mu x_2$ (μ is a positive scalar), the property is obvious; it follows from assumption (3). When $V(x_1) = V(x_2)$, the property follows from assumption (2). Indeed, if this property were not true, there would exist an $\bar{x}$ belonging to the segment $[x_1, x_2]$ such that $V(\bar{x}) < V(x_1) = V(x_2)$. Since the function $V(x)$ is continuous, we could then find an element $\tilde{x}$ of $[\bar{x}, x_2]$, for example, such that $V(\bar{x}) < V(\tilde{x}) < V(x_2)$. Thanks to assumption (2), and since $V(x_1) > V(\tilde{x})$, a contradiction would emerge.

We are left with the case where there exists no scalar such that $x_1 = \mu x_2$ and where $V(x_2) > V(x_1)$ to clarify our point. We define γ (strictly positive) as the ratio $V(x_1)/V(x_2)$, and we set $x_2^* = \gamma x_2$ and $x_1^* = (1/\gamma)x_1$. Let $y = \lambda x_1 + (1 - \lambda) x_2$. In Fig. 3.1 the vector Oy belonging to the cone determined by vectors Ox_1 and Ox_2 intersects the segments $[x_1, x_2^*]$ and $[x_1^*, x_2]$ in a and b respectively.

It follows immediately from assumption (3) that $V(x_1^*) = V(x_2)$ and that $V(x_2^*) = V(x_1)$. On the other hand, assumption (2) implies, as we have

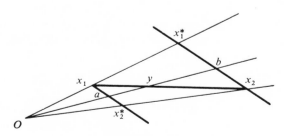

Figure 3.1

seen, that if two elements $\hat{x}_1$ and $\hat{x}_2$ are such that $V(\hat{x}_1) = V(\hat{x}_2)$, then for any scalar $\theta \in [0,1]$,

$$V[\theta\hat{x}_1 + (1 - \theta)\hat{x}_2] \geqslant V(\hat{x}_1) = V(\hat{x}_2). \tag{1}$$

We conclude from this that $V(a) \geqslant V(x_1)$ and $V(b) \geqslant V(x_2)$. Since the segments $[x_1, x_2^*]$ and $[x_1^*, x_2]$ are parallel, we derive

$$y = \lambda a + (1 - \lambda)b,$$

and, by assumption (2),

$$V(y) = \lambda V(a) + (1 - \lambda)V(b),$$

which finally becomes

$$V(y) \geqslant \lambda V(x_1) + (1 - \lambda)V(x_2).$$

A(3). Any element x of $\mathbb{R}^{\ell+}$ can be considered as the limit of a sequence of elements $x^n \gg 0$ of the form $x^n = x + 1/n$, where 1 designates the vector of $\mathbb{R}^\ell$ whose components are all equal to unity.

Let x_1 and x_2 be any two elements of $\mathbb{R}^{\ell+}$. Let $\{x_1^n\}$ and $\{x_2^n\}$ be the sequences associated with them. Given $\lambda \in [0, 1]$, by A(2) we have:

$$V[\lambda x_1^n + (1 - \lambda)x_2^n] \geqslant \lambda V(x_1^n) + (1 - \lambda)V(x_2^n).$$

Since the function V is continuous, this inequality continues to hold as n tends toward infinity.

B. The concavity of $V(x)$ implies that for each pair x_1, x_2 and for all $\theta \in [0, 1]$

$$V[\theta x_1 + (1 - \theta)x_2] \geqslant \theta V(x_1) + (1 - \theta)V(x_2).$$

Since f is increasing, we derive

$$f(V[\theta x_1 + (1 - \theta)x_2]) \geqslant f[\theta V(x_1) + (1 - \theta)V(x_2)].$$

Since f is concave:

$$f[\theta V(x_1) + (1 - \theta)V(x_2)] \geq \theta f[V(x_1)] + (1 - \theta)f[V(x_2)].$$

The combination of the two preceding inequalities shows that the function $f[V(x)]$ is concave.

Problem 2

We transform each function V^j by using a continuous monotonically increasing function, $U^j = [V^j]^{1/\lambda^j}$. The function U^j is continuous, satisfies assumption (2), and is homogeneous of degree one. Therefore it is concave, by properties (1) to (3) derived above.

The logarithmic function is both increasing and concave. Therefore $\log [V^j]^{1/\lambda^j} = W^j$ is concave. (W^j can be written $[1/\lambda^j] \log V^j$.)

Problem 3

In this problem we assume that the functions V^j are defined and positive on the nonnegative orthant:

$$X^j = \{x^j | x_i^j \geq 0 \quad \text{for} \quad i = 1, \ldots, \ell\}.$$

We look for the maximum of W^j over the domain defined by $X^j \cap \{x^j | px^j \leq \mu^j r\}$. This domain is closed and convex, since it is the intersection of closed, convex sets. Because all the components of the price vector are strictly positive, the domain is bounded and therefore compact. If W^j is assumed to be continuous, it attains its maximum on this domain. We assume that it is not only continuous but also differentiable over all X^j. Since W^j is concave, the Kuhn-Tucker conditions characterizing this maximum are necessary and sufficient. These conditions are written in the following way:

for all j, there exist η^j nonnegative scalars such that

$$\frac{\partial W^j}{\partial x_i^j} - \eta^j p_i \leq 0 \quad \text{for} \quad i = 1, \ldots, \ell;$$

$$x_i^j \geq 0 \quad \text{for} \quad i = 1, \ldots, \ell; \tag{2}$$

$$\sum_{i=1}^{\ell} \left[\frac{\partial W^j}{\partial x_i^j} - \eta^j p_i \right] x_i^j = 0; \tag{3}$$

and
$$\sum_{i=1}^{\ell} p_i x_i^j = \mu^j r. \tag{4}$$

Notice that we could write Eq. (4) directly, since W^j is increasing along the ray Ox^j. Taking Eq. (4) into account, Eq. (3) can then be written:

$$\sum_{i=1}^{\ell} \frac{\partial W^j}{\partial x_i^j} x_i^j = \eta^j \mu^j r.$$

However,

$$\sum_{i=1}^{\ell} \frac{\partial W^j}{\partial x_i^j} x_i^j = \frac{1}{\lambda^j V^j} \sum_{i=1}^{\ell} \frac{\partial V^j}{\partial x_i^j} x_i^j.$$

Since V^j is homogeneous of degree λ_j, we have the Euler equation

$$\sum_{i=1}^{\ell} \frac{\partial V^j}{\partial x_i^j} x_i^j = \lambda^j V^j,$$

and Eqs. (3) and (4) yield $\eta^j = 1/\mu^j r$.

The system of expressions (2), (3), (4) is therefore equivalent to the following system for all j:

$$\frac{\partial W^j}{\partial x_i^j} - \frac{p_i}{\mu^j r} \leq 0 \qquad i = 1, \ldots, \ell,$$

$$x_i^j \geq 0 \qquad i = 1, \ldots, \ell, \tag{5}$$

and
$$\sum_{i=1}^{\ell} \left(\frac{\partial W^j}{\partial x_i^j} - \frac{p_i}{\mu^j r} \right) x_i^j = 0.$$

Problem 4

Because W is the sum of concave functions, it also is concave. (Since a sum of quasi-concave functions is not necessarily quasi-concave, we transformed the V^j's into concave functions, thanks to the properties derived in the first problem.) The Kuhn-Tucker conditions are therefore necessary and sufficient to characterize the maximum of W and give the following system:

$$\frac{\partial W}{\partial x_i^j} - \eta p_i \leq 0 \qquad \text{for all } i = 1, \ldots, \ell$$

$$\text{and all } j = 1, \ldots, m;$$

$$x_i^j \geq 0 \qquad \text{for all } i = 1, \ldots, \ell$$

$$\text{and all } j = 1, \ldots, m;$$

$$\sum_{j=1}^{m} \sum_{i=1}^{\ell} \left(\frac{\partial W}{\partial x_i^j} - \eta p_i \right) x_i^j = 0; \tag{6}$$

and

$$\sum_{j=1}^{m} \sum_{i=1}^{\ell} p_i x_i^j = r.$$

As above, we can calculate the multiplier η: since $\Sigma_{j=1}^{m} \mu^j = 1$, the function W is the logarithm of a function that is homogeneous of degree one. Therefore we have

$$\sum_{j=1}^{m} \sum_{i=1}^{\ell} \frac{\partial W}{\partial x_i^j} x_i^j = 1$$

and then:

$$\eta = \frac{1}{\displaystyle\sum_{j=1}^{m} \sum_{i=1}^{\ell} p_i x_i^j} = \frac{1}{r}.$$

In order to solve for $\partial W / \partial x_i^j$, system (6) can be written:

$$\frac{\partial W^j}{\partial x_i^j} - \frac{p_i}{\mu^j r} \leq 0 \quad \text{for all } i = 1, \ldots, \ell$$

$$\text{and all } j = 1, \ldots, m;$$

$$x_i^j \geq 0 \quad \text{for all } i = 1, \ldots, \ell$$

$$\text{and all } j = 1, \ldots, m; \tag{7}$$

and
$$\sum_{j=1}^{m} \sum_{i=1}^{\ell} \left(\frac{\partial W^j}{\partial x_i^j} - \frac{p_i}{\mu^j r} \right) x_i^j = 0.$$

A necessary and sufficient condition for the sum of a group of nonpositive terms to be zero is that each term of the sum must be zero. When we take this remark into account, the equivalence of systems (7) and (5) follows immediately.

Problem 5

We propose an aggregation procedure as follows:

$$W = \sum_{j=1}^{m} \mu^j W^j(x^j),$$

where the W^j's are concave utility functions and where the μ^j's again characterize the chosen distribution of income. Maximizing W subject to the overall budget constraint obviously gives us system (6).

By taking $\eta^j = \eta/\mu^j$, (6) implies (2). So that Eqs. (3) and (4) hold, it is necessary that

$$\sum_{i=1}^{\ell} \frac{\partial W^j}{\partial x_i^j} x_i^j = \eta^j \mu^j r = \eta r.$$

Let $U^j = e^{W_j}$. The preceding equation then implies that

$$\sum_{i=1}^{\ell} \frac{\partial U^j}{\partial x_i^j} x_i^j = \eta r U^j.$$

This is the Euler equation, which we know to be a necessary and sufficient condition for a function to be homogeneous.

Therefore U^j is homogeneous of degree ηr. System (6) then allows us to calculate $\eta r = 1$. So that system (6) and Eqs. (2), (3), and (4) for any j will be equivalent, it is necessary for W^j to be the logarithm of a function that is homogeneous of degree one.

THE APPLICABILITY of this exercise is rather restricted, inasmuch as demand functions derived from a homogeneous utility function yield a structure of consumption that does not depend on income. However, in the study of intertemporal problems, if we aggregate the goods available at some date into a single aggregate good and assume that prices vary equiproportionally over time, then by applying the theorem of Hicks-Leontief, we may assume that the utility function defined over these aggregates is homogeneous. This assumption leads to interesting results concerning both savings and behavior under inflation. Finally, we note that the problems in this exercise do not contradict Arrow's theorem on the existence of a social welfare function, since we assume here that the given distribution of income is optimal. The optimal distribution of income would be a result of solving Arrow's problem, if such a solution existed.

Suggested Readings

Chipman, John S., and Moore, James C. 1980. "Real National Income with Homothetic Preferences and a Fixed Distribution of Income." *Econometrica* 48: 401–422.

Deaton, Angus, and Muellbauer, John. 1980. *Economics and Consumer Behavior.* Cambridge: Cambridge University Press.

Debreu, Gerard. 1959. *Theory of Value: An Axiomatic Analysis of Economic Equilibrium,* chap. 4. New Haven: Yale University Press.

Friedman, Milton, 1957. *A Theory of the Consumption Function.* New York: National Bureau of Economic Research.

Lau, Lawrence J. 1969. "Duality and the Structure of Utility Functions." *Journal of Economic Theory* 1: 374–396.

4

Integrability
of Demand Functions

Consider a consumer who allocates his income r between goods ℓ indexed by $h = 1, \ldots, \ell$. If the corresponding prices are p_h, assume that we observed demand functions of the form $x_h = f_h(p_1, \ldots, p_\ell, r)$. If these demand functions were assumed to be derivable from a utility function, what would be the necessary conditions for such a utility function to exist? In particular, show that if we wish to construct the indifference surfaces on which these demand functions are based, the latter must satisfy the Slutsky equations:

$$\forall i \text{ and } j, \qquad \frac{\partial x_i}{\partial p_j} + x_j \frac{\partial x_i}{\partial r} = \frac{\partial x_j}{\partial p_i} + x_i \frac{\partial x_j}{\partial r}.$$

The necessary conditions to be derived in this exercise will be shown to be sufficient for the existence of the utility function in the particular case to be studied in exercise 5.

PROPOSED SOLUTION

Consider a consumer whose set of feasible consumption bundles is given by $X \subset \mathbb{R}^\ell$. Let $S \subset \mathbb{R}^{\ell+1}$ be the set of price and income components (p, r) such that the intersection of the budget set and the consumption set $\gamma(p, r) = \{x \mid px \leq r\} \cap X$ is not empty. Assume that X is compact and convex.[1] Since $\gamma(p, r)$ is the intersection of closed sets, it is closed. And since $\gamma(p, r)$ is a subset of a compact set X, $\gamma(p, r)$ is compact. We assume that the consumer's choices may be represented by a continuous utility

---

1. An equivalent assumption leading to the demonstration that $\gamma(p, r)$ is compact is assumption (1) in note 1 of exercise 2—that is, X is convex, closed, and bounded from below. If all the components of the price vector are strictly positive, this assumption allows us to show that $\gamma(p, r)$ is compact.

function U, defined on X, which attains its maximum on $\gamma(p,r)$. If U is strictly quasi-concave (see assumption 4 in note 1 to exercise 2), this maximum is achieved at a unique point denoted $x(p,r)$. If, as we assume here, this point is not a saturation point, $\Sigma_{h=1}^{\ell} p_h x_h(p,r) \equiv r$. Therefore we have characterized a single-valued mapping of S into X, the components of which are called demand functions.

If $(p^0, r^0) \in S$ and $r^0 \neq \min(p^0 x)$ over X, that is if (p^0, r^0) belongs to the interior of S, the demand functions $x_h(p,r)$ can be shown to be continuous in (p^0, r^0). Moreover, if $x(p^0, r^0)$ belongs to the interior of X and if U is twice differentiable, $x(p,r)$ is differentiable in (p^0, r^0). Then the cross-partial derivatives of the demand functions satisfy the Slutsky equations:

$$\forall i \neq j, \quad \frac{\partial x_i}{\partial p_j} + x_j \frac{\partial x_i}{\partial r} \equiv \frac{\partial x_j}{\partial p_i} + x_i \frac{\partial x_j}{\partial r}.$$

If λ is any positive scalar, the set $\gamma(\lambda p, \lambda r)$ is identical to $\gamma(p,s)$. (S is a cone.) Therefore the demand functions are homogeneous of degree zero: $x(\lambda p, \lambda r) = x(p,r)$.

Is it possible to reverse the procedure—that is, to construct a utility function based on the observed demand functions? We look for the properties that the demand functions must satisfy for this to be possible.

A utility function (or, even more generally, a complete preordering defined on X) allows us to rank two consumption vectors independently of all prices and income. This is why demand functions derived from a utility function are homogeneous of degree zero (they exhibit no money illusion). To construct a utility function defined on X, it is necessary to assume that the observed demand functions are homogeneous of degree zero. In what follows, assume that $x(\lambda p, \lambda r) = x(p,r)$ and that $r > 0$.

Set

$$x(p,r) = x(\pi,1) = x(\pi),$$

where

$$\pi = \frac{p}{r} \qquad [\pi \in \mathbb{R}^{\ell}].$$

Assume as well that

$$\sum_{h=1}^{\ell} p_h x_h(p,r) \equiv r, \quad \text{or} \quad \sum_{h=1}^{\ell} \pi_h x_h(\pi) \equiv 1.$$

Now consider the function $x(\pi)$, which maps an open, simply connected set K of $(\mathbb{R}^\ell)^+$ into X. Assume that this function is continuously differentiable on K and has a continuous inverse function, denoted $\pi(x)$. Then we have a one-to-one mapping of K onto $Y = x(K) \subset X$. Note that $x(K)$ is an open set and therefore belongs to the interior of X, since the function π is continuous. Let $\mathring{x} \in x(K)$, and denote $\pi(\mathring{x})$ by $\mathring{\pi}$. Then $\mathring{\pi}x = 1$ defines the budget hyperplane passing through $\mathring{x}$ such that $\mathring{x}$ is the point preferred by the consumer in the closed half-space situated under this hyperplane—the set $\gamma(\mathring{\pi}, 1)$.

Since $\mathring{x}$ is interior to X, if a utility function U exists, the indifference surface passing through $\mathring{x}$ is tangent at $\mathring{x}$ to this hyperplane. The demand functions then allow us to define a field of supporting hyperplanes. Can we find surfaces characterized by equations of the type $S(x) = $ constant, which have all of their points in one such hyperplane as the tangent hyperplane? The hyperplane tangent at x to the surface $S(x) = S(\mathring{x})$ satisfies the equation

$$\left(\frac{dS}{dx}\right)\bigg|_{\mathring{x}} (x - \mathring{x}) = 0.$$

This hyperplane must be identical to the supporting hyperplane passing through x having the following equation:

$$\mathring{\pi}x = 1 \quad \text{or} \quad \mathring{\pi}(x - \mathring{x}) = 0.$$

Therefore it is necessary that $\pi(x)$ be, without specifying the factor, the gradient of a function—in other words, that there exists a scalar function $f(x_1, \ldots, x_\ell) = f(x)$, called the integrating factor, such that

$$f(x) \sum_{h=1}^{\ell} \pi_h(x) \, dx_h$$

is a total differential. If $\Sigma_j \, \pi_j(x) \, dx_j$ has an integrating factor and if $\Sigma_j \, \pi_j x_j \equiv 1$, the differential form $\Sigma_j \, x_j d\pi_j$ has an integrating factor $g(\pi) = f[x(\pi)]$ and vice versa, because of the invertibility of $x(\pi)$.

To say that the differential form $\Sigma_{j=1}^{\ell} x_j d\pi_j$ has an integrating factor is equivalent to saying that, with respect to the variables p and r, the form $\Sigma_{j=1}^{\ell} x_j dp_j - dr$ has an integrating factor. However, there is a theorem (given in the appendix to this exercise) which asserts that a necessary and sufficient condition for this last differential form to have an integrating factor is that

$$\forall i \neq j, \qquad \frac{\partial x_i}{\partial p_i} + x_j \frac{\partial x_i}{\partial r} = \frac{\partial x_j}{\partial p_i} + x_i \frac{\partial x_j}{\partial r}.$$

These are the Slutsky equations. In conclusion, demand functions that are homogeneous of degree zero, that satisfy the budget identity and the Slutsky equations, and that are invertible in the sense defined above, are derivable from a utility function.

Two further comments are in order:

(a) Mathematically, it is equivalent to say that the form $\Sigma_j \pi_j dx_j$ has an integrating factor $f(x)$ and to say that along any closed curve of the simply connected domain the integral of $f(x) \Sigma_j \pi_j dx_j$ (interpreted as a measure of the variation in utility) is zero. If we assume that the preference relation defined by the theory of revealed preference satisfies the weak axiom (asymmetry), the addition of the assumption of the strong axiom (transitivity) prevents us from constructing a sequence of comparisons beginning and ending at $\mathring{x}$, which indicates that x is revealed preferred to itself. Therefore, in some sense, the Slutsky equations are implied by the strong axiom of revealed preference theory.

(b) By remaining in the (p, r) space, we could have inquired directly into the conditions under which the differential form $\Sigma_{j=1}^l x_j(p, r)dp_j - dr$ has an integrating factor. These conditions, which are necessary and sufficient as long as the domain under consideration is simply connected, are obviously just the Slutsky equations. Such an approach, although somewhat artificial, allows us to define an "indirect utility function." To obtain a direct utility function (that is, a function defined on X), it is necessary to assume homogeneity of degree zero of the demand functions as well as invertibility. Then we notice that the weak axiom of revealed preference theory, which assumes a one-to-one correspondence between the price vector and the vector of chosen consumption bundles (for income fixed) and moreover defines a relation independently of any change in the monetary unit, implies both homogeneity of degree zero and invertibility of demand at the same time.

The equivalence between the theory of revealed preference strengthened by the strong axiom and the proposition of the existence of a utility function (an equivalence that has been proved rigorously by Houthaker and Uzawa) emerges clearly.

APPENDIX

Let $\sum_{j=1}^{n} A_j(y)dy_j$ be a differential form defined on an open, simply connected set. The expression $g(y)$ is an integrating factor if and only if

$$\forall i \neq j, \qquad \frac{\partial[g(y)A_j(y)]}{\partial y_i} = \frac{\partial[g(y)A_i(y)]}{\partial y_i}$$

by applying the theorem of Poincaré.

In these relations we can eliminate $g(y)$ and obtain the following conditions for $i \neq j \neq k \neq i$:

$$0 = A_i \left(\frac{\partial A_j}{\partial y_k} - \frac{\partial A_k}{\partial y_j} \right) + A_k \left(\frac{\partial A_i}{\partial y_j} - \frac{\partial A_j}{\partial y_i} \right) + A_j \left(\frac{\partial A_k}{\partial y_i} - \frac{\partial A_i}{\partial y_k} \right).$$

We can therefore show that, of the $n(n-1)(n-2)/6$ equations, only $(n-1)(n-2)/2$ are independent. It is possible to derive $(n-1)(n-2)/2$ independent equations by fixing one of the indices, for example $k = n$, and writing the conditions for the form $\sum_{j=1}^{n-1} (A_j/A_n) \, dy_j + dy_n$. Setting $n = \ell + 1, y_j = p_j$ for $j = 1, \ldots, \ell, y_n = r$, we have the Slutsky equations.

Suggested Readings

Boyce, William E., and DiPrima, Richard C. 1965. *Elementary Differential Equations and Boundary Value Problems,* chap. 2. New York: John Wiley.

Debreu, Gerard. 1959. *Theory of Value: An Axiomatic Analysis of Economic Equilibrium,* chap. 4. New Haven: Yale University Press.

Debreu, Gerard. 1972. "Smooth Preferences," *Econometrica* 40: 603–616.

Houthakker, Hendrik, 1961. "The Present State of Consumption Theory." *Econometrica* 29: 704–740.

Hurwicz, Leonid. 1971. "On the Problem of Integrability of Demand Functions." In *Preferences, Utility, and Demand,* ed. John S. Chipman, Leonid Hurwicz, Marcel K. Richter, and Hugo F. Sonnenschein. New York: Harcourt Brace Jovanovich.

Samuelson, Paul A. 1947. *Foundations of Economic Analysis,* chap. 5. Cambridge, Mass.: Harvard University Press.

Samuelson, Paul A. 1950. "The Problem of Integrability in Utility Theory." *Economica* 17: 355–385.

Uzawa, Hirofumi. 1960. "Preference and Rational Choice in the Theory of Consumption." In *Mathematical Methods in the Social Sciences, 1959,* ed. Kenneth J. Arrow, Samuel Karlin, and Patrick Suppes. Stanford, Calif.: Stanford University Press.

A Linear Expenditure Model

Econometric studies of demand sometimes use a simple model which assumes that the amount allocated to the purchase of a good is a linear function of income and prices. What restrictions are placed on these linear functions by consumer theory?

Consider a consumer whose income is $r > 0$. He buys good h in quantity x_h at price p_h, where h varies from 1 to ℓ. His demand functions are such that

$$p_h x_h = \sum_{i=1}^{\ell} a_{hi} p_i + b_h r + c_h.$$

Problem 1

What can we conclude from homogeneity of degree zero and the equality of expenditure and income—in other words, the budget constraint?

Problem 2

If the Slutsky equations are to hold, what additional restrictions are required?

Problem 3

Characterize the utility function from which these demand functions are derivable.

We suggest that the following variables be used for this integration: $z_h = x_h - d_h$, where $d_h = -a_{hh}/b_h - 1$.

PROPOSED SOLUTION

So that the proposed demand functions correspond to consistent choices, we want them to satisfy the strong axiom of revealed preference. Consumer choice theory shows the equivalence of this axiom and the assumption of the existence of a utility function. Therefore it is usual to impose the integrability conditions on the demand functions studied; specifically, satisfaction of the budget constraint with equality, homogeneity of degree zero, and satisfaction of the Slutsky equations. The restrictions generated by these integrability conditions effectively allow us to construct a utility function from which the demand functions are derivable.

Problem 1

Homogeneity of degree zero implies that $c_h = 0$ for all h. The equality of expenditure and income is written

$$\sum_{h=1}^{\ell} p_h x_h = \sum_{h=1}^{\ell} \sum_{i=1}^{\ell} a_{hi} p_i + r \sum_{h=1}^{\ell} b_h \equiv r.$$

This is an identity with respect to the independent variables p_h and r. Consequently, we must have

$$\sum_{h=1}^{\ell} b_h = 1 \tag{1}$$

and, for all h,

$$\sum_{j=1}^{\ell} a_{jh} = 0. \tag{2}$$

Problem 2

The Slutsky equations can be written:

$$\forall h, \forall k, \, h \neq k, \qquad \frac{\partial x_h}{\partial p_k} + x_k \frac{\partial x_h}{\partial r} = \frac{\partial x_k}{\partial p_h} + x_h \frac{\partial x_k}{\partial r}.$$

These equations must be satisfied by the demand functions for all values of prices and income. Therefore we have the following identities:

$$\frac{a_{hk}}{p_h} + \frac{b_h}{p_h p_k}\left(\sum_{i=1}^{\ell} a_{ki}p_i + b_k r\right) \equiv \frac{a_{kh}}{p_k} + \frac{b_k}{p_k p_h}\left(\sum_{j=1}^{\ell} a_{hj}p_j + b_h r\right).$$

From which

$$b_h a_{ki} = b_k a_{hi} \qquad i \neq h \neq k \neq i, \tag{3}$$

$$a_{hk} + b_h a_{kk} = b_k a_{hk} \qquad h \neq k. \tag{4}$$

Eq. (4) implies that $a_{hk} = b_h a_{kk}/(b_k - 1)$. Therefore it is possible to express all the nondiagonal terms as a function only of the diagonal terms—the a_{hh}'s—and of the b_h's.

If the a_{hk}'s satisfy Eq. (4), then they satisfy Eq. (3). Finally:

$$\sum_{h=1}^{\ell} a_{hk} = a_{kk} + \sum_{h \neq k} \frac{b_h a_{kk}}{b_k - 1}$$

$$= a_{kk}\left(1 + \frac{\sum_{h \neq k} b_h}{b_k - 1}\right)$$

$$= \frac{a_{kk}}{b_k - 1}\left(\sum_{h=1}^{\ell} b_h - 1\right)$$

$$= 0 \text{ because of Eq. (1).}$$

Therefore Eqs. (1) and (4) imply Eq. (2).

In summary, if we define the parameters

$$d_h = -\frac{a_{hh}}{b_h - 1} \qquad j = 1, \ldots, \ell,$$

the demand functions must necessarily be of the following form for them to be integrable:

$$x_h = \frac{1}{p_h}\left(-\sum_{i \neq h} b_h d_i p_i + a_{hh}p_h + b_h r\right)$$

$$x_h = \frac{1}{p_h}\left(-\sum_{i=h} b_h d_i p_i - [b_h - 1]d_h p_h + b_h r \right)$$

$$= \frac{1}{p_h}\left(-b_h \sum_{i=1}^{\ell} d_i p_i + b_h r + d_h p_h \right).$$

Problem 3

The equations characterizing the demand functions can be written

$$p_h x_h - p_h d_h = b_h \left(r - \sum_{i=1}^{\ell} d_i p_i \right). \tag{5}$$

Let $z_1, \ldots, z_\ell$ be the variables defined by $z_h = x_h - d_h$, where $h = 1, \ldots, \ell$. If $z_1(p,\rho), \ldots, z_\ell(p,\rho)$ are demand functions defined by maximizing $V(z_1, \ldots, z_\ell)$ subject to the constraint $\Sigma_{i=1}^{\ell} p_i z_i = \rho$, then

$$x_1(p,\rho) = z_1(p,\rho) + d_1, \ldots, x_\ell(p,\rho) = z_\ell(p,\rho) + d_\ell$$

maximizes

$$V[x_1 - d_1, \ldots, x_\ell - d_\ell] = U(x_1, \ldots, x_\ell)$$

subject to the constraint $\Sigma_i p_i x_i = \rho + \Sigma_i p_i d_i$.
We set $r = \rho + \Sigma_i p_i d_i$. Then the functions

$$x_1(p,r) = z_1\left(p,r - \sum_i p_i d_i \right) + d_1, \ldots, x_\ell(p,r)$$

$$= z_\ell\left(p,r - \sum_i p_i d_i \right) + d_\ell$$

are the demand functions associated with the maximization of U subject to the constraint $\Sigma_i p_i x_i = r$. Integration of the demand functions $x_h(p,r)$ characterized by Eq. (5) can then be undertaken by integrating the demand functions $z_h(p,\rho)$, defined by substituting the above in Eq. (5) and obtaining $z_h(p,\rho) = b_h \rho/p_h$.

If these new demand functions are derived from a utility function V, then $\Sigma_i p_i dz_i$ is equal to the total differential of V without specifying the coefficient (the integrating factor). Moreover,

$$\sum_{i=1}^{\ell} p_i dz_i = \rho \sum_{i=1}^{\ell} b_i \frac{dz_i}{z_i}.$$

An indifference curve where V = constant is defined by $dV = 0$ and therefore by

$$\sum_{i=1}^{\ell} b_i \frac{dz_i}{z_i} = 0 \quad \text{or} \quad \prod_{i=1}^{\ell} z_i^{b_i} = \text{constant}.$$

Then we have

$$U(x_1, \ldots, x_\ell) = V(x_1 - d_1, \ldots, x_\ell - d_\ell),$$

$$= \prod_{i=1}^{\ell} (x_i - d_i)^{b_i},$$

which is the utility function sought.

THIS IS Stone's model and the form of the utility function obtained suggests the following remarks:

(a) The set of consumption bundles associated with the demand functions of Stone's model is characterized by

$$X = \{x | x_h \geq d_h, \quad \forall h = 1, \ldots, \ell\}.$$

(b) The d_h's can be interpreted as the consumption bundles that the consumer considers to be minimal. The point in set X that has the coordinates $d_1, \ldots, d_h, \ldots, d_l$ would therefore be the "minimum standard of living."

Suggested Readings

Brown, Alan, and Deaton, Angus S. 1972. "Models of Consumer Behaviour: A Survey." *Economic Journal* 82: 1145–1236.

Phlips, Louis. 1974. *Applied Consumption Analysis*. Amsterdam: North-Holland.

Stone, Richard. 1954. "Linear Expenditure Systems and Demand Analysis: An Application to the Pattern of British Demand." *Economic Journal* 64: 511–527.

PART TWO

Optimal Enterprise Decision Making

6 The Search for Efficient Production Programs

Consider an economy consisting of four goods indexed by $i = 1, 2, 3, 4$.

The technology is represented by a set of eight primary activities indexed by $j = 1, \ldots, 8$. To the primary activity j corresponds a vector a^j of $\mathbb{R}^4$, and the matrix consisting of elements a_i^j ($i = 1, \ldots, 4$; $j = 1, \ldots, 8$) will be called the technology matrix. We specify A to be

$$A = \begin{bmatrix} -3 & -7 & -1 & -8 & -11 & -4 & -8 & -2 \\ -6 & -9 & -2 & -13 & -19 & -3 & -5 & -4 \\ 4 & 3 & 3 & 3 & 12 & -2 & 0 & 5 \\ 0 & 2 & -1 & 1 & 0 & 5 & 10 & -2 \end{bmatrix}.$$

Thus, to activity 3 corresponds the vector

$$a^3 = \begin{bmatrix} -1 \\ -2 \\ 3 \\ -1 \end{bmatrix},$$

which is interpreted in the following way: by combining one unit of good 1, two units of good 2, and one unit of good 4, we obtain three units of good 3.

Moreover, we make two fundamental assumptions: first, all the primary activities exhibit constant returns; if a^j represents a possible production level, so does $\lambda_j \alpha^j$; $\forall \lambda_j \geq 0$. Second, all activities can occur simultaneously at any scale.

Problem 1 The study of Y, the set of feasible output.

(a) Show that Y is a convex cone.

(b) Are the following three assumptions satisfied: free disposal, irreversibility, and the impossibility of free output?

Problem 2 The search for efficient points of Y.

(a) By a direct comparison of activities 1 and 5, 2 and 4, 3 and 8, 6 and 7, show that four of the proposed activities can be eliminated immediately.

(b) Consider the set E of the elements y^* of Y, with which we can associate a vector $p \in \mathbb{R}^4$, all the components of which are strictly positive, such that for all $y \in Y$, $py^* \geqslant py$. Show that the elements of E are necessarily efficient.

(c) Show that if $y^* \in E$, the vector p associated with y^* satisfies the following conditions: $pA \leqslant 0$; $pa^j < 0 \Rightarrow \lambda_j = 0$. Interpret these conditions from an economic point of view.

(d) To simplify the calculation, we specify that the matrix inverse of

$$\begin{bmatrix} -3 & -6 & 4 & 0 \\ -7 & -9 & 3 & 2 \\ -1 & -2 & 3 & -1 \\ -8 & -5 & 0 & 10 \end{bmatrix}$$

exists and is equal to

$$\frac{1}{189} \begin{bmatrix} 165 & -80 & -140 & 2 \\ -108 & 18 & 126 & 9 \\ 9 & -33 & 84 & 15 \\ 78 & -55 & -49 & 25 \end{bmatrix}.$$

Show that activities 1 and 2 cannot belong to E.

(e) To make sure that the two activities 1 and 2 should be eliminated, consider positive linear combinations of activities 3 and 7 that strictly dominate 1 and 2 (a two-dimensional geometric figure might be useful). What is the final set of efficient points of Y? To which production techniques does it correspond and what are its properties?

PROPOSED SOLUTION

This exercise is based on a representation of technical possibilities by so-called activity vectors. Such analysis lends itself particularly well to practical application and therefore to economic calculation. One of the most widely used techniques of operations research—linear programming—was developed from this methodology. The reader already familiar with linear programming will readily understand the approach that we follow here. In particular, we propose to establish a link between this method of technical constraints and the general analysis used in microeconomic theory, and to show that the study of efficient techniques (which we assume to have already been completed when we are given a production function) may not be quite so simple in certain cases.

Problem 1

(a) Our two assumptions imply that any output of the form $y = \sum_{j=1}^{8} \lambda_j a^j$ with $\forall j$, $\lambda_j \geq 0$ is possible.

The set Y of feasible output is therefore defined by

$$Y = \{y | y = \sum_j \lambda_j a^j \quad \text{and} \quad \forall j : \lambda_j \geq 0\}.$$

Let $y \in Y$ and consider $\mu \geq 0$ a scalar. We can write $\mu y = \sum_j \mu \lambda_j a^j$. Since, for all j, $\mu \lambda_j \geq 0$, μy belongs to Y and Y is a cone.

Let y^1 and $y^2 \in Y$ and $t \in [0, 1]: y^1 = \sum_j \lambda_j^1 a^j$, $y^2 = \sum_j \lambda_j^2 a^j$. Show that $ty^1 + (1 - t)y^2$ can be written as $\sum_j \eta_j a^j$ with, for all j, $\eta_j \geq 0$. It is sufficient to note that

$$ty^1 + (1 - t)y^2 = \sum_j [t\lambda_j^1 + (1 - t)\lambda_j^2]a^j$$

and to take $\eta_j = t\lambda_j^1 + (1 - t)\lambda_j^2$, which, by the given assumptions, is necessarily positive or zero. Therefore Y is convex.

It would be possible to assert this directly by noticing that Y is defined as the convex closure of the set formed by the eight half-spaces associated with each basic activity.

Also notice that the mapping that makes a vector of feasible output correspond to a vector of nonnegative coefficients $(\lambda_1, \ldots, \lambda_j, \ldots, \lambda_s)$ is a continuous, linear mapping from the nonnegative orthant of $\mathbb{R}^8$ into $\mathbb{R}^4$. Therefore the technology matrix defines a linear mapping from the space of activities into the space of goods.

(b) Let Ω be the nonnegative orthant of $\mathbb{R}^4$, that is, the set of all vectors with nonnegative components. The assumption of the impossibility of free output can be written $\Omega \cap Y \subset \{0\}$.

Notice that for all j, a^j has a strictly negative first component, a_1^j. Let $y \in Y$, with $y = \Sigma_{j=1}^8 \lambda_j a^j$ where, for all j, $\lambda_j \geq 0$. Its first component is

$$y_1 = \sum_{j=1}^{8} \lambda_j a_1^j.$$

Since all the terms are either negative or zero, the sum is necessarily negative or zero. However, so that $y \in \Omega$ it is necessary that $y_1 \geq 0$, which then implies that $\forall j \ \lambda_j = 0$. We have thus shown that the only point common to Ω and to Y is the origin. The assumption of the impossibility of free output is satisfied.

The assumption of irreversibility can be written $Y \cap \{-Y\} \subset \{0\}$. To show that this assumption is satisfied, we use a similar argument.

Let $y \in Y$; $y = \Sigma_j \lambda_j a^j$, $y_1 = \Sigma_j \lambda_j a_1^j$. The vector $-y$ has as a first coordinate $-y_1$. For $-y$ to belong to Y it is necessary that $-y_1 \leq 0$, or $y_1 \geq 0$, which implies that $\lambda_j = 0 \ \forall j$ and that $y = 0$.

The assumption of free disposal can only be satisfied by adding to the set of primary activities the four basic vectors with one as the diagonal coefficient and zeros elsewhere. Each of these vectors corresponds to an activity characterized by a single input and the absence of any output.

Problem 2

(a) We notice immediately that the activities introduced under the assumption of free disposal are not efficient because they are dominated by the null vector. Therefore we shall ignore them. The comparisons mentioned in the statement of the problem allow us to eliminate activities 4, 5, 6, and 8 because they are not efficient. Take activity 5, for example: it is dominated by the vector of possible output equal to λa^1 with $\lambda = 3$. Indeed, this output vector allows us to produce as much of each of the goods 2 and 3 as activity 5, but with lower inputs of goods 1 and 2.

(b) If $y^* \in E$ is not efficient, we can increase at least one of its coordinates without decreasing the others and still remain in Y. Since the vector p associated with y^* is strictly positive, the quantity py^* can then be increased in Y, which contradicts the fact that y^* maximizes py on Y. Therefore the set E is included in the set of efficient points of Y. This property is perfectly general, because we have not included in the proof any particular properties of Y.

(c) The statement $y^* \in E$ is equivalent to claiming that $\exists p$ strictly positive such that

$$py \leqslant py^* \qquad \forall y \in Y. \tag{1}$$

Since the origin belongs to Y, we have, whatever the value of y^*,

$$py^* \geqslant 0. \tag{2}$$

Because Y is a cone, we have necessarily

$$py^* \leqslant 0. \tag{3}$$

Indeed, in the contrary case, py^* could not maximize py on Y, because any vector $\lambda y^*(\lambda > 1)$ would yield $py^* \lambda > py^*$. Finally, we have

$$py^* = 0 \tag{4}$$

because of inequalities (2) and (3). Since $a^j \in Y$, $pa^j \leqslant 0$ because of expression (1) and Eq. (4). Therefore

$$pA \leqslant 0. \tag{5}$$

Since $y^* \in Y$, $\exists \lambda_j \geqslant 0$ such that $y^* = \Sigma_j \lambda_j a^j$. From Eq. (4) we derive $py^* = \Sigma_j \lambda_j \, pa^j = 0$.

For a sum of negative or zero terms to be zero, it is necessary, because of expression (5), that each term be zero. Therefore $\lambda_j pa^j = 0$, $\forall j$. This allows us to establish the specified result:

$$pa^j < 0 \Rightarrow \lambda^j = 0.$$

We interpret the vector p as a price vector. Then y^* achieves the maximum profit on Y, with this maximum being equal to zero because of constant returns. The profit associated with each primary activity is negative or zero. A primary activity is included in $y^* \in E$ only if the profit associated with this activity is not strictly negative.

(d) We assume that a^1 and a^2 belong to E. Then there exist p^1 and p^2 respectively, all components of which are strictly positive, such that

$$p^1 a^1 = 0 \qquad (p^2 a^2 = 0);$$

$$p^1 a^j \leqslant 0 \qquad \forall j \neq 1;$$

and
$$p^2 a^j \leqslant 0 \qquad \forall j \neq 2.$$

In particular, if we denote by B the matrix defined in the statement of the problem, the rows of which are the vectors a^1, a^2, a^3, and a^7, we have

$$p^1 B = [0, -x_2, -x_3, -x_7]$$

and
$$p^2 B = [-z_1, 0, -z_3, -z_7],$$

where x_2, x_3, x_7, z_1, z_3, z_7 are positive scalars or zero. For example, $x_3 = -p^1 a^3$. We derive from that

$$p^1 = [0, -x_2, -x_3, -x_7][B]^{-1}.$$

The second component of p^1 is equal to

$$-\frac{1}{189} [18x_2 + 126x_3 + 9x_7].$$

Therefore it cannot be strictly positive, which contradicts the initial assumption. The same applies to the third component of p^2, which is equal to

$$-\frac{1}{189} [9z_1 + 84z_3 + 15z_7].$$

Therefore activities a^1 and a^2 cannot belong to E.

(e) We seek a combination of activities 3 and 7

$$\lambda_3 a^3 + \lambda_7 a^7, \ \lambda_3 \geqslant 0, \ \lambda_7 \geqslant 0$$

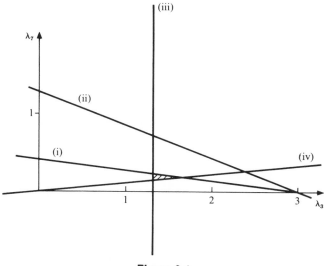

Figure 6.1

that dominates activity 1. For such a combination to exist, it is necessary and sufficient that in the quadrant $[\lambda_3, \lambda_7]$ the intersection of the following four half-planes

(i) $\qquad \lambda_3 a_1^3 + \lambda_7 a_1^7 \geq a_1^1$

(ii) $\qquad \lambda_3 a_2^3 + \lambda_7 a_2^7 \geq a_2^1$

(iii) $\qquad \lambda_3 \alpha_3^3 + \lambda_7 a_3^7 \geq a_3^1$

(iv) $\qquad \lambda_3 \alpha_4^3 + \lambda_7 a_4^7 \geq a_4^1$

and the positive orthant be nonempty. The geometric representation of these half-planes in Fig. 6.1 corroborates the existence of a nonempty intersection (the shaded area).

We could continue in the same way to show that activity 2 is not efficient. However, it suffices to point out that $6a^3 + a^7$ dominates $2a^2$.

What remains is the definition of the set of efficient points of Y.

Any combination of the form $\sum_{j=1}^{8} \lambda_j a^j$, with $\lambda_j > 0$ for at least one $j \neq 3$ and 7, cannot be efficient, since any activity $a_j (j \neq 3$ and 7) can be replaced by a positive linear combination of activities 3 and 7 that dominates it and thus allows us to obtain a vector of output that dominates the initial combination while still remaining in Y. Any efficient production vector is then of the form $\lambda_3 a^3 + \lambda_7 a^7$, with $\lambda_3 \geqslant 0$, $\lambda_7 \geqslant 0$.

Let Z be the set defined by

$$Z = \{y \,|\, y = \lambda_3 a^3 + \lambda_7 a^7, \lambda_3 \geqslant 0, \lambda_7 \geqslant 0\}.$$

The efficient set is included in Z. Therefore E is included in Z. We plan to show that Z is included in E, so that we can assert that the three sets E, Z, and the efficient set are identical. Accordingly, we look for a vector p with strictly positive coordinates p_1, p_2, p_3, p_4 such that

$$pa^3 = -p_1 - 2p_2 + 3p_3 - p_4 = 0$$

and $\qquad\qquad pa^7 = -8p_1 - 5p_2 + 10p_4 = 0.$

Setting $p_1 = p_2 = 1$ and solving the resulting linear system in p_3 and p_4, we find that $p_3 = 43/30$ and $p_4 = 13/10$.

For any $y \in Y$ there exists an efficient vector $\bar{y}$, which belongs to A, all the coordinates of which are greater than or equal to those of Y. Since $\bar{y} \in Z$, we have $p\bar{y} = 0$, where p is the strictly positive vector defined above. Therefore

$$\forall y \in Y, \qquad py \leqslant 0.$$

Any vector of Z then maximizes py on Y, and we have demonstrated that $Z \subset E$.

NOTE IN CONCLUSION that this property of the identity of set E and the set of efficient points of Y is always true when Y is a convex polyhedron, but

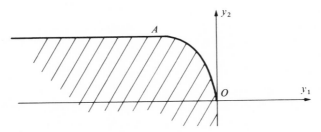

Figure 6.2

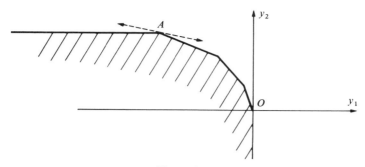

Figure 6.3

may no longer be true if Y is convex in some other way. Figs. 6.2 and 6.3 show this distinction concretely.

Arc OA corresponds to the set of efficient points in the shaded production set of Figs. 6.2 and 6.3. Point A is efficient, but only a system of prices in which $p_1 = 0$ allows us to obtain this point as a profit maximum in Fig. 6.2. On the contrary, in the case where Y is a convex polyhedron (Fig. 6.3), it is always possible to associate a strictly positive price vector with a point like A.

We have been able to treat in depth the problem at hand—that is, finding the efficient points of Y and their properties—using very simple methods, because of the particular numerical values given in the statement of the problem. A more generalized treatment requires the use of more complicated mathematical techniques, specifically linear programming. Attainment of the set of efficient points, which is assumed to be already solved when we are given a production function, may therefore necessitate solving first a relatively complicated optimization problem.

Suggested Readings

Debreu, Gerard. 1959. *Theory of Value: An Axiomatic Analysis of Economic Equilibrium,* chap. 3. New Haven: Yale University Press.

Dorfman, Robert, Samuelson, Paul A., and Solow, Robert M. 1958. *Linear Programming and Economic Analysis.* New York: McGraw-Hill.

Koopmans, Tjalling C., ed. 1951. *Activity Analysis of Production and Allocation: Proceedings of a Conference.* New York: John Wiley.

Koopmans, Tjalling C. 1975. *Three Essays on the State of Economic Science.* New York: McGraw-Hill.

Malinvaud, Edmond. 1972. *Lectures on Microeconomic Theory,* trans. A. Silvey, chap. 3. Amsterdam: North-Holland.

7

Cost Curves with an Indivisible Factor

A farm encompasses an area of 500 acres of land. The expected average annual production of wheat is given by

$$Q = KT^\alpha Z^\beta (X + HY)^\gamma,$$

where H and K are constants,

α, β, γ are constants and $\alpha + \beta + \gamma = 1$,

Q is the annual production of wheat (in hundreds of bushels),

T is the area allocated to the cultivation of wheat (in acres),

Z is the weight of fertilizer used (in tons),

X represents the hours of unskilled labor used during the year, and

Y represents the tractor-hours used during the year.

Moreover, we assume that the land can be used only for the production of wheat and nothing else.

Problem 1

Comment on the proposed production function. In particular, how would you interpret the coefficients α, β, γ, H?

Problem 2

As a first step in this problem, assume that tractors do not exist. Designate by x the price of an hour of unskilled labor and by z the price of a ton of fertilizer. If the land is already seeded with wheat ($T = 500$), determine the total variable cost curve.

Numerical example: $x = \$2$, $z = \$1000$, $\alpha = 1/2$, $\beta = 1/6$, $\gamma = 1/3$, $K = 6$. Under these conditions how much will be produced if the price per hundred bushels of wheat is \$30?

Problem 3

Retain the assumption that the land has been previously seeded with wheat, but assume that the enterprise can now rent tractors. The rental rate of one tractor for one year (including salaries of the required skilled personnel) represents an additional fixed charge of $15,000 per year for the enterprise. Each tractor can provide up to 2,500 hours of work during the year. Finally, studies have shown that one tractor does in 8 hours the equivalent of 125 hours of unskilled labor (so that $H = {}^{125}/_8$). Designate by y the price of a tractor-hour (essentially the fuel cost) and set $y = \$16$.

Without performing new calculations, construct the total variable cost curve for $Q \in [0; 15,000]$ when the enterprise uses only tractors to the exclusion of unskilled labor.

Problem 4

Assume that the enterprise has rented n tractors. Construct the total variable cost curve when for each level of output the enterprise combines inputs optimally—that is, chooses the best use of the n rented tractors and labor (for $Q \in [0; 15,000]$ and $n = 1, 2, 3,$ or 4).

Problem 5

For $Q \in [0; 15,000]$ construct the total variable cost curve when for each level of output the enterprise combines optimally tractors and labor (n becomes a parameter to be determined optimally for each level of output).

In this case what will be the optimum level of output when the sale price is $30 per hundred bushels?

PROPOSED SOLUTION

The purpose of this exercise is to study the cost curve in the case (frequently found in practice) where there is substitutability between two factors of production, but where at least one of these factors is indivisible (here the tractors). We should expect discontinuities in the marginal cost curve, so that we must compare local maxima to determine the enterprise's optimal policy.

This exercise is solved by applying the Kuhn-Tucker conditions. In the text of the solution we sometimes do not describe the economic significance of the calculations made, because this will be undertaken systematically in the solution of exercise 9.

We mention in passing the development of a particular mathematical programming technique known as integer programming, which aims for a more rapid solution of this type of problem, where indivisibilities are present.

Problem 1

The production function is homogeneous of degree one. The production set is therefore a cone and the assumption of constant returns holds. This function is the Cartesian product of concave functions (for example, $[X + HY]^\gamma$ is a concave function because $\gamma \leq 1$) and it is therefore quasi-concave. Homogeneity of degree one and quasi-concavity imply concavity (see exercise 3); hence, the production set is convex.

We consider $\Delta T/T$ as the rate of change of the area allocated to the cultivation of wheat. The rate of growth of output of wheat, considering first-order terms only, is then equal to $\Delta Q/Q = \alpha \, \Delta T/T$. The constant α is therefore interpreted as the output elasticity with respect to the area used. Similarly, β corresponds to the output elasticity with respect to the amount of fertilizer used, and γ is the output elasticity with respect to the combined number of tractor-hours and labor-hours used. The constant H is the marginal rate of substitution between the two variable factors, labor-hours and tractor-hours. We shall also call it the relative efficiency.

Problem 2

Since land is fixed, the only variables are X and Z. For a given output Q, it is necessary to minimize cost, which is equal to $xX + zZ$.

It is unnecessary to consider the nonnegativity constraints on the variables since, for a given positive Q, X and Z must be positive. The problem can then be written:

$$\min xX + zZ \quad \text{subject to} \quad KT^\alpha Z^\beta X^\gamma \geq Q.$$

We notice that for cost to be minimized the constraint is necessarily satisfied with equality, since the production function is strictly increasing with respect to each variable. Therefore there exists a $\lambda \geq 0$ such that, if the Lagrangian is given by $L = xX + zZ + \lambda(Q - K^\alpha Z^\beta X^\gamma)$, the gradient of L will equal 0 at the minimum.

This condition is sufficient as well, inasmuch as the Lagrangian is a convex function. To characterize X, Z, and λ we then have the following system:

$$\frac{\partial L}{\partial X} = x - \lambda \frac{\gamma Q}{X} = 0; \tag{1}$$

$$\frac{\partial L}{\partial Z} = z - \lambda \frac{\beta Q}{Z} = 0; \tag{2}$$

and

$$Q = KT^\alpha Z^\beta X^\gamma. \tag{3}$$

We calculate λ by substituting the values of X and Z obtained from Eqs. (1) and (2) into (3):

$$Q = KT^\alpha \left(\frac{BQ}{z}\right)^\beta \left(\frac{\gamma Q}{x}\right)^\gamma \lambda^{\beta+\gamma},$$

where

$$\lambda^{\beta+\gamma} = \frac{1}{KT^\alpha \left(\frac{\beta}{z}\right)^\beta \left(\frac{\gamma}{x}\right)^\gamma} Q^\alpha.$$

On the other hand, we derive from Eqs. (1) and (2) the minimum cost function:

$$C(Q) = xX + zZ = \lambda(\gamma + \beta)Q,$$

or

$$C(Q) = (\gamma + \beta) \left(\frac{x^\gamma z^\beta}{KT^\alpha \beta^\beta \gamma^\gamma}\right)^{\frac{1}{\beta+\gamma}} Q^{(1+\frac{\alpha}{\beta+\gamma})}.$$

For the values given in the numerical example $C(Q) = Q^2/600$. If the sale price of wheat is \$30 per hundred bushels, the chosen output is such that $dC/dQ = Q/300 = $ price of wheat $= \$30$. Therefore, $Q = 9,000$ bushels and $C(Q) = \$135,000$ (see Fig. 7.1).

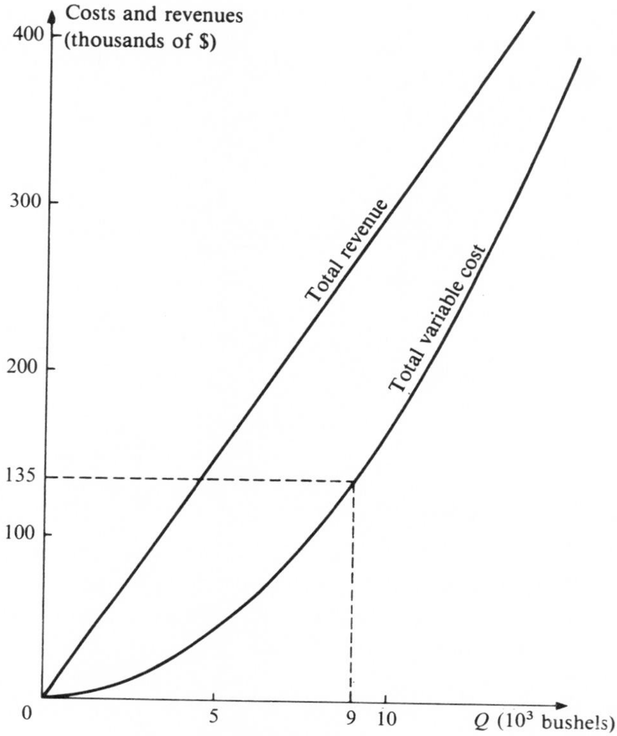

Figure 7.1

Problem 3

The problem is exactly the same as the one solved above: we look for

$$\min yY + zZ \quad \text{subject to} \quad KT^\alpha H^\gamma Z^\beta Y^\gamma \geq Q.$$

In the expression $C(Q)$ it is then sufficient to replace KT^α by $KT^\alpha H^\gamma$ and x by y.

$$C(Q) = (\gamma + \beta) \left(\frac{y^\gamma z^\beta}{KT^\alpha H^\gamma \beta^\beta \gamma^\gamma} \right)^{\frac{1}{\beta + \gamma}} Q^{(1 + \frac{\alpha}{\beta + \gamma})} = \frac{2Q^2}{1,875}.$$

When we use n tractors, the total cost is

$$C(Q, n) = n \times 15,000 + \frac{2Q^2}{1,875}.$$

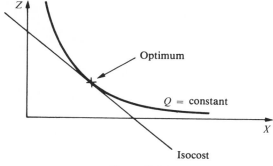

Figure 7.2

Problem 4

In the calculations above we did not have to take into account the non-negativity constraints on the variables. Indeed, in the case where only labor or tractors are used, the isoquants (in the quadrant XZ or YZ) are asymptotic to the axes, so that a cost minimum necessarily corresponds to a tangency between the isoquant and the isocost line (see Fig. 7.2). On the other hand, in the case where a tractor is used to its full capacity, the production function becomes

$$Q = KT^{\alpha}Z^{\beta}(X + H \times 2,500)^{\gamma}.$$

For such values of Q the isoquant cuts the X-axis and it is possible that the cost minimum occurs at a corner solution (Fig. 7.3). To search for the optimum, then, it is necessary to reintroduce the nonnegativity conditions on the variables.

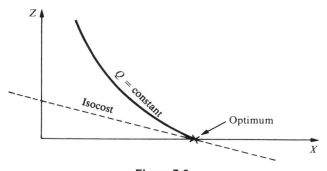

Figure 7.3

As a first step, assume that we have decided to rent n tractors and construct the cost curves corresponding to $n = 1, 2, 3, 4$. Later (in problem 5) we will compare the curves obtained in order to optimally combine tractors and labor.

The problem can be formalized in the following way: for Q and n given $(Q > 0)$, find the minimum of $xX + yY + zZ$ subject to the constraints

$$Q \leqslant 6(500)^{1/2} Z^{1/6} \left(X + \frac{125}{8} Y \right)^{1/3},$$

and $0 \leqslant Y \leqslant 2{,}500n,$ $X \geqslant 0,$ $Z \geqslant 0.$

By designating λ and μ as the dual variables, the Lagrangian is written

$$L = -(xX + yY + zZ) + \lambda \left[6(500)^{1/2} Z^{1/6} \left(X + \frac{125}{8} Y \right)^{1/3} - Q \right]$$

$$+ \mu(2{,}500n - Y).$$

Notice that $Q > 0$ implies that at the optimum $Z > 0$, which yields

$$\frac{\partial L}{\partial Z} = -z + \frac{\lambda Q}{6Z} = 0$$

and $X + HY > 0$ for the same reason. This limits to three the number of possible situations: (1) $X > 0$, $Y = 0$; (2) $X = 0$, $Y > 0$; or (3) $X > 0$, $Y > 0$.

Situation (1) cannot occur, because it would be necessary that we have simultaneously

$$X > 0 \Rightarrow \frac{\partial L}{\partial X} = 0 \quad \text{or} \quad -x + \frac{\lambda Q}{3(X + HY)} = 0,$$

and $\dfrac{\partial L}{\partial Y} \leqslant 0 \Leftrightarrow -y + \dfrac{1}{3} \dfrac{H\lambda Q}{(X + HY)} \leqslant 0.$

Taking into account the first condition, the second condition can be written

$$-y + Hx \leqslant 0 \quad \text{or} \quad -16 + \frac{125}{8} \times 2 \leqslant 0,$$

which cannot be true. Therefore, if we decide to rent a tractor, the optimal solution can never correspond to using only labor. At the optimum we will necessarily have

$$Q = 6(500)^{1/2} Z^{1/6} \left(X + \frac{125}{8} Y \right)^{1/3},$$

as in the preceding problems.

In summary, at the optimum the three following equations will necessarily hold:

$$-z + \frac{\lambda Q}{Z} = 0, \tag{4}$$

$$-y + \frac{\lambda H Q}{3(X + HY)} - \mu = 0, \tag{5}$$

and $$Q = 6(500)^{1/2} Z^{1/6} (X + HY)^{1/3}. \tag{6}$$

Thus only situations (2) and (3) are possible, so that four cases arise:

$$
\begin{array}{llll}
\text{a:} & X = 0, & Y < 2{,}500n, \\
\text{b:} & X > 0, & Y < 2{,}500n, \\
\text{c:} & X = 0, & Y = 2{,}500n, \\
\text{d:} & X > 0, & Y = 2{,}500n.
\end{array}
$$

Case b is impossible since

$$X > 0 \Rightarrow \frac{\partial L}{\partial X} = -x + \frac{\lambda Q}{3(X + HY)} = 0.$$

Taking Eq. (4) into account, we would have

$$8X + 125Y = 8{,}000Z.$$

On the other hand, taking Eq. (5) into account,

$$Y < 2{,}500n \Rightarrow \mu = 0 \Leftrightarrow 8X + 125Y = 5^6 Z.$$

This system has no solution except when $Z = 0$, a case that has already been eliminated.

Practically speaking, this indicates that we will never use unskilled labor if tractors are not operating at full capacity. Now let us examine each feasible case.

- Case a: $X = 0$, $Y < 2,500n$
  We must have

$$\mu = 0 \Leftrightarrow Y = 125Z. \tag{7}$$

Using Eq. (6), we obtain expressions for Y and Z as a function of Q:

$$Y = \frac{Q^2}{2^2 \times 3^2 \times 5^4}, \qquad Z = \frac{Q^2}{2^2 \times 3^2 \times 5^7}.$$

Total variable cost is written

$$C = yY + zZ = \frac{2Q^2}{1,875}.$$

On the one hand, this solution is valid for $\partial L/\partial X \leqslant 0 \Leftrightarrow 3xHY \geqslant Q\lambda$ or, taking Eq. (3) into account, $3xHY \geqslant 6zZ$, which always holds thanks to Eq. (7); but on the other hand, $Y < 2,500n$, which is equivalent to $Q < 7,500 \sqrt{n}$.

- Case c: $X = 0$, $Y = 2,500n$
  Only Z varies:

$$\text{Eqs. (4) and (6)} \Rightarrow Z = \frac{Q^6}{2^{10} \times 3^6 \times 5^{23}n^2}. \tag{8}$$

Variable cost is equal to $C = Q^6/2^7 \times 3^6 \times 5^{20}n^2$. On the one hand, this solution is valid if

$$\frac{\partial L}{\partial X} \leqslant 0 \Leftrightarrow xH \times 2,500 \, n \geqslant 2,000 \, Z,$$

or, taking Eq. (8) into account,

$$Q \leqslant 2 \times 3 \times 5^4 \sqrt{5n};$$

and, on the other hand,

$$\mu \geq 0 \Leftrightarrow \frac{125\ Z}{Y} \geq 1 \quad \text{or} \quad Q \geq 7{,}500\ \sqrt{n}.$$

• Case d: $X > 0$, $Y = 2{,}500\ n$

We have $\partial L/\partial X = 0$ or, taking Eq. (4) into account, $X + HY = 1{,}000\ Z$ which, from Eq. (6), yields

$$Z = \frac{Q^2}{2^6 \times 3^2 \times 5^5}, \qquad X = \frac{Q^2}{2^3 \times 3^2 \times 5^2} - \frac{5^7\ n}{2}.$$

Then variable cost is

$$C = \frac{Q^2}{2^3 \times 3 \times 5^2} + 5^4\ n(2^6 - 5^3).$$

On the one hand, this solution is valid for

$$X > 0 \Rightarrow Q > 2 \times 3 \times 5^4\ \sqrt{5\ n};$$

on the other hand:

$$\mu \geq 0 \Leftrightarrow 5^6\ Z \geq 8\ X + 125\ Y,$$

so that $5^6\ Z > 8{,}000\ Z$, which always holds.

Summary of results. By considering total variable cost as a function of n, denoted $C(n)$ for a given n, we can derive Table 7.1. It is evident that the total variable cost functions defined in this way are continuous. Similarly,

Case	$Q \in$	Variable cost	Total variable cost
a	$(0, 7{,}500\ \sqrt{n})$	$\dfrac{2\ Q^2}{1{,}875}$	$15{,}000\ n + \dfrac{2\ Q^2}{1{,}875}$
c	$(7{,}500\ \sqrt{n}, 2 \times 3 \times 5^4\ \sqrt{5\ n})$	$\dfrac{Q^6}{2^7 \times 3^6 \times 5^{20}\ n^2}$	$55{,}000\ n + 2^7 \times 3^6 \times 5^{20}\ n^2$
d	$(2 \times 3 \times 5^4\ \sqrt{5n}, +\infty)$	$\dfrac{Q^2}{600} - 61 \times 5^4\ n$	$\dfrac{Q^2}{600} - 37 \times 5^4\ n$

Table 7.1

we can verify from the table that the marginal cost functions are continuous for n fixed.

Problem 5

Until now, we have considered n fixed. The next problem is to determine, for a given level of output Q, the optimal number of tractors to be used. For this purpose n becomes a decision variable and we must relate the curves $C(n)$ to one another for different values of n.

- Case a

It can be shown that for $n = 1, 2, 3, 4$ and for $Q \leq 2 \times 3 \times 5^4 \sqrt{5} \, n$, we have $C(n) < C(n + 1)$. We know that

$$0 \leq Q \leq 7,500 \sqrt{n} \Rightarrow C(n) = 15,000 \, n + \frac{2Q^2}{1,875}$$

and $7,500 \sqrt{n} \leq Q \leq 2 \times 3 \times 5^4 \sqrt{5} \, n \Rightarrow C(n) = 55,000 \, n$

$$+ \frac{Q^6}{2^7 \times 3^6 \times 5^{20} n^2} .$$

On the other hand, we see immediately that, for $n = 1, 2, 3, 4$, we have

$$2 \times 3 \times 5^4 \sqrt{5} \, n \leq 7,500 \sqrt{n + 1}.$$

Therefore, for $Q \leq 2 \times 3 \times 5^4 \sqrt{5} \, n$,

$$C(n + 1) = 15,000(n + 1) + \frac{2Q^2}{1,875}.$$

Consequently, we must show that for

$$Q \in [2 \times 3 \times 5^4 \sqrt{5} \, n, \, 7,500 \sqrt{n}],$$

we have

$$55,000 \, n + \frac{Q^6}{2^7 \times 3^6 \times 5^{20} \, n^2} < 15,000(n + 1) + \frac{2Q^2}{1,875}.$$

Let $Q^2 = u$. Then we must show that the following holds over the interval $[2^2 \times 3^2 \times 5^9 n, 2^4 \times 3^2 \times 5^8(n + 1)]$:

$$g(u) = \frac{u^3}{2^7 \times 3^6 \times 5^{20} n^2} - \frac{2u}{1{,}875} + 40{,}000 \, n - 15{,}000 < 0.$$

However,

$$g'(u) = \frac{3u^2}{2^7 \times 3^6 \times 5^{20} n^2} - \frac{2}{3 \times 5^4}$$

vanishes for $u = 2^4 \times 3^2 \times 5^8 n < 2^2 \times 3^2 \times 5^9 n$. Therefore $g(u)$ is an increasing function of u over the interval considered. Then it is sufficient to show that $g[2^4 \times 3^2 \times 5^8(n + 1)] < 0$. As we can easily see, this holds for $n = 1, 2, 3, 4$.

- Case b

It can be shown that for $n = 1, 2, 3, 4$ and for $Q \geqslant 7{,}500 \sqrt{n + 1}$, we have $C(n) > C(n + 1)$. Now,

$$7{,}500 \sqrt{n + 1} \leqslant Q \leqslant 2 \times 3 \times 5^4 \sqrt{5(n + 1)} \Rightarrow C(n + 1)$$

$$= 55{,}000(n + 1) + \frac{Q^6}{2^7 \times 3^6 \times 5^{20}(n + 1)^2},$$

$$Q \geqslant 2 \times 3 \times 5^4 \sqrt{5(n + 1)} \Rightarrow C(n + 1) = \frac{Q^2}{600} - 37 \times 5^4(n + 1).$$

As we have already seen, since $7{,}500 \sqrt{n + 1} \geqslant 2 \times 3 \times 5^4 \sqrt{5n}$ for $Q \geqslant 7{,}500 \sqrt{n + 1}$, we will have $C_n = Q^2/600 - 37 \times 5^4 \times n$. Then it remains to show that we have the following if Q belongs to the interval $[7{,}500\sqrt{n + 1}, 2 \times 3 \times 5^4 \sqrt{5(n + 1)}]$:

$$\frac{Q^2}{600} - 37 \times 5^4 n > 55{,}000(n + 1) + \frac{Q^6}{2^7 \times 3^6 \times 5^{20}(n + 1)^2}.$$

As before, let $Q^2 = u$. We must show that the following holds if $u \in [2^4 \times 3^2 \times 5^8(n + 1), 2^2 \times 3^2 \times 5^9(n + 1)]$:

$$h(u) = \frac{u^3}{2^7 \times 3^6 \times 5^{20}(n+1)^2} - \frac{u}{2^3 \times 3 \times 5^2}$$
$$+ 55{,}000(n+1) + 37 \times 5^4 n < 0.$$

However,

$$h'(u) = \frac{3u^2}{2^7 \times 3^6 \times 5^{20}(n+1)^2} - \frac{1}{2^3 \times 3 \times 5^2}$$

vanishes for $u = 2^2 \times 3^2 \times 5^9(n+1)$.

The function $h(u)$ is therefore decreasing over the considered interval. It is sufficient to show that $h[2^4 \times 3^2 \times 5^8(n+1)] < 0$. As we can easily see, this is satisfied for $n = 1, 2, 3, 4$.

● Case c

It can be shown that $C(n)$ and $C(n+1)$ for $n = 1, 2, 3, 4$ have one and only one point of intersection over the following interval: $[2 \times 3 \times 5^4 \sqrt{5n}, 7{,}500 \sqrt{n+1}]$. This point of intersection is obtained directly as the positive root of the equation:

$$\frac{q^2}{600} - 37 \times 5^4 n = 15{,}000(n+1) + \frac{2Q^2}{1{,}875},$$

that is, where

$$Q = \frac{5^4 \times 2}{3} \sqrt{6} \sqrt{61n + 24}.$$

Table 7.2, to be used in conjunction with Fig. 7.4, lists the principal values of the total cost curve with the optimal production technique for each interval.

The total cost curve drawn in Fig. 7.5 is easily derived from Table 7.2 as the envelope of the curves in Fig. 7.4. Points A, B, C, and D correspond to the intersection points of curves $C(n)$ for varying n and have for an abscissa $Q = [(5^4 \times 2)/3] \sqrt{6} \sqrt{61n + 24}$.

The marginal cost curve is drawn in Fig. 7.6. This curve is discontinuous at the points which have the same abscissas as A, B, C, and D. The points corresponding to optimal output are found at the intersection of the marginal cost curve and the horizontal line indicating the price per bushel,

Value of Q	Numerical value of Q	Value of C	Production technique in interval
0	0	0	
			Labor only
$\dfrac{5^4 \times 2}{3}\sqrt{6}\sqrt{(61 \times 0) + 24}$	5,000	41,666	
			1 tractor without labor
$7,500\sqrt{1}$	7,500	75,000	
			1 tractor without labor
$2 \times 3 \times 5^4 \sqrt{5 \times 1}$	8,385	94,062	
			1 tractor with labor
$\dfrac{5^4 \times 2}{3}\sqrt{6}\sqrt{(61 \times 1) + 24}$	9,410	124,443	
			2 tractors without labor
$7,500\sqrt{2}$	10,610	150,000	
			2 tractors without labor
$2 \times 3 \times 5^4 \sqrt{5 \times 2}$	11,858	188,125	
			2 tractors with labor
$\dfrac{5^4 \times 2}{3}\sqrt{6}\sqrt{(61 \times 2) + 24}$	12,247	207,212	
			3 tractors without labor
$7,500\sqrt{3}$	13,000	225,000	
			3 tractors without labor
$2 \times 3 \times 5^4 \sqrt{5 \times 3}$	14,523	282,187	
			3 tractors with labor
$\dfrac{5^4 \times 2}{3}\sqrt{6}\sqrt{(61 \times 3) + 24}$	14,610	290,000	
			4 tractors
$7,500\sqrt{4}$	15,000	300,000	

Table 7.2

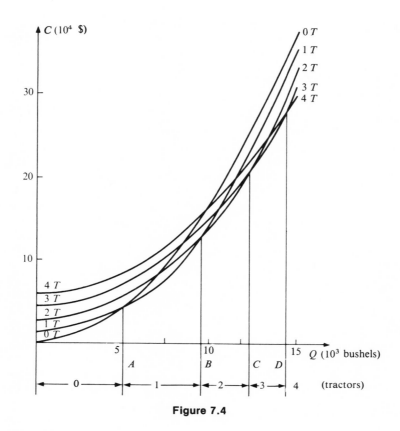

Figure 7.4

that is, at \$30 per hundred bushels. There are five such intersection points: E, F, G, K, and L.

Moreover, an optimum point has the following property: if in the neighborhood of the optimum we increase output slightly, marginal cost exceeds marginal revenue (here the sale price of wheat); on the contrary, if we reduce output a bit, marginal revenue exceeds marginal cost.

In summary, there will be an optimum only if to the right of such a point we have $p < dC/dQ$ and to the left $p > dC/dQ$ (mathematically this is equivalent to saying that every optimum corresponds to a local profit maximum). These considerations lead us to retain as possible optimal points only points E, F, and G. Point E corresponds to using one tractor at full capacity in addition to using unskilled labor. This is the optimum for the second problem. The associated output level satisfies $Q_E/300 = 30$, therefore $Q_E = 9,000$ bushels. Point F corresponds to using two tractors

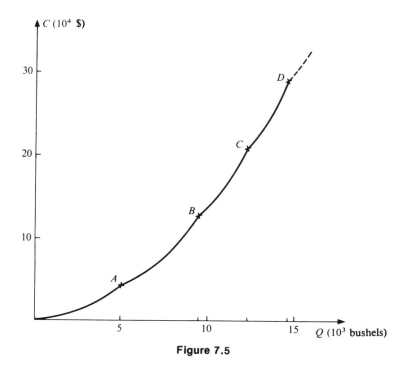

Figure 7.5

at full capacity without any unskilled labor. The associated output level satisfies

$$\frac{6Q^5}{2^7 \times 3^6 \times 5^{20}(2)^2} = 30 \quad \text{or} \quad Q_F = 5^4 \times 3 \times 2^2 \sqrt[5]{\frac{3 \times 5}{2}},$$

or $Q_F \simeq 11{,}220$ bushels. Point G corresponds to using three tractors at full capacity without unskilled labor. The associated level of output satisfies

$$\frac{6Q^5}{2^7 \times 3^6 \times 5^{20}(3)^2} = 30 \quad \text{or} \quad Q_G = 5^4 \times 3 \times 2 \sqrt[5]{20 \times 27},$$

so that $Q_G \simeq 13{,}200$ bushels.

To choose among E, F, and G, that is to define the global maximum from among the local maxima, it is necessary to compute explicitly the profit corresponding to each of the chosen outputs. The results are given in Table 7.3. The best solution proves to be the one that uses two tractors

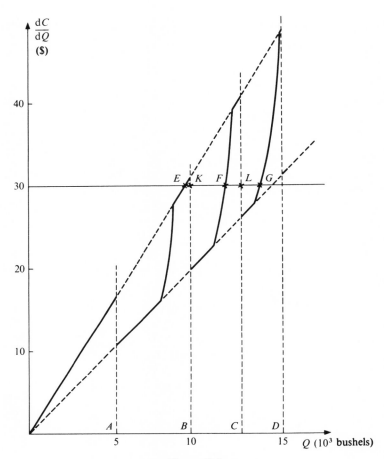

Figure 7.6

Point	Output (in bushels)	Expression for profit	Result (in dollars)
E	9,000	$30 \times 9,000 - \dfrac{(9,000)^2}{600} + 37 \times 5^4$	158,125
F	11,220	$30 \times 11,220 - \dfrac{(11,220)^6}{2^7 \times 3^6 \times 5^{20} \times 2^2} - 110,000$	170,500
G	13,200	$30 \times 13,200 - \dfrac{(13,200)^6}{2^7 \times 3^6 \times 5^{20} \times 3^2} - 165,000$	165,000

Table 7.3

full time and no unskilled labor. This corresponds to an output of approximately 11,220 bushels.

Suggested Readings

Luenberger, David G. 1969. *Optimization by Vector Space Methods*. New York: John Wiley.

Nadiri, Ishaq. 1982. "Producers' Theory." In *Handbook of Mathematical Economics*, Vol. 2, ed. Kenneth J. Arrow and Michael D. Intriligator. Amsterdam: North-Holland.

Shephard, Ronald. 1970. *Theory of Cost and Production Functions*. Princeton, N.J.: Princeton University Press.

Price Decentralization

This exercise treats several properties of convex production sets and of their dual cones, and considers the properties of a possible aggregation procedure for production functions. As a tool, we state without proving the following two properties:

(1) Let $Y \subset \mathbb{R}^n$ be a closed, convex set. To each boundary point y^* of Y we can associate a nonzero vector $p \in \mathbb{R}^n$ such that $py \leq py^*$, $\forall y \in Y$. This result is known as the separating hyperplane theorem (or Minkowski's theorem).

(2) Let $Y_1, \ldots, Y_m$ be m convex, closed subsets of $\mathbb{R}^n$. Let

$$Y = \sum_{j=1}^{m} Y_j = \left\{ y \mid y = \sum_{j=1}^{m} y_j, y_j \in Y_j \right\}.$$

If $Y \cap \{-Y\} = \{0\}$ (known in the literature as the assumption of irreversibility), Y is closed.

Problem 1

Let $Y_1, \ldots, Y_m$ be m subsets of $\mathbb{R}^n$, with $Y = \Sigma_{j=1}^{m} Y_j$, and p be an element of $\mathbb{R}^n$. Show the following property:

(3) Let $\hat{y}_1, \ldots, \hat{y}_m$ be points of $Y_1, \ldots, Y_m$ respectively, with $\hat{y} = \Sigma_{j=1}^{m} \hat{y}_j$. We have $\forall y \in Y$, $py \leq p\hat{y}$ if and only if for all $j \in \{1, \ldots, m\}$ $\forall y_j \in Y_j$, $py_j \leq p\hat{y}_j$.

Problem 2

Let $Y \subset \mathbb{R}^n$ be closed, convex, and different from $\mathbb{R}^n$. Let $\theta(Y)$ be the set of $p \in \mathbb{R}^n$ such that the linear functional py attains its maximum on Y.

Show that $\theta(Y)$ is a nontrivial cone. Under the same assumptions prove the following property:

(4) If to all p which belongs to $\theta(Y)$ we associate the set $A(p) = \{y|py \leq \max pu, u \in Y\}$, and furthermore if we define the set $\Phi(Y) = \cap_{p \in \theta(Y)} A(p)$, then $\Phi = Y$.

Problem 3

Let Y_1 and $Y_2 \subset \mathbb{R}^n$ be closed and convex. Let $\theta_1 = \theta(Y_1)$, $\theta_2 = \theta(Y_2)$, and $Y = Y_1 + Y_2$, and define $A(p)$ as above. Show that if Y satisfies the irreversibility assumption of property (2) and if the origin is feasible, we have $Y = \cap_{p \in \theta_1 \cap \theta_2} A(p)$.

Problem 4

Use the results above to characterize as a function of the price parameters the equation of the set of efficient points of the aggregate production set formed from the two production sets defined by

$$y_1 \leq (-y_2)^{1/2}(-y_3)^{1/4}, \qquad y_2 \leq 0, \qquad y_3 \leq 0;$$

and
$$y_1 \leq (-y_2)^{1/4}(-y_3)^{1/2}, \qquad y_2 \leq 0, \qquad y_3 \leq 0.$$

IN THIS EXERCISE we point out the general properties of the operation of aggregating sets. These properties allow us to define the sum of closed convex sets in a tangential way, while at the same time a decentralized procedure for determining the boundary of the aggregate set emerges. In exercise 9 we shall establish a link between determining an optimal allocation by applying Kuhn-Tucker conditions and using classical economic reasoning based on the comparison of marginal products.

Notice that the method used in exercise 9 (maximizing the unique output for fixed quantities of the inputs) may yield not only the efficient points but also , in certain cases, some nonefficient points of the aggregate set. Figure 8.1 illustrates this possibility.

There are two goods, input y_1 and output y_2. The production set is shaded. The set of efficient points corresponds to arc OA. Maximizing y_2 for $y_1 = y_1^0$ yields point B, which is not efficient. However, such a difficulty does not arise in exercise 9, because output is always a strictly increasing function of the quantities of each input.

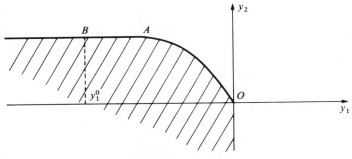

Figure 8.1

PROPOSED SOLUTION

Problem 1

First of all, we show that if $\hat{y}$ maximizes py over Y and if $\hat{y} = \Sigma_{j=1}^{m} \hat{y}_j$, with $\forall j$, $\hat{y}_j \in Y_j$, then $\forall j$, $\hat{y}_j$ maximizes py_j over Y_j. Indeed, if this were not the case, there would exist an index $h \in \{1, \ldots, m\}$ and an element $\bar{y}_h \in Y_h$ such that $p\bar{y}_h > p\hat{y}_h$. Then the element $\bar{y}$ of Y defined by $\bar{y} = \Sigma_{j \neq h} \hat{y}_j + \bar{y}_h$ would satisfy

$$p\bar{y} = \sum_{j \neq h} p\hat{y}_j + p\bar{y}_h > p\hat{y},$$

which would contradict the hypothesis.

We continue by showing that if $\forall j$, $\hat{y}_j \in Y_j$ maximizes py_j over Y_j, then $\hat{y} = \Sigma_j \hat{y}_j$ maximizes py over Y. Consider any arbitrary element of Y: $y = \Sigma_{j=1}^{m} y_j$.

Then

$$p(\hat{y} - y) = \sum_{j=1}^{m} p(\hat{y}_j - y_j).$$

Since, by hypothesis, $p(\hat{y}_j - y_j) \geq 0\ \forall j$, we have $p(\hat{y} - y) \geq 0$, which completes the proof.

This property, which is so easy to show, provides a foundation for the theory of decentralization using prices. Here is an example to help us understand it.

Assume that we know how to associate a price vector with any economic situation that is determined to be optimal, such that the aggregate net output corresponding to this situation maximizes the total value of output calculated by applying this price vector to the set of all possible outputs. Property (3), demonstrated above, ensures that optimal total output is achieved by the following procedure of decentralization: announce a system of prices associated with an optimal production program, and instruct each basic production unit to maximize its own profit taking into account this system of fixed prices. This property can be applied if we assume that the aggregate production set is the sum of the basic production sets, that is, if we rule out external economies.

Problem 2

The set $\theta(Y)$ is obviously a cone, since if $p \in \theta(Y)$, any linear functional $\lambda p y$ where λ is a nonnegative scalar achieves its maximum over Y. On the other hand, if Y is closed and different from $\mathbb{R}^n$, there exists at least one boundary point, $\bar{y}$. By the separating hyperplane theorem we can associate with $\bar{y}$ a nonzero vector $p \in \mathbb{R}^n$ such that $\bar{y}$ maximizes py over Y, inasmuch as Y is convex. This allows us to show the existence of at least one element of $\theta(Y)$ that is different from the origin, and $\theta(Y)$ is nontrivial.

To demonstrate property (4), notice that $A(p)$ contains Y, therefore $\Phi \supset Y$. We then show that $Y \supset \Phi$. If this were not the case, there would exist $\bar{y} \in \Phi$, which would not belong to Y. The fact that $\bar{y}$ does not belong to Y allows us to demonstrate the existence of a separating hyperplane

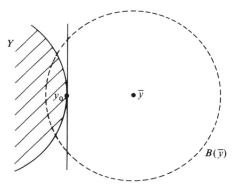

Figure 8.2

such that $\bar{y}$ is found strictly above this separating hyperplane of Y. The existence of such a separating hyperplane, which is shown below, contradicts the fact that $\bar{y}$ belongs to Φ; consequently we must have $Y = \Phi$.

To complete the proof, suppose that $\bar{y}$ does not belong to Y. Let $B(\bar{y})$ be a closed ball (Fig. 8.2) whose center is $\bar{y}$, where $B(\bar{y})$ intersects Y. The nonempty set $Y \cap B(\bar{y})$ is compact because $B(\bar{y})$ is compact and Y is closed. The continuous function $\|\bar{y} - y\|$ therefore attains its minimum on this set at a point y_0. Since $y_0 \in Y$, we have $\|\bar{y} - y_0\| > 0$.

We now show that the linear functional $(\bar{y} - y_0)y$ attains its maximum over Y at y_0. Let y be any arbitrary element of Y.

Let $a = (\bar{y} - y_0)y - (\bar{y} - y_0)y_0$, and assume that $a > 0$. Let t be a scalar such that $0 < t < 1$. The element $(1 - t)y_0 + ty$ belongs to Y, inasmuch as Y is convex. The distance between this element and point $\bar{y}$ is calculated as

$$\|(1 - t)y_0 + ty - \bar{y}\|^2 = \|\bar{y} - y_0\|^2 - 2t(1 - t)a + t^2[\|\bar{y} - y\|^2 - \|\bar{y} - y_0\|^2].$$

Since a is strictly positive, it is possible to choose t in such a way that

$$\frac{t}{1 - t}[\|\bar{y} - y\|^2 - \|\bar{y} - y_0\|^2] < 2\,a.$$

Then we have

$$\|(1 - t)y_0 + ty - \bar{y}\|^2 - \|y_0 - \bar{y}\|^2 < 0,$$

which contradicts the fact that y_0 minimizes the distance to $\bar{y}$ over Y.

Therefore the vector $\bar{y} - y_0$ belongs to $\theta(Y)$. The maximum of $(\bar{y} - y_0)y$ over Y is equal to $(\bar{y} - y_0)y_0$. However,

$$(\bar{y} - y_0)\bar{y} - (\bar{y} - y_0)y_0 = \|\bar{y} - y_0\|^2 > 0.$$

Consequently $\bar{y}$ cannot belong to Φ.

This property allows us to give a tangential definition of any closed convex set as the intersection of the half-spaces that are defined by its supporting hyperplanes and in which it is contained.

Problem 3

Because Y is the sum of convex sets, it is itself convex. The assumption of irreversibility can be written as $Y \cap \{-Y\} \subset \{0\}$, and since the origin belongs to Y because the zero activity is feasible, the conditions for applying property (2) are satisfied and Y is closed. Still, because of irreversibility, Y is different from $\mathbb{R}^n$. Therefore $\theta(Y)$ is a nontrivial cone and $Y = \cap_{p \in \theta(Y)} A(p)$.

It is sufficient to show that $\theta(Y) = \theta_1 \cap \theta_2$, which follows directly from property (4). Indeed, by this property all $p \in \theta(Y)$ belongs to θ_1 and to θ_2 and vice versa. Therefore we can write $Y = \cap_{p \in \theta_1 \cap \theta_2} A(p)$.

This property, which can be easily generalized to the sum of n closed convex sets, is the fundamental result of this exercise. Indeed, it allows a decentralized search for the boundary of the aggregate set Y since, on the one hand, determination of a boundary point of Y is achieved from maximizing the linear functional py over each basic production set (where p belongs to the intersection of the dual cones of the basic production sets) and, on the other hand, we know that in this way all the boundary points of Y are obtained. The direct characterization of the aggregate set Y by a central agent requires that this agent know each basic production set and make the often difficult analytical computation of the aggregate set (exercise 9 gives an example of such a computation). In the decentralized procedure, however, the central agent needs to know only the dual cones and then calculate their intersection, which is generally more simple. Moreover, for practical economic calculation, only a part of this intersection (which is defined a priori as a neighborhood of the market prices) may be of interest to the central agent.

Problem 4

The dual cones of the two production sets are identical and consist of the set of vectors with components p_1, p_2, p_3 such that $p_1 \geqslant 0$, $p_2 > 0$, $p_3 > 0$—to which it is convenient to add the origin. This dual cone is then also the dual cone of the aggregate set. The origin in output space corresponds to the section of this dual cone made up of the face $p_1 = 0$, $p_2 > 0$, $p_3 > 0$. The set of vectors $p_1 > 0$, $p_2 > 0$, $p_3 > 0$ then allows us to characterize all the other boundary points. We notice that all these boundary points, determined by maximizing a linear functional py, where p has strictly positive components, are efficient; compare for example, the proof of (b) in problem 2 of exercise 6. Since any linear functional is defined only up to a positive scalar multiple, we can set $p_1 = 1$. Maximization of $y_1 + p_2 y_2 + p_3 y_3$ over the closed convex set

$$y_1 \leq (-y_2)^{1/2}(-y_3)^{1/4}, \qquad y_2 \leq 0, \qquad y_3 \leq 0$$

yields the unique point

$$y_1 = \frac{1}{16p_2^2 p_3}, \qquad y_2 = -\frac{1}{32p_2^3 p_3}, \qquad y_3 = -\left(\frac{1}{8p_2 p_3}\right)^2.$$

Similarly, maximization of $y_1 + p_2 y_2 + p_3 y_3$ over the closed convex set

$$y_1 \leq (-y_2)^{1/4}(-y_3)^{1/2}, \qquad y_2 \leq 0, \qquad y_3 \leq 0$$

yields the unique point

$$y_1 = \frac{1}{16p_2 p_3^2}, \qquad y_2 = -\left(\frac{1}{8p_2 p_3}\right)^2, \qquad y_3 = -\frac{1}{32p_2 p_3^3}.$$

The set of efficient points of the aggregate set is therefore characterized, sufficiently close to the origin, as a function of strictly positive parameters p_2 and p_3 by

$$y_1 = \frac{1}{16p_2 p_3^2} + \frac{1}{16p_3 p_2^2}, \qquad y_2 = -\left(\frac{1}{8p_2 p_3}\right)^2 - \frac{1}{32p_2^3 p_3},$$

$$y_3 = -\frac{1}{32p_2 p_3^3} - \left(\frac{1}{8p_2 p_3}\right)^2.$$

In conclusion it is useful to give an example that indicates the importance of the assumption of convexity in everything above. In the space

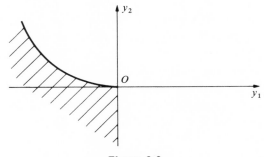

Figure 8.3

$\{y_1Oy_2\}$ let the production set be defined by $y_2 \leq (-y_1)^2$, $y_1 \leq 0$, which is represented by the shaded area in Fig. 8.3. The dual cone of this production set is reduced to the half-axis Oy_1. Maximizing the only linear functional that corresponds to this dual cone yields the origin and nothing but the origin.

Suggested Readings

Debreu, Gerard. 1959. *Theory of Value: An Axiomatic Analysis of Economic Equilibrium,* chap. 4. New Haven: Yale University Press.

Fisher, Frank. 1969. "Existence of Aggregate Production Functions." *Econometrica* 37: 553–577.

Hadley, George. 1961. *Linear Algebra,* chap. 6. Reading, Mass.: Addison-Wesley.

Koopmans, Tjalling C., ed., 1951. *Activity Analysis of Production and Allocation: Proceedings of a Conference.* New York: John Wiley.

Malinvaud, Edmond. 1972. *Lectures on Microeconomic Theory,* trans. A. Silvey, chap. 4. Amsterdam: North-Holland.

Nikaido, Hukukane. 1968. *Convex Structures and Economic Theory.* New York: Academic Press.

Takayama, Akira. 1974. *Mathematical Economics.* Hinsdale, Ill.: Dryden Press.

Aggregation of Production Sets

Consider an enterprise that produces good Z by using factors X and Y. This enterprise is composed of two plants, 1 and 2. Plant 1 produces quantity z_1 of good Z by using quantities x_1 and y_1 of the factors X and Y. The technical capabilities of plant 1 are limited by the following constraints (unlike exercises 6 and 8, we adopt here the convention that inputs are positive):

$$z_1 \leq (x_1 + 1)^{1/2}(y_1 + 1)^{1/2} - 1, \qquad x_1 \geq 0, \qquad y_1 \geq 0.$$

On the contrary, for plant 2 there is strict complementarity between the two factors; in other words,

$$z_2 \leq \min \{2x_2, 2y_2\}, \qquad x_2 \geq 0, \qquad y_2 \geq 0.$$

Problem 1

The enterprise is endowed with quantities $\bar{x}$ and $\bar{y}$ of the factors X and Y and allocates these factors to the two plants in order to maximize its production of good Z. Determine the optimal allocation between the two plants as a function of total resources $\bar{x}$ and $\bar{y}$. Derive the aggregate production function for the enterprise and show that it is continuous. (Because of the symmetry of this problem, we shall limit our consideration to the case where $\bar{y} \geq \bar{x} > 0$.)

We can use either the Kuhn-Tucker conditions expressed in the variables x_1, y_1, and x_2 only, or an argument based on the comparison of marginal products when $\bar{y}$ varies from $\bar{x}$ to infinity.

Problem 2

Assume that the enterprise has quantities $\bar{x} = 1$ and $\bar{y} = 2$ of the factors of production at its disposal. Moreover, it can buy unlimited quantities of goods X and Y at the prices $p_x = 5$ and $p_y = {}^1\!/_{10}$, but it cannot sell any of these. Finally, it can sell unlimited quantities of good Z at a price $p_z = 1$.

Characterize the profit maximum for the enterprise. What is the consequence of the assumed factor market imperfections?

PROPOSED SOLUTION

Problem 1

The optimal allocation of resources between the two plants is achieved by solving the following problem:

$$\max z_1 + z_2$$

subject to $z_1 \leq (x_1 + 1)^{1/2}(y_1 + 1)^{1/2} - 1, \qquad x_1 \geq 0, \quad y_1 \geq 0;$ (1)

$$z_2 \leq \min \{2x_2, 2y_2\}, \qquad x_2 \geq 0, \qquad y_2 \geq 0;$$ (2)

$$x_1 + x_2 \leq \bar{x};$$ (3)

and $y_1 + y_2 \leq \bar{y}.$ (4)

Presented in this fashion, the problem cannot be solved using classical methods—because the function $\min \{2x_2, 2y_2\}$ is not differentiable. In fact, in searching for the maximum, we can always revert to the case where $y_2 = x_2$. For example, in the case where $y_2 > x_2$ it is possible to transfer the quantity $y_2 - x_2$ of good Y from plant 1 to plant 2 without reducing aggregate output.

If we draw a box diagram (Fig. 9.1) in which the opposing axes correspond to the respective inputs of the two plants, we see clearly that $y_2 = x_2$ if an allocation is optimal.

Consider a point like M and draw the isoquants for the two plants that pass through this point (see the dotted isoquants). Obviously point B corresponds to an allocation which yields more aggregate output than that corresponding to point M. Therefore an optimal allocation must correspond to a point on the segment O_2A. Depending on the respective values of $\bar{y}$ and $\bar{x}$ (the dimensions of the box), the optimal allocation will be found either along the interior of this segment or at one of its extremities. Constraint (2) above then becomes

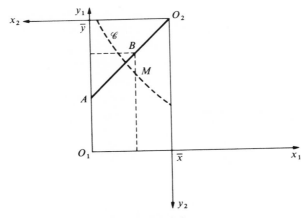

Figure 9.1

$$z_2 \leq 2x_2 \tag{2}$$

and wherever it occurs we can replace the variable y_2 by the variable x_2.

Presented in this way, the problem can be solved by applying the Kuhn-Tucker conditions, and a few preliminary remarks will greatly simplify the solution.

To begin with, since the function to be maximized is strictly increasing, constraints (1) and (2) above will necessarily be satisfied with equality at the maximum. The function to be maximized is concave because it is linear. The set characterized by constraint (1) is a convex cone whose vertex is given by $x_1 = -1$, $y_1 = -1$, and $z_1 = -1$. Since all the other constraints are linear, the set over which we seek the maximum of $z_1 + z_2$ is convex. Therefore the Kuhn-Tucker conditions will be necessary and sufficient.

Taking into account the preceding remarks, we can write the problem in the following form:

$$\max (x_1 + 1)^{1/2}(y_1 + 1)^{1/2} - 1 + 2x_2$$

subject to $\qquad\qquad x_1 + x_2 \leq \bar{x},$ $\qquad\qquad$ (3)

$$y_1 + x_2 \leq \bar{y} \tag{4}$$

for $\qquad\qquad x_1 \geq 0, \qquad y_1 \geq 0, \qquad x_2 \geq 0.$

The Lagrangian is written

$$L = (x_1 + 1)^{1/2}(y_1 + 1)^{1/2} - 1 + 2x_2 + \lambda(\bar{x} - x_1 - x_2) + \mu(\bar{y} - y_1 - x_2).$$

Since the function to be maximized is strictly increasing with respect to each of its arguments, constraints (3) and (4) will necessarily be binding in an optimal allocation. The Kuhn-Tucker conditions are written:

$$\frac{\partial L}{\partial x_1} \leq 0, \quad \text{with} \quad x_1 \frac{\partial L}{\partial x_1} = 0;$$

$$\frac{\partial L}{\partial y_1} \leq 0, \quad \text{with} \quad y_1 \frac{\partial L}{\partial y_1} = 0;$$

and
$$\frac{\partial L}{\partial x_2} \leq 0, \quad \text{with} \quad x_2 \frac{\partial L}{\partial x_2} = 0.$$

In principle, there are eight different cases to consider. Because of the symmetry of the problem, we shall analyze only the cases consistent with levels of total resources satisfying $\bar{y} \geq \bar{x} > 0$. What are these cases? The following are obviously ruled out:

$$x_1 = y_1 = x_2 = 0;$$

$$x_1 = x_2 = 0, \qquad \frac{\partial L}{\partial y_1} = 0;$$

and
$$y_1 = 0, \qquad x_2 = 0, \qquad \frac{\partial L}{\partial x_1} = 0.$$

The case where $y_1 = 0$, $x_1 > 0$, $x_2 > 0$—that is, $y_1 = 0$, $\partial L/\partial x_1 = 0$, $\partial L/\partial x_2 = 0$—is also inconsistent with $\bar{y} \geq \bar{x} > 0$.

Then only four cases are left to be analyzed:

$$\text{Case 1:} \quad x_1 = y_1 = 0, \qquad \frac{\partial L}{\partial x_2} = 0;$$

$$\text{Case 2:} \quad x_1 = 0, \qquad \frac{\partial L}{\partial y_1} = 0, \qquad \frac{\partial L}{\partial x_2} = 0;$$

Case 3: $\dfrac{\partial L}{\partial x_1} = 0,$ $\dfrac{\partial L}{\partial y_1} = 0,$ $\dfrac{\partial L}{\partial x_2} = 0;$

Case 4: $\dfrac{\partial L}{\partial x_1} = 0,$ $\dfrac{\partial L}{\partial y_1} = 0,$ $x_2 = 0.$

● Case 1

This case is possible only if $\bar{y} = \bar{x}$. The Kuhn-Tucker conditions are then satisfied, since it is possible to find positive values of λ and μ such that

$$\frac{\partial L}{\partial x_1} = \frac{1}{2} - \lambda \leqslant 0,$$

$$\frac{\partial L}{\partial y_1} = \frac{1}{2} - \mu \leqslant 0,$$

and $\dfrac{\partial L}{\partial x_2} = 2 - \lambda - \mu = 0.$

Then we have:

$$x_1 = y_1 = 0,$$

$$x_2 = y_2 = \bar{x} = \bar{y},$$

and $z = z_1 + z_2 = 2\bar{x} = 2\bar{y}.$

● Case 2

Converted to equalities, (3) and (4) yield $x_1 = 0$, $x_2 = \bar{x} = y_2$, and $y_1 = \bar{y} - \bar{x}$.

The following equations allow us to calculate λ:

$$\frac{\partial L}{\partial y_1} = \frac{1}{2}\left(\frac{1}{\bar{y} - \bar{x} + 1}\right)^{1/2} - \mu = 0,$$

$$\frac{\partial L}{\partial x_2} = 2 - \lambda - \mu = 0,$$

or $\lambda = 2 - \dfrac{1}{2}\left(\dfrac{1}{\bar{y} - \bar{x} + 1}\right)^{1/2}$

This case is possible only if $\partial L/\partial x_1 \leqslant 0$, that is, if

$$2 \geqslant \frac{1}{2}(\bar{y} - \bar{x} + 1)^{1/2} + \frac{1}{2}\left(\frac{1}{\bar{y} - \bar{x} + 1}\right)^{1/2} \tag{5}$$

Taking into account that $\bar{y} \geqslant \bar{x}$, this inequality of the second degree in $t = (\bar{y} - \bar{x} + {}^1\!/_2)^{1/2}$ yields

$$\bar{y} \leqslant \bar{x} + (2 + \sqrt{3})^2 - 1.$$

In summary, for $\bar{x} < \bar{y} \leqslant \bar{x} + (2 + \sqrt{3})^2 - 1$, we have

$$x_1 = 0, \qquad x_2 = y_2 = \bar{x}, \qquad y_1 = \bar{y} - \bar{x},$$

and

$$z = 2\bar{x} + (\bar{y} - \bar{x} + 1)^{1/2} - 1.$$

Case 1 emerges as the limit of case 2 when $\bar{y}$ tends toward $\bar{x}$.

- Case 3

We need to solve the following system of equations:

$$\frac{\partial L}{\partial x_1} = \frac{1}{2}\left(\frac{y_1 + 1}{x_1 + 1}\right)^{1/2} - \lambda = 0,$$

$$\frac{\partial L}{\partial y_1} = \frac{1}{2}\left(\frac{x_1 + 1}{y_1 + 1}\right)^{1/2} - \mu = 0,$$

$$\frac{\partial L}{\partial x_2} = 2 - \lambda - \mu = 0,$$

$$x_1 + x_2 = \bar{x}, \tag{3'}$$

$$y_1 + x_2 = \bar{y}. \tag{4'}$$

By eliminating λ and μ, we derive the following equation:

$$2 = \frac{1}{2}\left(\frac{y_1 + 1}{x_1 + 1}\right)^{1/2} + \frac{1}{2}\left(\frac{x_1 + 1}{y_1 + 1}\right)^{1/2}. \tag{6}$$

This equation is solved by defining $u = \left(\dfrac{y_1 + 1}{x_1 + 1}\right)^{1/2}$.

Choosing the solution that is greater than one, we find

$$y_1 + 1 = (2 + \sqrt{3})^2(x_1 + 1).$$

Since from Eqs. (3)' and (4)', $y_1 = x_1 = \bar{y} - \bar{x}$, we have:

$$x_1 = \frac{\bar{y} - \bar{x} - (2 + \sqrt{3})^2 + 1}{(2 + \sqrt{3})^2 - 1},$$

$$x_2 = \frac{(2 + \sqrt{3})^2(\bar{x} + 1) - \bar{y} - 1}{(2 + \sqrt{3}) - 1},$$

$$y_1 = \frac{(2 + \sqrt{3})^2(\bar{y} - \bar{x} - 1) + 1}{(2 + \sqrt{3})^2 - 1}.$$

And since the variables are positive, we have the following condition:

$$(2 + \sqrt{3})^2(\bar{x} + 1) - 1 > \bar{y} > \bar{x} + (2 + \sqrt{3})^2 - 1.$$

Aggregate output is equal to

$$z = \frac{(2 + \sqrt{3})(\bar{y} - \bar{x})}{(2 + \sqrt{3})^2 - 1} - 1 + \frac{2(2 + \sqrt{3})^2(\bar{x} + 1) - 2\bar{y} - 2}{(2 + \sqrt{3})^2 - 1}$$

$$= \frac{\sqrt{3}(\bar{y} - \bar{x})}{(2 + \sqrt{3})^2 - 1} + 1 + 2\bar{x}.$$

When $\bar{y}$ tends toward $\bar{x} + (2 + \sqrt{3})^2 - 1$, z tends toward $2\bar{x} + 1 + \sqrt{3}$. However, in case 2, when $\bar{y} \rightarrow \bar{x} + (2 + \sqrt{3})^2 - 1$, we find the same limit for z. Therefore the aggregate production function is continuous when we go from case 2 to case 3.

- Case 4
    Here $x_2 = 0$ and Eqs. (3)' and (4)' yield $x_1 = \bar{x}, y_1 = \bar{y}, x_2 = y_2 = 0$. Aggregate output is then equal to

$$z = (\bar{x} + 1)^{1/2}(\bar{y} + 1)^{1/2} - 1.$$

Taking into account that $\partial L/\partial x_1 = \partial L/\partial y_1 = 0$, the condition $\partial L/\partial x_2 \leq 0$ is written

$$2 \leq \frac{1}{2}\left(\frac{\bar{y}+1}{\bar{x}+1}\right)^{1/2} + \frac{1}{2}\left(\frac{\bar{x}+1}{\bar{y}+1}\right)^{1/2}. \tag{7}$$

Because $\bar{y} \geq \bar{x}$, this condition yields

$$\bar{y} \geq (2+\sqrt{3})^2(\bar{x}+1) - 1.$$

When $\bar{y} \rightarrow (2+\sqrt{3})^2(\bar{x}+1) - 1$, aggregate output

$$z \rightarrow (2+\sqrt{3})(\bar{x}+1) - 1.$$

However, in case 3 we found the same limit for z when $\bar{y}$ tended toward $(2+\sqrt{3})^2(\bar{x}+1) - 1$ from below. Therefore we have derived the aggregate production function of the enterprise over the entire domain $\bar{y} \geq \bar{x} > 0$.

Figure 9.2 shows the domains corresponding to the various cases in the $\bar{x}$, $\bar{y}$ plane where case 1 is given by the 45-degree line along which $\bar{x} = \bar{y}$.

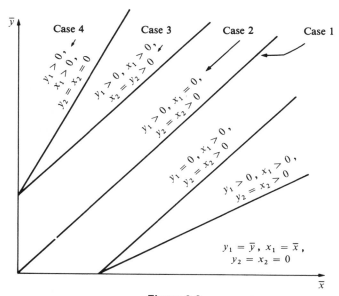

Figure 9.2

Let us derive all these results again, this time using economic intuition.

An initial allocation that comes to mind involves distributing $y_2 = x_2 = \bar{x}$ to plant 2 and the rest (that is, $y_1 = \bar{y} - \bar{x}$ and $x_1 = 0$) to plant 1. Since marginal products are nonincreasing, this allocation is optimal as long as a transfer of resources from plant 2 to plant 1 does not lead to increased output.

Taken as a first-order approximation with respect to the variations $\triangle x_1 = -\triangle x_2 = -\triangle y_2 = \triangle y_1 > 0$, the gain in output is equal to

$$\frac{1}{2} \left(\frac{1}{\bar{y} - \bar{x} + 1} \right)^{1/2} \triangle y_1 + \frac{1}{2} (\bar{y} - \bar{x} + 1)^{1/2} \triangle x_1 - 2 \triangle x_1.$$

This is not positive as long as

$$\frac{1}{2} \left(\frac{1}{\bar{y} - \bar{x} + 1} \right)^{1/2} + \frac{1}{2} (\bar{y} - \bar{x} + 1)^{1/2} - 2 \leqslant 0.$$

This is inequality (5), and we return again to the domain corresponding to case 2. As $\bar{y}$ increases for a fixed $\bar{x}$, and if we retain the allocation given above, the marginal product of factor X increases in plant 1, since it is equal to $1/2(\bar{y} - \bar{x} + 1)^{1/2}$. Inequality (5) is no longer satisfied when $\bar{y}$ exceeds the value $\bar{x} + (2 + \sqrt{3})^2 - 1$. This indicates that a transfer of resources from plant 2 to plant 1 leads to increased output. Then the optimal allocation is given by

$$y_2 = x_2 > 0, \qquad y_1 > 0, \qquad x_1 > 0.$$

To characterize this allocation it is sufficient to write, in addition to constraints (3) and (4), that the gain in output resulting from a transfer of resources defined by $\triangle x_1 = -\triangle x_2 = -\triangle y_2 = \triangle y_1$ compensates exactly for the loss:

$$\frac{1}{2} \left(\frac{x_1 + 1}{y_1 + 1} \right)^{1/2} \triangle y_1 + \frac{1}{2} \left(\frac{y_1 + 1}{x_1 + 1} \right)^{1/2} \triangle x_1 - 2 \triangle x_1 = 0.$$

This gives the following equation:

$$2 = \frac{1}{2} \left(\frac{x_1 + 1}{y_1 + 1} \right)^{1/2} + \frac{1}{2} \left(\frac{y_1 + 1}{x_1 + 1} \right)^{1/2},$$

which is Eq. (6). Therefore we can retrieve the characteristics of case 3. In this case the value of x_2 decreases when $\bar{y}$ increases for $\bar{x}$ fixed. It vanishes for $\bar{y} = (2 + \sqrt{3})^2(\bar{x} + 1) - 1$. Beyond this limiting value the optimal allocation is given by

$$x_1 = \bar{x}, \qquad y_1 = \bar{y}, \qquad y_2 = x_2 = 0.$$

Such an allocation is optimal as long as a transfer of resources from plant 1 to plant 2 would not lead to increased output. That is, as long as

$$2 \leqslant \frac{1}{2}\left(\frac{\bar{y} + 1}{\bar{x} + 1}\right)^{1/2} + \frac{1}{2}\left(\frac{\bar{x} + 1}{\bar{y} + 1}\right)^{1/2},$$

which is Eq. (7).

In conclusion, when the production sets are convex, classical economic reasoning based on the comparison of marginal products leads to the definition of an allocation satisfying the Kuhn-Tucker conditions, which is itself the optimal allocation, since these conditions are sufficient as well.

Problem 2

To determine the optimal policy of the enterprise, we must seek the profit maximum under various constraints. We can do this by applying the Kuhn-Tucker conditions, which are necessary and sufficient. Given our equivalence results between a direct economic argument and application of Kuhn-Tucker conditions, which we demonstrated in problem 1, we need to choose now between two possible methods.

Beginning with the prices of the factors, we could calculate the marginal cost curve as a function of output and then, by applying the traditional method, equate marginal cost to the selling price of good Z. Unfortunately, when the enterprise is endowed with certain initial quantities of the factors and at the same time can only purchase (but not sell) from factor markets, the marginal cost function is difficult to calculate. (A similar situation arises in the real-world economy when no-resale markets exist for certain equipment.) Moreover, the results obtained in problem 1 would not be useful for such a calculation. Consequently, we shall use another method.

Beginning with the selling price of the output and some fixed quantities of the inputs, it is possible to determine the value, or shadow price, that the enterprise attributes to an additional unit of any input. If the factor market allows, profit maximization yields the equalization of this shadow price and the market price.

How do we calculate this shadow price? The shadow price of factor X, for example, is equal to its marginal product multiplied by the price of good Z—in other words, it is equal to the partial derivative of the aggregate production function $z = f(\bar{x}, \bar{y})$ with respect to $\bar{x}$, since the price of good Z is equal to one. It is interesting to note that in this case the shadow prices for the factors are equal to the multipliers λ and μ introduced in problem 1. As an example, we shall prove it for case 3 of problem 1, where

$$z = 2\bar{x} + 1 + \frac{\sqrt{3}(\bar{y} - \bar{x})}{(2 + \sqrt{3})^2 - 1}.$$

The marginal product of factor X, or the shadow price, is equal to

$$\frac{\partial z}{\partial \bar{x}} = 2 - \frac{\sqrt{3}}{(2 + \sqrt{3})^2 - 1} = 1 + \frac{\sqrt{3}}{2}.$$

The equation $\partial L/\partial x_1 = 0$ allows us to calculate λ:

$$\lambda = \frac{1}{2}\left(\frac{y_1 + 1}{x_1 + 1}\right)^{1/2} = \frac{1}{2}(2 + \sqrt{3}) = 1 + \frac{\sqrt{3}}{2}.$$

This is a general property: in the search for an optimal allocation, the multipliers associated with the scarcity constraints are equal to marginal products and can therefore be interpreted as shadow prices when the numéraire is chosen appropriately.

Finally, we point out that shadow prices are not defined at the points where we pass from one case to another, that is, at the points where the aggregate production function is not differentiable.

If $\bar{x} = 1$ and $\bar{y} = 2$, we are in case 2. The shadow prices are equal respectively to

$$2 - \frac{1}{2(\bar{y} - \bar{x} + 1)^{1/2}} = 2 - \frac{1}{2\sqrt{2}} < p_x = 5$$

and

$$\frac{1}{2(\bar{y} - \bar{x} + 1)^{1/2}} = \frac{1}{2\sqrt{2}} > p_y = \frac{1}{10}.$$

To equate the shadow prices to the market prices, the enterprise should sell factor X and buy factor Y. Since factors can be purchased only, the enterprise can only equate the shadow price of factor Y to p_y. Similarly, the shadow price for Y corresponding to case 3 is equal to the expression $1 - \sqrt{3}/2 > 1/10$.

Only case 4 can yield an initial value of y that equates its shadow price to its market price. If y is the optimal quantity to buy, we must have

$$\frac{1}{2}\left(\frac{\bar{x}+1}{\bar{y}+y+1}\right)^{1/2} = \frac{1}{10}, \quad \text{or} \quad \frac{1}{2}\left(\frac{2}{y+3}\right)^{1/2} = \frac{1}{10},$$

and $y = 47$.

To ensure that we have determined the optimal policy for the enterprise, it is sufficient to show that after such a purchase the shadow price of factor X cannot rise above $p_x = 5$.

As a consequence of the imperfection in factor markets, the possibilities of substitution among factors of production will be restricted; for enterprises are led to use greater quantities than they would otherwise wish of certain relatively less productive factors. If we exclude from the analysis the difficult problem of durable production goods, we point out that such possibilities can arise in real-world economic situations only along a dynamic decision path. These situations require earlier events (for example, an incorrect prediction of price fluctuations) to explain why the enterprise holds factors of production that are not fully used.

Suggested Readings

Koopmans, Tjalling C. 1957. *Three Essays on the State of Economic Science.* New York: McGraw-Hill.

Malinvaud, Edmond. 1972. *Lectures on Microeconomic Theory*, trans. A. Silvey, chap. 4. Amsterdam: North-Holland.

PART THREE

General Equilibrium Theory

Comparative Statics and Multiple Equilibria

The following exercise is designed to present a complete general equilibrium model and to study the properties of this equilibrium. The various optimization exercises solved in problems 1 and 2 are handled with the help of simple representations in two-dimensional space or by applying Kuhn-Tucker conditions.

The economy that we consider here is a private-property economy consisting of only three goods: good 1 is a consumption good, with price p_1; good 2 is labor, with price p_2 (wage); good 3 is land, with price p_3 (rent). We assume that the total amount of land, T, is owned by one group, the capitalists. A second group, all of whom are equally skilled (so as not to complicate the analysis), makes up a proletariat whose only resource is labor power.

For each group there exists a minimum subsistence level of consumption, which we choose equal to one, such that consumption of good 1 by the capitalists and workers respectively[1] meets the conditions $x_1^c \geq 1$ and $x_1^p \geq 1$.

Finally, there exists a ceiling on labor for each group, which cannot be exceeded; we set this at 3 such that labor supplied by the capitalists and workers respectively meets the conditions $x_2^c \leq 3$ and $x_2^p \leq 3$.

Problem 1

(a) The workers' preferences are representable by a utility function:

$$V(x_1^p, x_2^p) = 2 \log x_1^p + \log (3 - x_2^p).$$

---

1. *Translators' note:* We use here the more customary term "capitalists," even though the meaning is more closely "landowners"; and we choose to employ the word "workers" rather than "proletariat" (which is reflected in the equations by the index p).

What must the real wage be to assure a minimum subsistence level? Show that two cases can be distinguished depending on whether $x_1^p = 1$ or $x_1^p > 1$. Why is this single distinction sufficient? In each of these cases write the functions expressing the demand for good 1 and the supply of labor, good 2. (It will be convenient to express these functions by denoting $p_1/p_2 = \pi_1$, or labor value price.)

(b) The mentality of the capitalists is different from that of the workers. Their utility function is

$$W(x_1^c, x_2^c) = \log x_1^c + \log (3 - x_2^c).$$

Furthermore, we shall adopt the following notations:

$$\frac{p_1}{p_2} = \pi_1, \qquad \frac{p_3}{p_2} = \pi_3, \qquad T\frac{p_3}{p_2} = \rho.$$

(1) What condition must be satisfied by π_1, π_2, and ρ so that the capitalists are assured a minimum subsistence level?

(2) Show that we must distinguish four cases depending on whether or not the capitalists work and on whether or not they are at the minimum subsistence level. Are all these cases equally realistic?

(3) In each of the above cases write the functions for the supply of labor, good 2, and the demand for good 1 by the capitalists.

(c) For each basic case determine aggregate demand and aggregate supply each as a function of π_1 and ρ. Show that we need retain only seven cases and that to each of these cases corresponds an area in the space π_1, ρ. Represent these various regions graphically.

Problem 2

Two production techniques are known: both exhibit constant returns and both require strict complementarity between manpower and labor.

The intensive technique yields one unit of good 1 using two units of labor, good 2, and one unit of land, good 3.

The extensive technique allows us to obtain one unit of good 1 using one unit of good 2 and two units of good 3.

(a) Depending on the value of π_3, discuss the technique to be chosen.

(b) Is the given system of prices sufficient to allow the entrepreneur to determine a production program?

(c) Show that if an equilibrium exists for the entrepreneur, it requires that the corresponding profit be zero.

(d) Deduce from this the position of the points corresponding to an eventual equilibrium of the enterprises in the space π_1, ρ.

Problem 3

(a) By combining the results of problems 1 and 2, show that the intensive technique alone cannot lead to an equilibrium.

(b) Solve for and discuss the various equilibria that can be established when T varies. What happens when T is small?

(c) What happens if $1 + \sqrt{13} \leqslant T < 6$?

PROPOSED SOLUTION

The preceding exercises have approached the behavior of consumers and the behavior of producers separately. Here we propose to integrate the two in a general equilibrium model of a private-property economy. This exercise therefore illustrates the descriptive aspect of microeconomic theory, that is, its oldest and most classic aspect. Remember that a general equilibrium model purports to describe and explain the fundamental phenomena of economic life—the formation of prices and profits. The equilibrium that we seek to determine here is a competitive equilibrium. The ability of a competitive general equilibrium model to describe realistically the functioning of an economy is debatable, inasmuch as many phenomena are not considered. However, the complete treatment of such a model is of great interest because, on the one hand, it allows us to take into account the interdependency between the decisions of various agents and, on the other hand, the general equilibrium model serves as an indispensable benchmark in many other microeconomic studies.

Problem 1

(a) Faced with a system of prices p_1, p_2, the workers can survive only if their budget constraint intersects their consumption set X^p, that is:

$$\{x^p | p_1 x_1^p \leqslant p_2 x_2^p\} \cap \{x^p | x_1^p \geqslant 1, x_2^p \leqslant 3\} \neq \varnothing,$$

which obviously implies $p_1 \leqslant 3p_2$, or $\pi_1 \leqslant 3$.

The problem of finding equilibrium situations is written

$$\max V(x_1^p, x_2^p) = 2 \log x_1^p + \log (3 - x_2^p).$$

with conditions

(1) $$x_1^p \geqslant 0,$$

(2) $$x_2^p \geqslant 0,$$

(3) $$3 - x_2^p \geqslant 0 \quad \text{(maximum labor supply)},$$

(4) $$x_1^p - 1 \geqslant 0 \quad \text{(minimum subsistence level)},$$

(5) $$-p_1 x_1^p + p_2 x_2^p \geqslant 0 \quad \text{(budget constraint)}.$$

Applying the Kuhn-Tucker conditions, we define

$$L^p(x^p, u^p) = V(x^p) + u_1^p(3 - x_2^p) + u_2^p(x_1^p - 1) + u_3^p(-p_1 x_1^p + p_2 x_2^p).$$

With a few remarks we can solve the problem by differentiating eventually only two cases:

(i) It can be easily shown that at equilibrium the budget constraint is necessarily satisfied with equality.

(ii) We further note that labor supplied, x_2^p, can never reach 3 (except in the case where the survival condition is satisfied with equality, a case that we ignore and that could be treated directly by considering $x_1^p = 1, x_2^p = 3$). Indeed, when $x_2^p \to 3$, $V(x) \to -\infty$. Therefore a couplet $[x_1^p, 3]$ can never be an optimum: instead the worker would prefer $x_1^p - \epsilon, 3 - \epsilon'$ so that equality occurs only if $x_1^p - \epsilon$ falls outside of X^p, that is, if we are at the minimum subsistence level.

(iii) Condition (4) implies $x_1^p > 0$.

(iv) If we also take condition (5) into account, we see further that $x_2^p > 0$.

Finally, there are only two cases left to differentiate: either $x_1^p > 1$ or $x_1^p = 1$. A geometric interpretation is given in Fig. 10.1. Since the indifference curves $V(x_1^p, x_2^p)$ are asymptotic to the line $x_2^p = 3$, only the following can occur: either the optimum is represented as a tangency (as in Fig. 10.1), or the optimum is a corner solution corresponding to the minimum subsistence level $x_1^p = 1$.

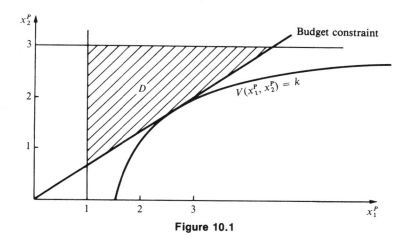

Figure 10.1

THE KUHN-TUCKER conditions yield in a quasi-evident way the solutions illustrated geometrically above.

● Case 1

If $x_1^p > 1$, then we have $u_2^p = 0$ and

$$(i) \Rightarrow p_1 x_1^p = p_2 x_2^p,$$

$$(ii) \Rightarrow x_2^p < 3 \Rightarrow u_1^p = 0,$$

$$(iii) \Rightarrow \frac{\partial L^p}{\partial x_1^p} = 0 = \frac{2}{x_1^p} - u_3^p p_1,$$

$$(iv) \Rightarrow \frac{\partial L^p}{\partial x_2^p} = 0 = -\frac{1}{3 - x_2^p} + u_3^p p_2.$$

Predictably, we retrieve the equations that correspond to the case where we can use the Lagrangian multipliers:

$$p_1 x_1^p = p_2 x_2^p,$$

and

$$u_3^p = \frac{2}{p_1 x_1^p} = \frac{1}{p_2 (3 - x_2^p)}.$$

We deduce immediately that

$$x_1^p = \frac{2}{\pi_1}, \qquad x_2^p = 2.$$

This solution is valid for $x_1^p > 1$, that is, for $\pi_1 < 2$.

- Case 2
   If $x_1^p = 1$,

$$\text{(i)} \Rightarrow x_2^p = \pi_1,$$

$$\text{(ii)} \Rightarrow u_1^p = 0,$$

$$\text{(iii)} \Rightarrow 2 + u_2^p - u_3^p p_1 = 0,$$

$$\text{(iv)} \Rightarrow \frac{1}{3 - \pi_1} + u_3^p p_2 = 0.$$

From the last two equations we derive:

$$u_3^p = \frac{1}{3p_2 - p_1}, \quad \text{nonnegative, since } \pi_1 \leqslant 3,$$

and $\qquad u_2^p = \dfrac{3(p_1 - 2p_2)}{3p_2 - p_1}, \quad$ nonnegative only if $\pi_1 \geqslant 2$.

Finally, we see that we can represent the functions of the demand for good 1 and the supply of labor (good 2) as shown in Fig. 10.2.

The representation obtained is not far from reality. If the real wage is low (π_1 large), the workers maintain their consumption at the subsistence level and must work a great deal. If the real wage increases, they maintain a normal workday and increase their consumption. (If the maximum workday were 12 hours per person, we would consider 8 hours per person to be normal.)

(b) Since the analysis for the behavior of the capitalists is the same in principle, we stress only significant differences from the preceding case.

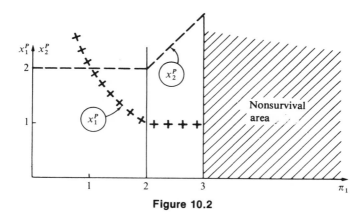

Figure 10.2

Inasmuch as the capitalists do not wish to consume land directly (land, good 3, is not an argument in their utility function), they rent all their land to the enterprises. Under these conditions the budget constraint becomes

$$p_1 x_1^c = p_2 x_2^c + p_3 T,$$

and the survival condition of the capitalists is

$$\{x | p_1 x_1^c \leq p_2 x_2^c + p_3 T\} \cap \{x | x_1^c \geq 1, x_2^c \leq 3\} \neq \emptyset.$$

This can also be written as

$$3 p_2 + p_3 T \geq p_1 \quad \text{or} \quad 3 + \pi_3 T \geq \pi_1.$$

The functions of the demand for good 1 and the supply of good 2 will be solutions of the system

$$\max W(x^c) = \log x_1^c + \log (3 - x_2^c),$$

with (1') $x_1^c \geq 0,$

(2') $x_2^c \geq 0,$

(3') $3 - x_2^c \geq 0,$

$$(4') \qquad\qquad\qquad x_1^c - 1 \geqslant 0,$$

$$(5') \qquad\qquad -p_1 x_1^c + p_2 x_2^c + p_3 T \geqslant 0.$$

Remarks (i), (ii), and (iii) continue to hold for the capitalists, but remark (iv) must be reconsidered since nonzero consumption x_1^c does not imply nonzero work (consumption expenses may be covered in full by the rent earned on the land). Four cases are to be distinguished:

	$x_1^c > 1$	$x_1^c = 1$
$x_2^c > 0$	Case 1	Case 2
$x_2^c = 0$	Case 3	Case 4

As above, the case where the feasible set is reduced to a single point $(3 + \pi_3 T = \pi_1)$ poses no problem. We then have $x_1^c = 1$ and $x_2^c = 3$.

To study the various cases for the capitalists we define, as we did above,

$$L^c(x^c, u^c) = W(x^c) + u_1^c[3 - x_2^c] + u_2^c[x_1^c - 1]$$

$$+ u_3^c[-p_1 x_1^c + p_2 x_2^c + p_3 T].$$

In all the cases:

(i) $\Rightarrow -p_1 x_1^c + p_2 x_2^c + p_3 T = 0,$ \hfill (6)

(ii) $\Rightarrow u_1^c = 0,$ \hfill (7)

(iii) $\Rightarrow x_1^c > 0 \Rightarrow \dfrac{\partial L^c}{\partial x_1^c} = \dfrac{1}{x_1^c} + u_2^c - p_1 u_3^c = 0.$ \hfill (8)

For each of the cases considered we obtain two additional equations that allow us to calculate the variables x_1^c and u_1^c, and we specify the conditions under which the solutions obtained are valid.

● Case 1:

The capitalists work and are above their minimum subsistence level. Additional conditions are

$$x_1^c > 1 \Rightarrow u_2^c = 0 \qquad\qquad\qquad (9)$$

and
$$x_2^c > 0 \Rightarrow \frac{\partial L}{\partial x_2^c} = 0 = -\frac{1}{3 - x_2^c} + u_3^c p_2. \tag{10}$$

From Eqs. (6) and (7) we deduce

$$u_3^c = \frac{1}{p_1 x_1^c} = \frac{1}{p_2(3 - x_2^c)} = \frac{2}{3p_2 + p_3 T},$$

which is the classical Lagrangian case.

Using the notation given in the introduction, we derive

$$x_1^c = \frac{3p_2 + p_3 T}{2p_1} = \frac{3 + \rho}{2\pi_1}$$

and
$$x_2^c = 3 - \frac{3p_2 + p_3 T}{2p_2} = \frac{3p_2 - p_3 T}{2p_2} = \frac{3}{2} - \frac{\rho}{2}.$$

The feasibility conditions are

$$x_2^c > 0 \Rightarrow \rho < 3$$

and
$$x_1^c > 1 \Rightarrow \rho + 3 > 2\pi_1.$$

- Case 2:

The capitalists work and are at their minimum subsistence level. The equations that determine the equilibrium are (6), (7), (8), and

$$x_1^c = 1, \tag{11}$$

$$x_2^c > 0 \Rightarrow \frac{\partial L^c}{\partial x_2^c} = 0 = -\frac{1}{3 - x_2^c} + u_3^c p_2. \tag{12}$$

We derive immediately

$$x_1^c = 1, \qquad x_2^c = \pi_1 - \rho.$$

Feasibility conditions, after combining Eqs. (12) and (8), are

$$x_2^c > 0 \Rightarrow \rho < \pi_1,$$

$$u_2^c \geq 0 \Rightarrow \frac{2\pi_1 - \rho - 3}{3 + \rho - \pi_1} \geq 0.$$

Taking into account the survival condition, we must have

$$\rho + 3 \leq 2\pi_1.$$

- Case 3:

  The capitalists do not work and are above their minimum subsistence level.

  To Eqs. (6), (7), and (8) we must add

$$x_2^c = 0, \tag{13}$$

$$x_1^c > 1 \Rightarrow u_2^c = 0. \tag{14}$$

The solution is immediate:

$$x_1^c = \frac{\rho}{\pi_1}, \qquad x_2^c = 0.$$

This solution is feasible if

$$x_1^c > 1 \Rightarrow \rho > \pi_1,$$

$$\frac{\partial L^c}{\partial x_2^c} \leq 0 \Rightarrow -\frac{1}{3 - x_2^c} + p_2 u_3^c \leq 0,$$

or, taking Eq. (8) into account:

$$-\frac{1}{3} + \frac{1}{\rho} \leq 0 \Rightarrow \rho \geq 3.$$

- Case 4:

  The capitalists do not work and are at their minimum subsistence level. Then

$$x_1^c = 1, \qquad x_2^c = 0.$$

This solution is feasible if

$$\pi_1 = \rho \quad \text{(budget constraint)},$$

$$\frac{\partial L^c}{\partial x_2^c} \leqslant 0 \Rightarrow -\frac{1}{3} + u_3^c p_2 \leqslant 0 \quad \text{or} \quad u_3^c \leqslant \frac{1}{3p_2},$$

$$u_2 \geqslant 0 \Rightarrow p_1 u_3^c - 1 \geqslant 0 \quad \text{or} \quad u_3^c \geqslant \frac{1}{p_1}.$$

It is consistent if

$$\frac{1}{p_1} \leqslant \frac{1}{3p_2}, \ 3 \leqslant \pi_1.$$

Taking the various constraints into account, we can summarize by Fig. 10.3 the feasible regions of the four cases considered. Case 4 emerges as intermediate between cases 2 and 3.

(c) If we take sections (a) and (b) into account, aggregate demand is

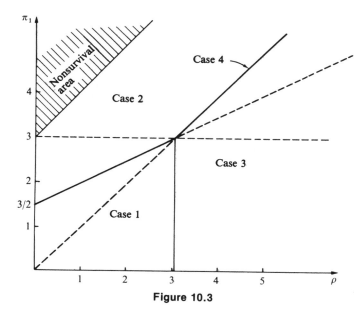

Figure 10.3

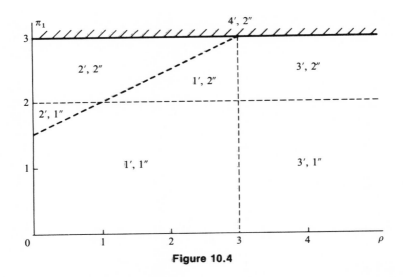

Figure 10.4

defined only for $\pi_1 \leqslant 3$. Then we can simplify Fig. 10.3 and partition the region $\{\pi_1 \leqslant 3\}$ according to the form of the functions of demand for good 1 and supply of good 2. In Fig. 10.4 a prime indicates the parameters related to the capitalists and a double prime those related to the workers. It is apparent that there are seven cases to consider. In each, the functions of the demand for good 1 and the supply of labor (good 2) emerge as the sums of the demands and the supplies of each group. Table 10.1 summarizes all the possible results in the form x_1^D = aggregate demand of good 1 and x_2^S = aggregate supply of good 2. Primes and double primes have the same meanings as in Fig. 10.4.

Problem 2

We wish now to study the supply of goods. Since the two production techniques are known, all the entrepreneurs have the same production set. It is a cone Y defined by

$$Y = \{y | y = \lambda_1 V_1 + \lambda_2 V_2, \lambda_1 \geqslant 0, \lambda_2 \geqslant 0\} - \Omega,$$

where Ω is the nonnegative orthant of $\mathbb{R}^3$ and where we have assumed

$$V_1 = \begin{bmatrix} 1 \\ -2 \\ -1 \end{bmatrix} \quad \text{(intensive technique)}$$

		Workers	
		1″	2″
		$x_1^p = \dfrac{2}{\pi_1},\ x_2^p = 2$	$x_1^p = 1,\ x_2^p = \pi_1$
Capitalists: 1′:	$x_1^c = \dfrac{3+\rho}{2\pi_1}$, $x_2^c = \dfrac{3-\rho}{2}$	$x_1^D = \dfrac{7+\rho}{2\pi_1}$, $x_2^S = \dfrac{7-\rho}{2}$	$x_1^D = \dfrac{3+\rho+2\pi_1}{2\pi_1}$, $x_2^S = \dfrac{3-\rho+2\pi_1}{2}$
2′:	$x_1^c = 1$, $x_2^c = \pi_1 - \rho$	$x_1^D = \dfrac{\pi_1+2}{\pi_1}$, $x_2^S = 2 + \pi_1 - \rho$	$x_1^D = 2$, $x_2^S = 2\pi_1 - \rho$
3′:	$x_1^c = \dfrac{\rho}{\pi_1}$, $x_2^c = 0$	$x_1^D = \dfrac{2+\rho}{\pi_1}$, $x_2^S = 2$	$x_1^D = \dfrac{\pi_1+\rho}{\pi_1}$, $x_2^S = \pi_1$
4′:	$x_1^c = 1$, $x_2^c = 0$		$x_1^D = 2$, $x_2^S = \pi_1$

Table 10.1

and
$$V_2 = \begin{bmatrix} 1 \\ -1 \\ -2 \end{bmatrix} \quad \text{(extensive technique).}$$

Therefore we allow free disposal and the aggregate production set is obviously Y. This allows us to focus on set Y and presume that production is undertaken by a single entrepreneur who takes the prices as given and maximizes his profit on Y. If many enterprepreneurs were involved, nothing would change.

The assumptions of exercise 6 are satisfied and we can use its conclusions here.

First, if a profit maximum exists, profit is necessarily zero inasmuch as Y is a cone (this justifies our lack of consideration earlier of the eventual distribution of profit). There are three possible cases:

● Case 1:

  Only the extensive technique is used.

  If $pV_2 = 0$, $pV_1 < 0$. Then

$$\pi_1 - 1 - 2\pi_3 = 0 \quad \text{and} \quad \pi_1 - 2 - \pi_3 < 0,$$

which implies

$$\pi_1 - 1 - 2\pi_3 = 0 \quad \text{and} \quad 0 \leqslant \pi_3 < 1.$$

● Case 2:

  The two techniques are used concurrently.

  If $pV_2 = 0$, $pV_1 = 0$. Then

$$\pi_1 = 3 \quad \text{and} \quad \pi_3 = 1.$$

● Case 3:

  Only the intensive technique is used.

  If $pV_1 = 0$, $pV_2 < 0$. Then

$$\pi_1 - 2 - \pi_3 = 0 \quad \text{and} \quad \pi_1 - 1 - 2\pi_3 < 0,$$

which implies

$$\pi_1 - 2 - \pi_3 = 0 \quad \text{and} \quad \pi_3 > 1.$$

In summary, it is sufficient to compare π_3 to one to find out which case should be considered. If we draw an isoquant in y_2, y_3 space corresponding to the level of production y^* (Fig. 10.5), it is clear that cost minimization by the entrepreneur leads to the choice of point I (intensive technique) if $\pi_3 > 1$, the choice of any point on segment IE if $\pi_3 = 1$, and the choice of point E (extensive technique) if $\pi_3 < 1$.

We can represent as follows the locus of possible equilibria for the producer in the space $[\pi_1, \pi_3]$ as in Fig. 10.6, or in the space $[\pi_1, \rho]$, as in Fig. 10.7.

A given vector of possible prices is not sufficient to determine output for the entrepreneur because if y^* is a solution, then any λy^* with $\lambda \geqslant 0$ is a solution as well; that is, it also yields a profit maximum for the entrepreneur (where profits are zero at the maximum).

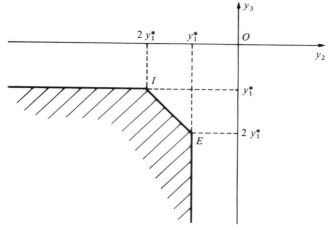

Figure 10.5

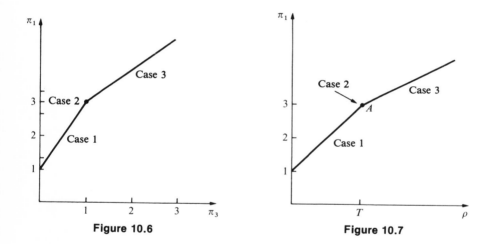

Figure 10.6   **Figure 10.7**

Problem 3

We turn now to a study of the equilibrium. Combining Figs. 10.4 and 10.7 allows us to state immediately that only the productive combinations corresponding to cases 1 and 2 of Fig. 10.7 can lead to an equilibrium. Using the intensive technique alone (case 3) will never be appropriate because for $\pi_1 > 3$, the survival of the workers is not guaranteed. We shall therefore distinguish two types of equilibria corresponding to cases 1 and 2.

(a) Equilibria of type A, corresponding to case 2 of Fig. 10.6: here $\pi_1 = 3$ and $\pi_3 = 1$.

Since the price of land is not zero, the "market for land" must be equilibrated in physical units, so that $x_3^D = T = x_3^S$. When point A in Fig. 10.7, which has an abscissa T, varies, from Fig. 10.4 we have the following three cases: 2′,2″; 4′,2″; 3′,2″.

- Case A_I: $T < 3$, corresponding to the case 2′,2″.

Because of Walras' Law, if the markets corresponding to the first two goods are in equilibrium, the third market will be in equilibrium as well. Table 10.1 yields

$$x_1^D = 2, \qquad x_2^S = 2\,\pi_1 - \rho = 6 - T.$$

On the other hand, if activities V_1 and V_2 are operating at levels λ_1 and λ_2 respectively, we have

$$x_1^S = \lambda_1 + \lambda_2, \qquad x_2^D = 2\lambda_1 + \lambda_2.$$

Algebraic manipulation and equilibrium in the first two markets yield

$$\lambda_1 = x_2^S - x_1^D = 4 - T, \qquad \lambda_2 = 2x_1^D - x_2^S = T - 2.$$

Consequently $x_3^D = \lambda_1 + 2\lambda_2 = T = x_3^S$ is satisfied. This case is possible only if λ_1 and λ_2 are positive; that is, if $T \le 4$ (which is satisfied, since $T < 3$) and if $T \ge 2$ (which corresponds to the survival condition).

In this case the workers are at their minimum subsistence level and work to their maximum limit. The capitalists remain at their minimum subsistence level. Their rent lies between 2 and 3. They provide an amount of work equal to $3 - \rho = 3 - T$ in order to make up the difference between their expenses and their rent.

- Case A_{II}: $T = 3$, corresponding to the case 4′,2″.

This is a limiting case of the preceding one, when T tends toward 3. The capitalists are at their minimum subsistence level and live off their rent. The workers are at their minimum subsistence level and work to their maximum limit.

- Case A_{III}: $T > 3$, corresponding to the case 3′,2″.

Table 10.1 yields

$$x_1^D = 1 + \frac{T}{3}, \qquad x_2^S = 3.$$

We derive as before

$$\lambda_1 = x_2^S - x_1^D = 2 - \frac{T}{3}, \qquad \lambda_2 = 2x_1^D - x_2^S = \frac{2T}{3} - 1.$$

Here $\lambda_1 \geq 0$ implies $T \leq 6$ and $\lambda_2 \geq 0$ implies $T \geq 3/2$, which is satisfied since $T > 3$.

The workers are always at their minimum subsistence level and work to their maximum limit. The capitalists still do not work, but their rent $\rho = T > 3$ allows them to rise above their minimum subsistence level.

(b) Equilibrium of type B, corresponding to case 1 of Fig. 10.7.

The survival condition implies that the extensive technique can be operating alone only if $T \geq 4$. Case 1 can then coexist only with cases $1',1''$; $1',2''$; $3',2''$; and $3',1''$ of Fig. 10.4.

Since the extensive technique is used by itself, we have necessarily

$$x_1^S = \lambda_2;$$

$$x_2^D = \lambda_2, \quad \text{with} \quad \lambda_2 \geq 0;$$

$$x_3^D = 2\lambda_2.$$

So that equilibrium in the first two markets is achieved, it is necessary and sufficient that $x_1^D = x_3^S$. If $\pi_3 > 0$, the last market is then automatically in equilibrium. It may not be in equilibrium if $\pi_3 = 0$. In this case it is sufficient to show that $x_3^D \leq x_3^S = T$. On the other hand, we have as the zero-profit condition of the enterprise:

$$\pi_1 = 1 + 2\pi_3.$$

• Case B_I, corresponding to the case $1'$, $1''$.

We have

$$x_1^D = \frac{7 + \rho}{2\pi_1}, \qquad x_2^S = \frac{7 - \rho}{2}.$$

From $x_1^D = x_2^S$ and market equilibrium, $7(\pi_1 - 1) = T\pi_3(1 + \pi_1)$.
  Since $\pi_1 = 1 + 2\pi_3$, we calculate the solutions:

$$\pi_3 = 0 \qquad \text{and} \quad \pi_1 = 1,$$

$$\pi_3 = \frac{7}{T} - 1 \quad \text{and} \quad \pi_1 = \frac{14}{T} - 1.$$

The first of these solutions belongs to the region of the case $1',1''$. It leads to an aggregate demand: $x_1^D = 7/2$. The required supply of labor is guaranteed, because the workers provide 2 units and the capitalists provide $3/2$ units. Since $\pi_3 = 0$, it is necessary to show that the demand for land does not exceed the supply. This demand is equal to $2\lambda_2$, with $\lambda_2 = x_1^D = x_2^S = 7/2$. This case is therefore possible only if

$$T \geqslant 7.$$

For $T \geqslant 7$, land is a free good.
  The second solution belongs to the region of this same case $1',1''$ if

$$0 \leqslant \pi_1 \leqslant 2,$$

which implies that $14/3 \leqslant T \leqslant 14$, and if

$$0 \leqslant T\pi_3 \leqslant 3,$$

which implies that $4 \leqslant T \leqslant 7$. By combining the two,

$$\frac{14}{3} \leqslant T \leqslant 7.$$

• Case B_{II}, corresponding to the case $1',2''$.
  We have

$$x_1^D = \frac{3 + \rho + 2\pi_1}{2\pi_1}, \qquad x_2^S = \frac{3 - \rho + 2\pi_1}{2}.$$

Now, $x_1^D = x_2^S$ implies $T\pi_3(1 + \pi_1) = (\pi_1 - 1)(2\pi_1 + 3)$.
  Since $\pi_1 = 1 + 2\pi_3$, we calculate the solutions:

$$\pi_3 = 0 \qquad \text{and} \quad \pi_1 = 1,$$

$$\pi_3 = \frac{5 - T}{T - 4} \quad \text{and} \quad \pi_1 = \frac{6 - T}{T - 4}.$$

The first solution does not belong to the region of the case $1', 2''$.
For the second solution to belong to this region, it is necessary that

$$2 \leqslant \pi_1 \leqslant 3 \quad \text{and} \quad 1 \leqslant T\pi_3 \leqslant 3.$$

We derive:

$$\frac{9}{2} \leqslant T \leqslant \frac{14}{3} \quad \text{and} \quad 1 + \sqrt{13} \leqslant T \leqslant 2(1 + \sqrt{2}).$$

Combining the two, cases B_{II} arises if

$$1 + \sqrt{13} \leqslant T \leqslant \frac{14}{3}.$$

- Case B_{III}, corresponding to the case $3', 2''$.
  We have

$$x_1^D = \frac{\pi_1 + \rho}{\pi_1}, \qquad x_2^S = \pi_1.$$

Now, $x_1^D = x_2^S$ implies $\pi_1(\pi_1 - 1) = \pi_3 T$.
Since $\pi_1 = 1 + 2\pi_3$, we calculate the solutions:

$$\pi_3 = 0 \qquad \text{and} \quad \pi_1 = 1,$$

$$\pi_3 = \frac{T - 2}{4} \quad \text{and} \quad \pi_1 = \frac{T}{2}.$$

The first solution is outside the region. The second belongs to the region of the case $3', 2''$ if

Solution		Case A$_\text{I}$		Case A$_\text{II}$	Case A$_\text{III}$		
Land:	$T =$	2		3	$1 + \sqrt{13}$	$\dfrac{14}{3}$	6
Price:	$\pi_1 =$	3	3	3		3	3
	$\pi_3 =$	1	1	1		1	1
Technique:	$\lambda_2 =$	0	$\dfrac{3T-6}{3}$	1		$\dfrac{2T-3}{3}$	3
	$\lambda_1 =$	2	$\dfrac{12-3T}{3}$	1		$\dfrac{6-T}{3}$	0
Aggregate: $x_1^D = x_1^S =$		2	2	2		$\dfrac{T+3}{3}$	3
of which	$x_1^p =$	1	1	1		1	1
	$x_1^c =$	1	1	1		$\dfrac{T}{3}$	2
Labor: $x_2^S = x_2^D =$		4	$6-T$	3		3	3
of which	$x_2^p =$	3	3	3		3	3
	$x_2^c =$	1	$3-T$	0		0	0
Rent of capitalists:	$\rho =$	2	T	3		T	6
Utility:	$e^V =$	0	0	0		0	0
	$e^W =$	2	T	3		T	6

Table 10.2a

$$2 \leqslant \pi_1 \leqslant 3 \quad \text{and} \quad \rho = T\pi_3 \geqslant 3,$$

which yields

$$1 + \sqrt{13} \leqslant T \leqslant 6.$$

- Case B$_\text{IV}$, corresponding to the case $3', 1''$.
  We have

$$x_1^D = \frac{2 + \rho}{\pi_1}, \qquad x_2^S = 2.$$

Solution		Case B$_{\text{III}}$		
Land:	$T =$	$1 + \sqrt{13}$	$\dfrac{14}{3}$	6
Price:	$\pi_1 =$	$\dfrac{1 + \sqrt{13}}{2}$	$\dfrac{T}{2}$	3
	$\pi_3 =$	$\dfrac{\sqrt{13} - 1}{4}$	$\dfrac{T - 2}{4}$	1
Technique: $\lambda_2 = x_1^D = x_1^S =$		$\dfrac{1 + \sqrt{13}}{2}$	$\dfrac{T}{2}$	3
of which	$x_1^p =$	1	1	1
	$x_1^c =$	$\dfrac{\sqrt{13} - 1}{2}$	$\dfrac{T - 2}{2}$	2
Labor:	$x_2^S = x_2^D =$	$\dfrac{1 + \sqrt{13}}{2}$	$\dfrac{T}{2}$	3
of which	$x_2^p =$	$\dfrac{1 + \sqrt{13}}{2}$	$\dfrac{T}{2}$	3
	$x_2^c =$	0	0	0
Rent of capitalists:	$\rho =$	3	$\dfrac{T(T - 2)}{4}$	6
Utility:	$e^V =$	$\dfrac{5 - \sqrt{13}}{2}$	$3 - \dfrac{T}{2}$	0
	$e^W =$	$\dfrac{3(\sqrt{13} - 1)}{2}$	$\dfrac{3}{2}(T - 2)$	6

Table 10.2b

The only solution to the system of equations

$$x_1^D = x_2^S \quad \text{and} \quad \pi_1 = 1 + 2\pi_3$$

is $\pi_3 = 0$, $\pi_1 = 1$, a solution that does not belong to the region of the case $3', 1''$. This case is therefore impossible.

TABLE 10.2 ALLOWS US to synthesize the various cases studied as T varies from 2 to ∞. In particular, it shows that for $1 + \sqrt{13} \leqslant T \leqslant 6$ there are multiple equilibria (see Table 10.2a, case A$_{\text{III}}$, Table 10.2b, and Table 10.2c). The set of equilibria is made up of the union of disjoint sets.

Solution		Case B$_{II}$			Case B$_{I}$		
Land:	$T =$	$1+\sqrt{13}$		$\dfrac{14}{3}$	6	7	∞
Price:	$\pi_1 =$	$\dfrac{1+\sqrt{13}}{2}$	$\dfrac{6-T}{T-4}$	2	$\dfrac{14}{T}-1$	1	1
	$\pi_3 =$	$\dfrac{\sqrt{13}-1}{4}$	$\dfrac{5-T}{T-4}$	$\dfrac{1}{2}$	$\dfrac{7}{T}-1$	0	0
Technique:	$\lambda_2 = x_1^D = x_1^S =$	$\dfrac{1+\sqrt{13}}{2}$	$\dfrac{T}{2}$	$\dfrac{7}{3}$	$\dfrac{T}{2}$	$\dfrac{7}{2}$	$\dfrac{7}{2}$
of which	$x_1^p =$	1	1	1	$\dfrac{2T}{14-T}$	2	2
	$x_1^c =$	$\dfrac{\sqrt{13}-1}{2}$	$\dfrac{T-2}{2}$	$\dfrac{4}{3}$	$\dfrac{1}{2}\dfrac{T(10-T)}{14-T}$	$\dfrac{3}{2}$	$\dfrac{3}{2}$
Labor:	$x_2^S = x_2^D = \lambda_2 =$	$\dfrac{1+\sqrt{13}}{2}$	$\dfrac{T}{2}$	$\dfrac{7}{3}$	$\dfrac{T}{2}$	$\dfrac{7}{2}$	$\dfrac{7}{2}$
of which	$x_2^p =$	$\dfrac{1+\sqrt{13}}{2}$	$\dfrac{6-T}{T-4}$	2	2	2	2
	$x_2^c =$	0	$\dfrac{T^2-2T-12}{2(T-4)}$	$\dfrac{1}{3}$	$\dfrac{T}{2}-2$	$\dfrac{3}{2}$	$\dfrac{3}{2}$
Rent of capitalists:	$\rho =$	3	$\dfrac{T(5-T)}{T-4}$	$\dfrac{7}{3}$	$7-T$	0	0
Utility:	$e^V =$	$\dfrac{5-\sqrt{13}}{2}$	$2\dfrac{2T-9}{T-4}$	1	$\dfrac{4T^2}{(14-T)^2}$	4	4
	$e^W =$	$\dfrac{3(\sqrt{13}-1)}{2}$	$\dfrac{(T-2)^2(6-T)}{4(T-4)}$	$\dfrac{32}{9}$	$\dfrac{T(10-T)^2}{4(14-T)}$	$\dfrac{9}{4}$	$\dfrac{9}{4}$

Table 10.2c

The choice of one system of equilibrium prices rather than another has important distributional consequences for the agents, as Table 10.3 shows for possible equilibria when $T = 5$. Moreover, it is easy to show that each equilibrium is a Pareto optimum.

Figure 10.8 shows the levels achieved in equilibrium by the utility functions e^V and e^W as a function of T in the various possible cases. This figure suggests an interpretation of our results in terms of comparative statics. Indeed, it is interesting to study the effect of changes in T on the situation of the agents. Such a study is relevant only if the various equilibria are locally stable, which is doubtful in certain cases such as B_{III}, since there the

Cases for T = 5	Prices	Utility	Economic consequences
A_{III}	$\pi_1 = 3$ $\pi_3 = 1$	$e^V = 0$ $e^W = 5$	The workers are at their minimum subsistence level and work at their maximum possible physiological limit. Living exclusively off their rents, the capitalists are above their minimum subsistence level.
B_{III}	$\pi_1 = \dfrac{5}{2}$ $\pi_3 = \dfrac{3}{4}$	$e^V = \dfrac{1}{2}$ $e^W = \dfrac{9}{2}$	The workers are always at their minimum subsistence level. They provide an amount of labor less than the physiological maximum but greater than that judged to constitute a normal day. Although still living off their rents, the capitalists have a level of consumption less than that in A_{III}.
B_I	$\pi_1 = \dfrac{9}{5}$ $\pi_3 = \dfrac{2}{5}$	$e^V = \dfrac{100}{81}$ $e^W = \dfrac{125}{36}$	The workers are above their minimum subsistence level and work for a normal day, taking into account their needs. The capitalists work (although very little!) and have a level of consumption less than that in B_{III}.

Table 10.3

aggregate supply of labor x_2^S is equal to π_1, that is, it decreases as the wage increases.

Suppose enough technical progress occurs so that we observe an improvement in the units of output for each isoquant, that is, the same quantity of a good can be produced with a smaller quantity of land. This is equivalent to T increasing over time in this economy, while all other things remain the same. Consider the effect of a change in T starting at $T = 2$. At first the equilibrium moves along segments A of the curves. Prices do not change. The real wage is kept at the minimum consistent with survival of the workers. The only ones who benefit from this change are the capitalists. This movement can be continued until $T = 6$. When T exceeds 6, however, there is a dramatic change in the circumstances of the workers and the capitalists, for the equilibrium jumps from segments A_{III} to segments B_I of the curves. It might, then, be appropriate to consider

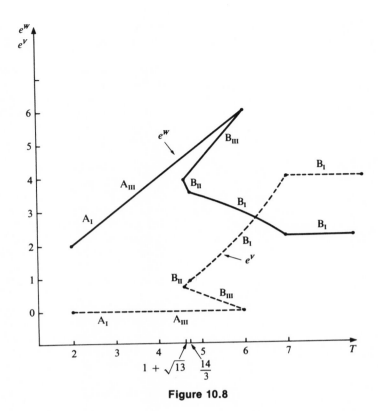

Figure 10.8

a policy of price intervention (such as lowering π_1—that is, raising the real wage) as soon as T exceeds $1 + \sqrt{13}$. In this way we would displace the equilibrium so that the resulting path of movement would take place along segments B_{II} and B_I.

As this model seems to suggest, if the existence of multiple equilibria in a private-property economy is not unrealistic, a policy of direct price intervention by the government can be justified both to attain distributive justice and to regulate the path of movement of the economy.

Suggested Readings

Arrow, Kenneth J., and Hahn, Frank H. 1971. *General Competitive Analysis*. San Francisco: Holden-Day.

Debreu, Gerard. 1970. "Economies with a Finite Set of Equilibria." *Econometrica* 38: 387–392.

Hicks, John R. 1946. *Value and Capital,* ed. 2. London: Oxford University Press.

Malinvaud, Edmond. 1972. *Lectures on Microeconomic Theory,* trans. A. Silvey, chap. 5. Amsterdam: North-Holland.

Quirk, James, and Saposnik, Rubin. 1968. *Introduction to General Equilibrium Theory and Welfare Economics.* New York: McGraw-Hill.

Samuelson, Paul. A. 1947. *Foundations of Economic Analysis.* Cambridge, Mass.: Harvard University Press.

The Existence and Stability of Equilibrium

Consider an exchange economy consisting of ℓ goods indexed by $h = 1, \ldots, \ell$ and m consumers each represented by an index i. For each consumer the set of feasible consumption bundles X_i is the nonnegative orthant of $\mathbb{R}^\ell$. The preferences of consumer i are represented by a utility function $U^i(x^i)$, which is continuous and strictly quasi-concave. Moreover, for each i $U^i(x^i)$ is increasing as in assumption 2 of note 1, exercise 2.

The vector of initial resources in this economy is denoted ω (where $\forall h, \omega_h > 0$), and from it each consumer receives a fraction $r^i\omega$ where $\forall i, r^i > 0$ and $\sum_{i=1}^{m} r^i = 1$. We denote by P the set of vectors p of $\mathbb{R}^\ell$ such that $p > 0$ and $\sum_h p_h\omega_h = 1$. P is compact and convex. Any price vector considered hereafter will belong to P.

Let $\xi^i(p)$ be the vector of demand functions of consumer i for $p \in P$. Consider

$$\xi(p) = \sum_{i=1}^{m} \xi^i(p).$$

Let φ be the mapping of P into $\mathbb{R}^\ell$, which is defined as

$$\forall p \in P, \qquad \varphi(p) = p + \mu[\xi(p) - \omega],$$

where μ is a strictly positive scalar.

Let u be the mapping of $\mathbb{R}^\ell$ into P, so that to every element of R^ℓ there corresponds a unique projection onto P. This is written:

$$\forall x \in \mathbb{R}^\ell, \qquad u(x) \in P,$$

$$\forall y \in P, y \neq x, \qquad \|y - x\| > \|u(x) - x\|.$$

This, of course, is the Euclidean norm.

Problem 1

Show that this economy has at least a competitive equilibrium.

Problem 2

In searching for a system of equilibrium prices, consider the iterative procedure defined by

$$p(t + 1) = u \circ \varphi[p(t)].$$

Under assumptions H_1 and H_2, given below, show that it is possible to find $\mu > 0$ such that this procedure converges to a system of equilibrium prices.

H_1: $\exists \epsilon > 0$ such that for $\forall (p^1, p^2) \in P \times P, p^1 \neq p^2$ we have

$$[\xi(p^1) - \xi(p^2)][p^1 - p^2] < - \epsilon(p^1 - p^2)^2.$$

H_2: The demand functions are Lipschitzian: $\exists M > 0$ such that for $\forall (p^1, p^2) \in P \times P, p^1 \neq p^2$ we have

$$[\xi(p^1) - \xi(p^2)]^2 \leq M^2(p^1 \times p^2)^2.$$

We remind the reader of the version of Brouwer's theorem: any continuous mapping of a convex, compact subset of $\mathbb{R}^\ell$ into itself has at least one fixed point.

The following mathematical properties will be useful as well:

(1) If $f^i(p)$ is a function mapping P into $\mathbb{R}^\ell$—characterized as follows:

$$\forall p \in P, \qquad f^i(p) \text{ maximizes } U^i$$

over $X_i \cap \{x \in \mathbb{R}^\ell | px \leq r^i p\omega$, and $\forall h, x_h \leq 2\omega_h\}$—then $f^i(p)$ is continuous on P.

(2) Let $\psi(p)$ be a mapping of a convex, compact subset of $\mathbb{R}^\ell$ into itself. If ψ is a contraction, that is, if $\exists A \in (0, 1)$ such that

$$\forall (p^1, p^2) \in P \times P, \qquad \|\psi(p^1) - \psi(p^2)\| < A\|p^1 - p^2\|,$$

then ψ has a unique fixed point, and the sequence defined by $p(t + 1) = \psi[p(t)]$ converges and has a fixed point in the limit.

PROPOSED SOLUTION

In this exercise, we seek a mapping—the mapping $\mu \circ \varphi$ in the statement of the problem—that allows us to treat simultaneously the problems of the existence and the stability of the equilibrium.

The mapping φ is clearly based on the notion of Walrasian tatonnement, which involves correcting each price depending upon the excess of demand over supply for the corresponding good.

Following this correction defined by the mapping φ, certain prices can become negative and the system of corrected prices may no longer satisfy the initial normalization condition. Therefore we must relocate the system of prices in P; this is the role of the mapping u. For this purpose we could have used another mapping v defined in the following way:

$$\forall h, \qquad v_h(\varphi) = \frac{1}{\lambda(\varphi)} \max \{0, \varphi_h\},$$

with
$$\lambda(\varphi) = \sum_h \omega_h \{\max 0, \varphi_h\}.$$

Although the mapping v is more natural from an economic viewpoint than the mapping u, we have chosen the latter because of our particular approach to the problem of stability.

Problem 1

The mapping $u \circ \varphi$ maps P into itself. We prove that any fixed point of this mapping is a system of equilibrium prices. Suppose that there exists p^* such that

$$p^* > 0, \qquad \sum_h p_h^* \omega_h = 1, \qquad u[\varphi(p^*)] = p^*.$$

We denote $\varphi^* = \varphi(p^*)$ and $u^* = u(\varphi^*)$. Two cases are possible:

(a) $\varphi^* \in P$ and $u^* = \varphi^*$. Then we have:

$$\forall h, \qquad p_h^* + \mu[\xi_h(p^*) - \omega_h] = p_h^*;$$

$$\text{therefore } \forall h, \qquad \xi_h(p) = \omega_h.$$

In this case p^* is truly a system of equilibrium prices.

(b) φ^* does not belong to P.

Then u^* is a solution to the following problem:

$$\min \frac{1}{2} \sum_{h=1}^{\epsilon} [u_h - \varphi_h^*]^2,$$

subject to the constraints $\Sigma_h u_h \omega_h = 1$ and $u_h \geq 0, \forall h$.

IF WE DENOTE by α the dual variable associated with the first constraint, the Kuhn-Tucker conditions (necessary and sufficient in this case) can be written:

$$\forall h, \qquad -u_h^* + \varphi_h^* + \alpha\omega_h \leq 0, \tag{1}$$

$$u^*(-u^* + \varphi^* + \alpha\omega) = 0, \tag{2}$$

$$u^*\omega = 1. \tag{3}$$

Equations (2) and (3) yield $\alpha = u^*(u^* - \varphi^*)$. However, by definition, $u^* = p^*$. Therefore:

$$\alpha = p^*(p^* - \varphi^*).$$

Since $\varphi^* = p^* + \mu[\xi(p^*) - \omega]$, we derive

$$\alpha = -\mu p^*[\xi(p^*) - \omega].$$

However, because the utility functions are increasing, we have

$$p^*\xi(p^*) = p^*\omega$$

and, as a consequence, $\alpha = 0$.

Expressions (1) and (2) can be written finally as

$$\forall h, \qquad \xi_h(p^*) \leq \omega_h, \tag{4}$$

$$\sum_h p_h^* [\xi_h(p^*) - \omega_h] = 0. \tag{5}$$

These are the equations that characterize a competitive equilibrium.

In summary, to demonstrate the existence of an equilibrium it is sufficient to show that the mapping $u \circ \varphi$ has a fixed point. We naturally use Brouwer's theorem. Unfortunately, even if u is continuous, there is no reason why φ should be continuous. Property (1) suggests a strategy that allows us to obtain a continuous mapping of P into itself.

Let $f^i(p) \in X^i$ be the function characterized in property (1). We have $f^i(p) = \xi^i(p)$ as long as $\forall h, f_h(p) < 2\omega_h$.

Consider now

$$f(p) = \sum_{i=1}^m f^i(p) \quad \text{and} \quad \tilde{\varphi}(p) = p + \mu[f(p) - \omega].$$

Surely, if $\forall h, f_h(p) < 2\omega_h$, we have

$$\tilde{\varphi}(p) = \varphi(p).$$

Because of property (1) $\tilde{\varphi}$ is continuous. The same applies to $u \circ \tilde{\varphi}$.

Brouwer's theorem allows us to assert the existence of a fixed point for $u \circ \tilde{\varphi}$ at least. It is sufficient to prove that any fixed point of $u \circ \tilde{\varphi}$ is a fixed point for $u \circ \varphi$ as well.

We have seen that a fixed point of $u \circ \varphi$ is rendered by expressions (4) and (5). Likewise, if p^* is a fixed point of $u \circ \tilde{\varphi}$ we have

$$\forall h, \qquad f_h(p^*) \leq \omega_h,$$

and

$$\sum_h p_h[f_h(p^*) - \omega_h] = 0.$$

Therefore

$$\forall h, \qquad f_h(p^*) < 2\omega_h$$

and

$$\forall h, \qquad f_h(p^*) = \xi_h(p^*).$$

We conclude that p^* is a fixed point for $u \circ \varphi$ and therefore it is a system of equilibrium prices.

Problem 2

As the statement of the problem suggests, we shall use property (2) to demonstrate the convergence toward a system of equilibrium prices of the procedure defined by

$$p(t + 1) = u \circ \varphi[p(t)]. \tag{6}$$

So that property (2) can be applied, it is necessary that $u \circ \varphi$ be a contraction. Figure 11.1 clarifies the meaning of property (2).

First we prove that if φ is a contraction, then $u \circ \varphi$ must be a contraction. Therefore we must show that

$$\forall (\varphi^1, \varphi^2) \in \mathbf{R}^\ell \times \mathbf{R}^\ell,$$

$$\|u(\varphi^1) - u(\varphi^2)\| \leqslant \|\varphi^1 - \varphi^2\|. \tag{7}$$

We set $u(\varphi^1) = u^1$ and $u(\varphi^2) = u^2$. In the case where $(\varphi^1, \varphi^2) \in P \times P$, expression (7) is obviously satisfied. Consider the case where $\varphi^1 \in P$ but φ^2 is not. Then we must show that

$$\|\varphi^1 - u^2\| \leqslant \|\varphi^1 - \varphi^2\|.$$

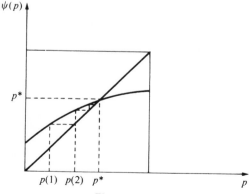

Figure 11.1

Assume the contrary:

$$\|\varphi^1 - u^2\| > \|\varphi^1 - \varphi^2\|.$$

By the definition of u and since $\varphi^1 \in P$, we have

$$\|u^2 - \varphi^2\| < \|\varphi^2 - \varphi^1\|.$$

Therefore:

$$\|\varphi^1 - u^2\| > \|\varphi^1 - \varphi^2\| > \|u^2 - \varphi^2\|. \tag{8}$$

Consider the triangle $\{\varphi^1, \varphi^2, u^2\}$. If we take inequality (8) into account, the projection z of φ^2 onto the line segment $[\varphi^1, u^2]$ belongs to the interior of this segment. Because P is convex, $z \in P$. Therefore we have

$$z \in P, \qquad \|\varphi^2 - z\| < \|\varphi^2 - u^2\|,$$

which contradicts the definition of u.

We are left with only the case where neither φ^1 nor φ^2 belongs to P. Let B_1 and B_2 be open balls defined by

$$B_1 = \{x \in \mathbf{R}^\ell | \|x - \varphi^1\| < \|u^1 - \varphi^1\|\},$$

$$B_2 = \{x \in \mathbf{R}^\ell | \|x - \varphi^2\| < \|u^2 - \varphi^2\|\},$$

Let π_1 (or π_2) be the plane that separates B_1 (or B_2) from P. Indeed P, B_1, and B_2 are convex and, by definition of u,

$$B_1 \cap P = \varnothing, \qquad B_2 \cap P = \varnothing.$$

The equation for π_1 is

$$(\varphi^1 - u^1)x = (\varphi^1 - u^1)u^1$$

and for π_2 is

$$(\varphi^2 - u^2)x = (\varphi^2 - u^2)u^2.$$

For all $p \in P$,

$$(\varphi^1 - u^1)p \leqslant (\varphi^1 - u^1)u^1$$

and
$$(\varphi^2 - u^2)p \leqslant (\varphi^2 - u^2)u^2.$$

Since u^1 and u^2 belong to P, we have

$$(\varphi^1 - u^1)(u^2 - u^1) \leqslant 0, \qquad (\varphi^2 - u^2)(u^1 - u^2) \leqslant 0. \tag{9}$$

Consider $(\varphi^1 - \varphi^2)^2$:

$$(\varphi^1 - \varphi^2)^2 = [(\varphi^1 - u^1) + (u^1 - u^2) + (u^2 - \varphi^2)]^2$$

$$= (u^1 - u^2)^2 + 2(u^1 - u^2)(\varphi^1 - u^1)$$

$$+ 2(u^1 - u^2)(u^2 - \varphi^2) + (\varphi^1 - u^1 + u^2 - \varphi^2)^2.$$

Then inequality (9) implies inequality (7), which is the result we were seeking.

Thus, if there exists $\mu > 0$ such that the associated function φ is a contraction, by property (2) there exists a system of unique equilibrium prices $p^* \in P$, since any system of equilibrium prices belonging to P is a fixed point of $u \circ \varphi$.

Moreover, for the value of μ considered, the procedure defined by Eq. (6) converges to p^*. For such a value of μ there exists $A \in (0, 1)$ such that

$$\forall (p^1, p^2) \in P \times P, \qquad [(p^1 - p^2) + \mu(\xi(p^1) - \xi(p^2))]^2 \leqslant A^2(p^1 - p^2)^2,$$

or, by algebraic manipulation,

$$\mu^2[\xi(p^1) - \xi(p^2)]^2 + 2\mu(p^1 - p^2)[\xi(p^1) - \xi(p^2)]$$

$$+ (1 - A^2)(p^1 - p^2)^2 \leqslant 0. \tag{10}$$

A necessary condition is that $\forall (p^1, p^2) \in P \times P$, $p^1 \neq p^2$, we have

$$(p^1 - p^2)[\xi(p^1) - \xi(p^2)] < 0.$$

Although its necessity is apparent, this condition is not sufficient; therefore we have strengthened it to lead to assumptions H_1 and H_2. When we take these assumptions into account, so that expression (10) is satisfied for all (p^1, p^2) of $P \times P$, it is sufficient that

$$(\mu^2 M^2 - 2\mu\epsilon + 1 - A^2) \leq 0. \tag{11}$$

We conclude from that, for any value of μ belonging to the interval $(0, 2\epsilon/M^2)$, the mapping φ is a contraction. This completes the proof.

How should we choose μ in this interval? Obviously we must choose it in such a way that the convergence of the procedure is as rapid as possible. Furthermore, the smallest value of A associated with a value of μ satisfying inequality (11) is given by $A = \sqrt{1 + g(\mu)}$, where $g(\mu) = \mu^2 M^2 - 2\mu\epsilon$. The smaller the value of A, the more rapid will be the convergence of the procedure. Therefore we choose μ so as to minimize $g(\mu)$; that is, $\mu = \epsilon/M^2$. The minimum value of A is

$$A = \sqrt{1 - \frac{\epsilon^2}{M^2}}.$$

We note in passing that for assumptions H_1 and H_2 to be consistent, we require that $\epsilon^2/M^2 < 1$. Therefore we must expect the convergence to be more rapid as ϵ is larger (which means that the property of gross substitutability, which provides the basis for assumption H_2, is stronger) and as M is smaller (which means that the demand functions are more regular).

We can interpret the procedure defined by Eq. (6) as a decentralized procedure designed to search for the Pareto optimum associated with the distribution of income given by the r^i's. In such a procedure, at step t, the central planning bureau announces a system of prices $p(t)$. Taking into account the income allocated to them, the consumers respond with their demands $\xi^i[p(t)]$. The central bureau can then calculate

$$u \circ \varphi[p(t)] = p(t + 1),$$

the system of prices to be announced in step $t + 1$. Realistically, a problem would then arise in choosing a value of μ—that is, in determining the important correction factor to be used at each step. Indeed, too small a value of μ leads to too slow a convergence, whereas too large a value can jeopardize the convergence toward a system of equilibrium prices.

Suggested Readings

Arrow, Kenneth J., and Hahn, Frank H. 1971. *General Competitive Analysis,* chap. 11. San Francisco: Holden-Day.

Debreu, Gerard. 1959. *Theory of Value: An Axiomatic Analysis of Economic Equilibrium,* chap. 5. New Haven: Yale University Press.

Fisher, Frank. 1976. "The Stability of General Equilibrium: Results and Problems." In *Essays in Economic Analysis,* ed. Michael J. Artis and Avelino R. Nobay. Cambridge: Cambridge University Press.

Hahn, Frank H. 1982. "Stability." In *Handbook of Mathematical Economics,* vol. 2., ed. Kenneth J. Arrow and Michael D. Intriligator. Amsterdam: North-Holland.

Karlin, Samuel. 1959. *Mathematical Methods and Theory in Games, Programming and Economics,* vol. 1, chap. 9. Reading, Mass.: Addison-Wesley.

Malinvaud, Edmond. 1972. *Lectures on Microeconomic Theory,* trans. A. Silvey, chaps. 5 and 8. Amsterdam: North-Holland.

Rudin, Walter. 1976. *Principles of Mathematical Analysis,* ed. 3, chap. 9. New York: McGraw-Hill.

Uzawa, Hirofumi. 1960. "Walras Tatonnement in the Theory of Exchange." *Review of Economic Studies* 27: 182–194.

PART FOUR

Pareto Optimality:
The Production Optimum

12

The Substitution Theorem

Consider an economy in which there are three goods—1, 2, and 3—with good 3 being labor (a primary factor of production). There are two enterprises (or sectors), enterprise 1 produces good 1 according to the production function

$$y_{11} = 3(-y_{12})^{1/3}(-y_{13})^{2/3}.$$

Enterprise 2 produces good 2 according to the production function:

$$y_{22} = 2(-y_{21})^{1/2}(-y_{23})^{1/2}.$$

The vector (y_{i1}, y_{i2}, y_{i3}) is the vector of net output of enterprise i, $i = 1$, 2. Notice that inputs are negative (that is, $y_{i3} < 0$).

(a) Show that the vectors of "technical coefficients" of each enterprise associated with a production optimum are independent of the characteristics of this optimum and calculate these vectors. This result is known as the substitution theorem. (Remember that the components of the vector of technical coefficients corresponding to the production of good 1 are, for example, $a_{11} = 0$, $a_{21} = -y_{12}/y_{11}$, $a_{31} = -y_{13}/y_{11}$.)

(b) By solving the linear system that expresses the price of each good as equal to its cost of production, calculate the prices associated with the technical coefficients defined in (a). (We consider good 3 as the numéraire). Taking the quantity of available labor to be ω, determine the set of possible consumption bundles of goods 1 and 2.

(c) Generalize the substitution theorem to the case where all of the following are satisfied:

(1) There are ℓ goods, of which one is a primary factor;

(2) There are $(\ell - 1)$ enterprises (or sectors) producing each of the $(\ell - 1)$ produced goods using the other $(\ell - 2)$ goods and the primary factor;

129

(3) The output of each enterprise is subject to a constant return-to-scale production function, which is differentiable and quasi-concave.

Will the substitution theorem continue to hold if there is more than one primary factor?

PROPOSED SOLUTION

The aim of this exercise is to generalize the assumptions on which Leontief's open model rests by proving a substitution theorem. In such a model production is subject to constant returns and a single technique is used, which means that there is strict complementarity between the factors, one of which (labor) is not produced. What happens if we keep the assumption of constant returns and have a single nonproduced factor (labor), but allow the possibility of substitution between the various factors?

The proposed solution treats rigorously the particular model specified; then it outlines a more general proof of the substitution theorem, valid in the case where the production functions are not differentiable; but it is limited always to an economy with three goods. Finally, a proof for ℓ goods is sketched in the case where we assume again the existence of differentiable production functions.

(a) A production optimum corresponds to the maximum of $y_{13} + y_{23}$ (that is, the minimum total labor requirement) subject to the constraints

$$y_{12} + y_{22} \geqslant y_2^0, \tag{1}$$

$$y_{11} + y_{21} \geqslant y_1^0, \tag{2}$$

$$y_{11} \leqslant 3(-y_{12})^{1/3}(-y_{13})^{2/3}, \quad \text{for} \quad y_{12} \leqslant 0, y_{13} \leqslant 0, \tag{3}$$

$$y_{22} \leqslant 2(-y_{21})^{1/2}(-y_{23})^{1/2}, \quad \text{for} \quad y_{21} \leqslant 0, y_{23} \leqslant 0. \tag{4}$$

The objective function is linear and therefore concave. Only constraints (3) and (4) are nonlinear. These constraints characterize the production sets, which are convex cones. The domain over which we maximize $y_{13} + y_{23}$ is therefore convex and the Kuhn-Tucker conditions are necessary and sufficient. Thus, it is sufficient to find a single solution satisfying these conditions.

The objective function is strictly increasing with respect to y_{13} and y_{23}, whereas the production functions are strictly decreasing functions of each of the respective variables. At the optimum, constraints (3) and (4) are satisfied with equality. Consequently we use the Lagrangian:

$$L = y_{13} + y_{23} + \lambda_1[y_{21} + 3(-y_{12})^{1/3}(-y_{13})^{2/3} - y_1^0]$$

$$+ \lambda_2[y_{12} + 2(-y_{21})^{1/2}(-y_{23})^{1/2} - y_2^0].$$

Since the isoquants approach the axes asymptotically, consider the case where the variables $-y_{13}$, $-y_{23}$, $-y_{12}$, $-y_{21}$ are strictly positive.
Then the Kuhn-Tucker conditions are written:

$$\frac{\partial L}{\partial y_{13}} = 1 - 2\lambda_1 \left(\frac{-y_{12}}{-y_{13}}\right)^{1/3} = 0, \tag{5}$$

$$\frac{\partial L}{\partial y_{23}} = 1 - \lambda_2 \left(\frac{-y_{21}}{-y_{23}}\right)^{1/2} = 0, \tag{6}$$

$$\frac{\partial L}{\partial y_{12}} = \lambda_2 - \lambda_1 \left(\frac{-y_{13}}{-y_{12}}\right)^{2/3} = 0, \tag{7}$$

$$\frac{\partial L}{\partial y_{21}} = \lambda_1 - \lambda_2 \left(\frac{-y_{23}}{-y_{21}}\right)^{1/2} = 0. \tag{8}$$

If we find a solution to the system of Eqs. (1) through (8) such that $y_{13} < 0$, $y_{23} < 0$, $y_{12} < 0$, $y_{21} < 0$, we are assured that this solution is the production optimum sought.
If we now introduce the technical coefficients, Eqs. (3) through (8) become:

$$3a_{21}^{1/3} a_{31}^{2/3} = 1, \tag{3'}$$

$$2a_{12}^{1/2} a_{32}^{1/2} = 1, \tag{4'}$$

$$1 - 2\lambda_1 \left(\frac{a_{21}}{a_{31}}\right)^{1/3} = 0, \tag{5'}$$

$$1 - \lambda_2 \left(\frac{a_{12}}{a_{32}}\right)^{1/2} = 0, \tag{6'}$$

$$\lambda_2 - \lambda_1 \left(\frac{a_{31}}{a_{21}}\right)^{2/3} = 0, \tag{7'}$$

$$\lambda_1 - \lambda_2 \left(\frac{a_{32}}{a_{12}}\right)^{1/2} = 0. \tag{8'}$$

This new system of six equations and six unknowns allows us to determine the values of the variables a_{21}, a_{31}, a_{12}, a_{32}, λ_1, λ_2 independently of Eqs. (1) and (2), which serve only to determine the value of the variables y_{11} and y_{22}. Then it is possible to calculate the values of the technical coefficients which characterize the optimum studied above independently of y_1^0 and y_2^0.

Eliminate λ_1 and λ_2 from Eqs. (5') through (8'):

$$\left(\frac{a_{21}}{a_{31}}\right)^{2/3} = \frac{1}{2}\left(\frac{a_{12}}{a_{32}}\right)^{1/2}\left(\frac{a_{31}}{a_{21}}\right)^{1/3},$$

$$\left(\frac{a_{32}}{a_{12}}\right)^{1/2} = \frac{1}{2}\left(\frac{a_{12}}{a_{32}}\right)^{1/2}\left(\frac{a_{31}}{a_{21}}\right)^{1/3},$$

or

$$\frac{a_{21}}{a_{31}} = \frac{1}{2}\left(\frac{a_{12}}{a_{32}}\right)^{1/2} \quad \text{and} \quad \frac{a_{32}}{a_{12}} = \frac{1}{2}\left(\frac{a_{31}}{a_{21}}\right)^{1/3},$$

and

$$\frac{a_{32}}{a_{12}} = \frac{1}{2}\left[2\left(\frac{a_{32}}{a_{12}}\right)^{1/2}\right]^{1/3} \quad \text{and} \quad \frac{a_{21}}{a_{31}} = \frac{1}{2}\left[2\left(\frac{a_{21}}{a_{31}}\right)^{1/3}\right]^{1/2}.$$

It follows that

$$\frac{a_{32}}{a_{12}} = 2^{-4/5}, \qquad \frac{a_{21}}{a_{31}} = 2^{-3/5}.$$

When we take into account Eqs. (3') and (4'), the values of the technical coefficients are

$$a_{31} = \frac{1}{3}\, 2^{1/5}, \qquad a_{21} = \frac{1}{3}\, 2^{-2/5},$$

$$a_{32} = \frac{1}{4}\, 2^{3/5}, \qquad a_{12} = 2^{-3/5}.$$

If y_1^0 and y_2^0 are positive, which is what we assumed when we said that good 3 is the only primary factor, these technical coefficients and Eqs. (1) and (2) allow us to calculate the negative values of the variables y_{13}, y_{23}, y_{12}, y_{21}, that is, the solution to the system of Eqs. (1) through (8).

In spite of the possibility of substitution among the various factors, we have shown in this particular example that to obtain all the possible production optima it is sufficient to use one and only one technique of production defined by a vector of fixed technical coefficients for each good; in other words, it is possible to represent the technical possibilities by an open Leontief model.

It is useful at this point to look for a geometric representation of this result in the case of three goods. Accordingly, we set the quantity of available labor equal to one (it is always possible to do this by changing units) and we try to define the set of net achievable outputs of goods 1 and 2. Consider the plane (y_1, y_2) consisting of the outputs of goods 1 and 2 taking the output of good 1 as the abscissa and the output of good 2 as the ordinate. Choose a distribution of labor between the two sectors defined by the scalar $\lambda \in [0, 1]$. Then the technical possibilities of sector 1 are defined in the plane (y_1, y_2) by a convex set $P_1(\lambda)$. For example, in the particular case already studied $P_1(\lambda)$ is defined by $y_{11} \leqslant 3(-y_{12})^{1/3}\lambda^{2/3}$ and $y_{12} \leqslant 0$.

In the same way we define the set $P_2(1 - \lambda)$ for sector 2. For a fixed λ the set of the vectors of net outputs technically obtainable from a given unit of labor is equal to the sum of the sets $P_1(\lambda)$ and $P_2(1 - \lambda)$. The set of technically feasible outputs achievable by varying λ from 0 to 1 is given by

$$\bigcup_{\lambda \in [0,1]} [P_1(\lambda) + P_2(1 - \lambda)].$$

Thus, if constant returns is assumed, we have

$$P_1(\lambda) = \lambda P_1(1), \qquad P_2(1 - \lambda) = (1 - \lambda)P_2(1).$$

The set of technically feasible outputs achievable from one unit of labor is identical to the set of vectors y such that:

$$y = \lambda y^1 + (1 - \lambda)y^2, \qquad y^1 \in P_1(1), y^2 \in P_2(1);$$

that is, it is identical to the convex closure of the union of $P_1(1)$ and

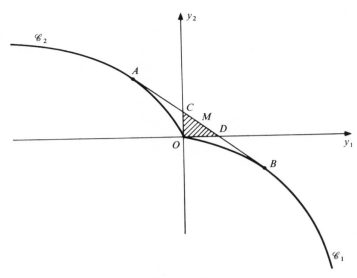

Figure 12.1

$P_2(1)$. In the (y_1, y_2) plane, this result is diagrammed in Fig. 12.1. Curve $O\mathscr{C}_1$ represents the boundary of set $P_1(1)$, and curve $O\mathscr{C}_2$ represents the boundary of $P_2(1)$. Curve $\mathscr{C}_2 AB \mathscr{C}_1$ represents the boundary of the convex closure of $P_1(1) \cup P_2(1)$. The set of achievable outputs of goods 1 and 2, given one unit of labor, is equal to the intersection of this set and the non-negative orthant $y_1 O y_2$, which is the triangle OCD.

Segment CD represents the set of production optima. Any production optimum such as point M can be represented by a linear combination of points A and B. Thus with each of these points we can associate an activity, that is, a vector of technical coefficients. The technical coefficients are independent of both the position of point M on CD and the quantity of available labor (because of the assumption of constant returns). This result is the substitution theorem.

Notice the role played by the assumption of no joint production, which implies that the sets $P_1(1)$ and $P_2(1)$ have an empty intersection with the positive orthant. This assumption permits us to eliminate the case where either A or B is found interior to the positive orthant.

Rigorously formulating such an approach allows us to demonstrate this result without the assumption of differentiability of the curves $\mathscr{C}_1$ and $\mathscr{C}_2$. In addition to the assumptions already made (existence of a single primary factor, constant returns, and convexity), it is sufficient to assume that the set of feasible points is nonempty and compact for a fixed quantity of labor.

(b) Let p_1, p_2, 1 be the price vector associated with the production optimum defined in (a). For this price vector the profit of each enterprise using the optimal production vectors (the profit maximum) is zero because of constant returns.

Zero profits for enterprise 1 yields the equation

$$p_1 = a_{21}p_2 + a_{31}. \tag{9}$$

For enterprise 2 we have

$$p_2 = a_{12}p_1 + a_{32}. \tag{10}$$

The linear system consisting of Eqs. (9) and (10) allows us to calculate p_1 and p_2:

$$p_1 = \frac{a_{31}}{1 - a_{12}a_{21}} + \frac{a_{32}a_{21}}{1 - a_{12}a_{21}} = \frac{1}{2} \, 2^{1/5},$$

$$p_2 = \frac{a_{32}}{1 - a_{12}a_{21}} + \frac{a_{31}a_{12}}{1 - a_{12}a_{21}} = \frac{1}{2} \, 2^{3/5}.$$

Note that the multipliers associated with the binding constraints in (a)—λ_1 and λ_2—can be interpreted as the prices of goods 1 and 2. For example, we calculate λ_1 from Eq. (5):

$$\lambda_1 = \frac{1}{2} \left(\frac{a_{31}}{a_{21}} \right)^{1/3} = \frac{1}{2} \, 2^{1/5}.$$

The value of p_1 is retrieved.

The system of prices associated with any production optimum is fixed and independent of the characteristics of this production optimum, as is shown in Fig. 12.1. In effect, the price vector associated with the optimum given by point M is normal to M and to the line segment AB. Its direction does not change as M varies along CD or as the quantity of labor varies.

To define the set of feasible consumption points, we use an approach that allows our reasoning to proceed independently of the number of goods considered. We have seen that it is sufficient to use one and only one activity in the production of each good to obtain all the production optima. Therefore let a_i be the vector (column) of technical coefficients for the production of good i by enterprise i. The components of a_i are a_{hi}, h varying from 1 to ℓ, where ℓ is the index given to the only primary factor available in quantity ω. Let y_i be the production of good i by enterprise i and y the vector (column) of dimension $(\ell - 1)$, since there are $(\ell - 1)$ enterprises. The vector x of consumption points, with components x_h, $h = 1, \ldots, \ell - 1$, is equal to

$$x = y - Ay = (I - A)y, \tag{11}$$

where I is the identity matrix and A the matrix of elements a_{hi}, with h and i varying from 1 to $\ell - 1$. For this vector x to be feasible, the amount of labor required (good ℓ) must not exceed the available quantity ω:

$$a_\ell y \leqslant \omega, \tag{12}$$

where a_ℓ is the row-vector of components $a_{\ell i}$. Taking Eq. (11) into account, (12) can be written:

$$a_\ell (I - A)^{-1}x \leqslant \omega.$$

This inequality, along with the condition $x \geqslant 0$, characterizes the set of feasible consumption points. The set is a simplex, and triangle OCD of Fig. 12.1 illustrates this set for the case where $\ell = 3$.

Returning now to the price vector, we let p be the row-vector of elements p_h, where h varies from 1 to $\ell - 1$. The price of good ℓ is equal to one, since this good is the numéraire. Then p is defined by the following system of equations showing that the profit of each enterprise is zero, a generalization of Eqs. (9) and (10):

$$p(I - A) = a_\ell, \tag{13}$$

from which we derive

$$p = a_\ell (I - A)^{-1}.$$

Then Eq. (12) takes the following very simple form

$$px \leqslant \omega.$$

Consequently, p_h is interpreted as the quantity of labor necessary to make one unit of good h available for consumption. Perhaps one could interpret this result as a labor theory of value.

(c) We now have ℓ goods designated by an index h or i. There are m enterprises designated by the index i. Let y_h^i be the output of good h from enterprise i:

$$y_h^i \leq 0, \qquad \forall h \neq i.$$

Suppose that the ith enterprise has a production function that is homogeneous of degree one, concave, and differentiable:

$$y_i^i = f_i(y_1^i, \ldots, y_\ell^i).$$

The last $\ell - m$ goods are primary factors of production.

A production optimum can be characterized by

$$\max \sum_{i=1}^{m} y_\ell^i$$

subject to the constraints

$$\sum_{i=1}^{m} y_h^i = \bar{y}_h \quad \text{for} \quad h = m + 1, \ldots, \ell - 1$$

$$(14)$$

and $\quad \sum_{i \neq h}^{m} y_h^i + f_h(\ldots, y_j^h, \ldots) = \bar{y}_h \quad \text{for} \quad h = 1, \ldots, m.$

The Lagrangian conditions are necessary to characterize the desired production optimum. The Lagrangian is written

$$L = \sum_{i=1}^{m} y_\ell^i + \sum_{h=1}^{m} \lambda_h \left[\bar{y}_h - \sum_{i \neq h} y_h^i - f_h(\ldots, y_j^h, \ldots) \right]$$

$$+ \sum_{h=m+1}^{\ell-1} \lambda_h \left[\bar{y}_h - \sum_{i=1}^{m} y_h^i \right].$$

The optimum is defined by the following system of equations: (14) and

$$\frac{\partial L}{\partial y_h^i} = 0 \qquad \forall i \quad \text{and} \quad \forall h, \quad \text{with} \quad i \neq h. \tag{15}$$

Equations (15) are homogeneous of degree zero with respect to the variables y_h^i and therefore depend only on the $m(\ell - 1)$ technical coefficients $a_{hi} = -y_h^i/y_{ii}$ and the $\ell - 1$ multipliers. There are $m(\ell - 1)$ of these equations. On the other hand, the equations characterizing the production functions yield m equations that relate the technical coefficients to one another:

$$f_i(a_{1i}, \dots, a_{\ell i}) = 1 \quad \text{for} \quad i = 1, \dots, m. \tag{16}$$

If $m = \ell - 1$ (that is, if there is only one primary factor), in principle the $m(\ell - 1) + m$ equations given by Eqs. (15) and (16) allow us to calculate the values of the technical coefficients and the multipliers (which can be interpreted as prices as long as the last good is taken to be the numéraire). Therefore, the technical coefficients and the associated prices are fixed and independent of the characteristics of the production optimum considered. Representing technical possibilities by an open Leontief model allows us to obtain all the possible production optima. The set of these optima in the space of net outputs of the $\ell - 1$ first goods is, as we have seen, a simplex.

However, if $m < \ell - 1$, that is, if there is more than one primary factor, there are not enough equations given by (15) and (16) to determine the $m(\ell - 1) + \ell - 1$ variables consisting of the technical coefficients and the multipliers (or prices). Then the values of these variables at the optimum depend on the characteristics of the particular optimum, since the equations in (14) are necessary to calculate them. The transition from one optimum to another (following, say, a change in final demand) is effectively rendered by substitutions among the various factors (produced or not)—that is to say, by a change in the technical coefficients.

The importance of the assumption of constant returns in all the above is obvious.

Suggested Readings

Arrow, Kenneth J. 1951. "Alternative Proof of the Substitution Theorem for Leontief Models in the General Case." In Koopmans, 1951b.
Dorfman, Robert, Samuelson, Paul A., and Solow, Robert M. 1958. *Linear Programming and Economic Analysis*. New York: McGraw-Hill.

Karlin, Samuel. 1959. *Mathematical Methods and Theory in Games, Programming and Economics,* vol. 1, chap. 8. Reading, Mass.: Addison-Wesley.

Koopmans, Tjalling C. 1951a. "Alternative Proof of the Substitution Theorem for Leontief Models in the Case of Three Industries." In Koopmans, 1951b.

Koopmans, Tjalling C., ed. 1951b. *Activity Analysis of Production and Allocation: Proceedings of a Conference.* New York: John Wiley.

Samuelson, Paul A. 1951. "Abstract of a Theorem Concerning Substitutability in Open Leontief Models." In Koopmans, 1951b.

13 Equilibrium and Pareto Optimality

In this exercise we study an economy made up of two agents, 1 and 2. We assume that there exist only two goods, X and Y. The variable X denotes a final consumption good that cannot be used also as a primary resource, whereas Y is a good that can be either consumed directly by the agents or used as an input in the production of X. The prices of X and Y are given by x and y.

The economy under consideration is a centralized economy, by which we mean that the "state" formed by the two individuals attempts to allocate optimally the available amount of good Y between final consumption and use as an input in the production of X. The production of X from Y is undertaken by a public enterprise E. This production is subject to the law of diminishing returns, with the only technical constraint assumed to take the form $X = kY^n$ with $n < 1$.

We assume that the preferences of the agents are represented by utility functions of the form

$$U_1 = X_1^{(1-m_1)} Y_1^{m_1} \quad \text{with} \quad 1 > m_1 > 0,$$

$$U_2 = X_2^{(1-m_2)} Y_2^{m_2} \quad \text{with} \quad 1 > m_2 > 0,$$

where X_i and Y_i are the quantities of the goods X and Y consumed by agent i, $i = 1, 2$.

We plan to study two methods of allocating available resources and to compare these methods for a particular example.

Problem 1

To study our first method of allocating resources, we require that the public enterprise E have a *balanced budget*. Distribution within the economy is subject to the rules of private ownership. If $\bar{Y}$ is the quantity of good Y available in the economy, we assume that agent 1 is endowed with $\lambda_1 \bar{Y}$, and agent 2 is endowed with $\lambda_2 \bar{Y}$, with $\lambda_1 > 0$, $\lambda_2 > 0$, $\lambda_1 + \lambda_2 = 1$. For each agent we set the simple behavioral rule of maximizing his utility function for given prices, subject to the budget constraint that relates his expenditure to his income.

(a) Construct an aggregate economic table for such an economy. Write the set of equations that determines the general equilibrium and verify that the number of independent equations is equal to the number of unknowns.

(b) For the equilibrium values of these variables, express the levels $\hat{U}_1$ and $\hat{U}_2$ attained by the utility functions of each of the agents. Show that there exists a functional dependence beteeen $\hat{U}_1$ and $\hat{U}_2$ when the distribution of resources within the economy changes. What is the form of this functional dependence when the agents have the same utility functions and we set $k = 2$ and $n = \frac{1}{2}$? For this particular case construct the "contract curve" $\hat{U}_1 = g(\hat{U}_2)$. Determine the extreme levels $\hat{U}_1$ if $\hat{U}_2 = 0$, and $\hat{U}_2$ if $\hat{U}_1 = 0$.

(c) A priori, what is your opinion of such a method of allocation?

Problem 2

To study the second method, we now allow the budget of enterprise E to be unbalanced. From the operation of E either a profit or a loss, R, occurs. This amount R is distributed between the agents ($R > 0$) or is financed by them ($R < 0$), and E is assigned the behavioral rule of maximizing R, *taking the prices as given.*

Here the profit of enterprise E will determine the distribution of income. In other words, in this entire second problem we consider agent i as disposing of a fixed quantity $\bar{Y}_i$ of Y, with $\bar{Y}_1 + \bar{Y}_2 = \bar{Y}$, while R is distributed between agents 1 and 2 in the proportions α_1 and α_2, with $\alpha_1 + \alpha_2 = 1$. Furthermore, we assume that α_1 and α_2 can take negative values, so that any distribution of primary resources can always be altered by the distribution of profit.

The behavioral rule assigned to agents 1 and 2 is the same as in the first problem.

(a) Construct the aggregate economic table of such an economy. Show the equality between the number of independent equations and the number of unknowns. Determine the system of equilibrium prices.

(b) Express the levels U_1^* and U_2^* achieved in equilibrium by the utility function of the agents for the values $m_1 = m_2 = m$, $k = 2$, $n = \frac{1}{2}$.

Construct the contract curve $U_1^* = h(U_2^*)$ when α_1 and α_2 vary; specify the extreme values.

Problem 3

(a) For the particular example studied show that the set of possible utility values of problem 2 includes the set of possible utility values of problem 1. Should we have anticipated this result? What is its economic significance and what can one conclude about the management of public enterprises under diminishing returns? Compare the two methods for the case $n = 1$.

(b) Suppose that $n > 1$. It is possible then to retain the behavioral rules defined above? How must we modify the objective assigned to E if we want to attain an equilibrium that is Pareto optimal?

(c) The preceding questions lead us to the determination of an optimal behavioral rule for enterprise E. What happens if there are two enterprises E and E' having identical production functions $X = kY^n$, with $n > 1$, and if these two enterprises conform to the behavioral rules defined above? Specifically, is the equilibrium attained a Pareto optimum? What can we conclude from this?

PROPOSED SOLUTION

This exercise is based on the optimality criterion of Pareto. We plan to compare different behavioral rules assigned to the economic agents. This leads us to the determination of a behavioral rule which, when applied, yields a Pareto optimal economic situation. A normative analysis, in which one strives to classify various types of economic organization, emerges. From this perspective the example considered here marks a turning point in this set of exercises. We shall deal quickly with the computation of various equilibria, since we have given the details of these calculations in previous exercises.

Problem 1

(a) In constructing the aggregate economic table, remember that there are three agents—the two individuals and the enterprise (Table 13.1). There is no distribution calculation because the profit or loss of the

	Expenditures			Income		
	Agent 1	Agent 2	Enterprise E	Agent 1	Agent 2	Enterprise E
Good Y	yY_1	yY_2	yY	$\lambda_1 y\bar{Y}$	$\lambda_2 y\bar{Y}$	
Good X	xX_1	xX_2				xX

Table 13.1

enterprise is zero at first. There are only two rows, one for each good; and there are five equations, the two rows that express the balance of demand and supply and the three columns that express the financial balances of the agents. It is well known that these five equations are not independent, since by Walras' Law if any four of them are satisfied, the fifth is also satisfied. In what follows, we shall consider the following four independent equations:

$$yY_1 + xX_1 = \lambda_1 y\bar{Y}, \tag{1}$$

$$yY_2 + xX_2 = \lambda_2 y\bar{Y} \tag{2}$$
(budget constraints of the agents),

$$yY = xX \tag{3}$$
(budget constraint of the enterprise E),

$$X_1 + X_2 = X \tag{4}$$
(market equilibrium for good X).

The reader can verify that the equation of market equilibrium for good Y is satisfied automatically.

The technical constraint faced by the enterprise yields this equation:

$$X = kY^n. \tag{5}$$

Maximization of U_1 subject to constraint (1) yields a supplementary equation—for example, the equation determining agent 1's demand for good X is

$$X_1 = \lambda_1(1 - m_1)\bar{Y}\frac{y}{x}. \tag{6}$$

Similarly, for agent 2, we determine

$$X_2 = \lambda_2(1 - m_2)\,\bar{Y}\frac{y}{x}. \tag{7}$$

The seven equations obtained depend only on the following seven variables: X_1, Y_1, X_2, Y_2, X, Y, y/x.

In principle, then, we can solve this system. However, the equilibrium obtained is not a competitive equilibrium because enterprise E is not a profit maximizer.

(b) Algebraic manipulation of Eqs. (3) and (5) yields

$$X = k^{\frac{1}{1-n}}\left(\frac{x}{y}\right)^{\frac{n}{1-n}}.$$

If we take the demand functions given by Eqs. (6) and (7) into account, the market equilibrium for good X, Eq. (4), allows us to calculate the equilibrium price ratio:

$$\lambda_1(1 - m_1)\,\bar{Y}\frac{y}{x} + \lambda_2(1 - m_2)\,\bar{Y}\frac{y}{x} = k^{\frac{1}{1-n}}\left(\frac{x}{y}\right)^{\frac{n}{1-n}}$$

or

$$\frac{y}{x} = k[\lambda_1(1 - m_1) + \lambda_2(1 - m_2)]^{n-1}\bar{Y}^{n-1}.$$

Equations (1) and (6) enable us to calculate U_1 as a function of y/x:

$$U_1 = \lambda_1 \bar{Y} m_1^{m_1}(1 - m_1)^{1-m_1}\left(\frac{y}{x}\right)^{1-m_1};$$

similarly,

$$U_2 = \lambda_2 \bar{Y} m_2^{m_2}(1 - m_2)^{1-m_2}\left(\frac{y}{x}\right)^{1-m_2}.$$

We can then calculate $\hat{U}_1$ and $\hat{U}_2$ as functions of the parameter λ_1, which characterizes the distribution of Y within the economy:

$$\hat{U}_1 = \lambda_1[1 + \lambda_1(m_2 - m_1) - m_2]^{(n-1)(1-m_1)} \bar{Y}m_1^{m_1}(1 - m_1)k^{1-m_1}\bar{Y}^{(1-m_1)(n-1)}$$

$$\hat{U}_2 = (1 - \lambda_1)[1 + \lambda_1(m_2 - m_1) - m_2]^{(n-1)(1-m_2)}$$

$$\times \bar{Y}m_2^{m_2}(1 - m_2)^{1-m_2}k^{1-m_2}\bar{Y}^{(1-m_2)(n-1)}.$$

By eliminating λ_1, we obtain a functional relationship between $\hat{U}_1$ and $\hat{U}_2$. For example, when $m_1 = m_2 = m$, $k = 2$, and $n = \frac{1}{2}$, we have

$$\hat{U}_1 = \lambda_1 A, \qquad \hat{U}_2 = (1 - \lambda_1)A$$

and $\qquad \hat{U}_1 + \hat{U}_2 = A$, with $A = 2^{(1-m)}m^m(1 - m)^{\frac{1-m}{2}}\bar{Y}^{\frac{1+m}{2}}.$

Then A is the value of the extreme level sought.

(c) For the consumers, the marginal rate of substitution between goods X and Y is equal to the price ratio. On the other hand, for enterprise E, this rate is equal to nkY^{n-1}, that is to say, taking Eqs. (3) and (5) into account, equal to ny/x. Since $n < 1$, this marginal rate of substitution is not equal to that of the consumers. Because the necessary conditions for Pareto optimality are not satisfied, it is possible to increase the satisfaction of one consumer (while leaving the satisfaction of the other consumer constant) by an appropriate exchange with the enterprise.

Problem 2

(a) Since the profit (or loss) R of enterprise E is no longer automatically zero, an additional row in the economic table is necessary to describe the distribution calculations. Table 13.2 again yields four independent equations:

	Expenditures			Income		
	Agent 1	Agent 2	E	Agent 1	Agent 2	E
Good Y	yY_1	yY_2	yY	$y\bar{Y}_1$	$y\bar{Y}_2$	
Good X	xX_1	xX_2				xX
Distribution			R	$\alpha_1 R$	$\alpha_2 R$	

Table 13.2

$$y Y_1 + x X_1 = y \bar{Y}_1 + \alpha_1 R, \tag{1'}$$

$$y Y_2 + x X_2 = y \bar{Y}_2 + \alpha_2 R, \tag{2'}$$

$$x X = y Y + R, \tag{3'}$$

$$X_1 + X_2 = X. \tag{4}$$

Equations (6) and (7) become

$$X_1 = (1 - m_1) \frac{y \bar{Y}_1 + \alpha_1 R}{x} \tag{6'}$$

and

$$X_2 = (1 - m_2) \frac{y \bar{Y}_2 + \alpha_2 R}{x}. \tag{7'}$$

Finally, maximization of $R = xX - yY$ subject to the technical constraint

$$X = k Y^n \tag{5}$$

yields a supplementary equation:

$$\frac{y}{x} = nk Y^{n-1}. \tag{8}$$

The eight equations thus obtained depend on eight variables: X_1, Y_1, X_2, Y_2, X, Y, R, y/x. They determine a competitive equilibrium in a private-ownership economy.

To calculate the equilibrium price ratio, we see that Eqs. (5) and (8) yield

$$X = k \left(\frac{nkx}{y} \right)^{\frac{n}{1-n}}.$$

Equation (3') allows us to calculate R:

$$R = \frac{(1-n)}{n} y \left(\frac{nkx}{y} \right)^{\frac{1}{1-n}},$$

and we substitute this expression in the demand equations determined by Eqs. (6') and (7'). Equation (4) determines the equilibrium price ratio as

$$k \left(\frac{nkx}{y} \right)^{\frac{n}{1-n}} = \frac{y}{x} [(1 - m_1) \bar{Y}_1 + (1 - m_2) \bar{Y}_2]$$

$$+ \frac{y}{x} [\alpha_1(1 - m_1) + \alpha_2(1 - m_2)] \frac{(1 - n)}{n} \left(\frac{nkx}{y} \right)^{\frac{1}{1-n}}$$

where

$$\frac{x}{y} = \frac{1}{kn^n} \left\{ \frac{(1 - m_1) \bar{Y}_1 + (1 - m_2) \bar{Y}_2}{1 - (1 - n)[\alpha_1(1 - m_1) + \alpha_2(1 - m_2)]} \right\}^{1-n}.$$

(b) In the given example where $m_1 = m_2 = m$, $k = 2$, $n = 1/2$, we have

$$\frac{x}{y} = \frac{\sqrt{2}}{2} \left[\frac{(1 - m) \bar{Y}}{1 - (1 - n)(1 - m)} \right]^{1-n}$$

and

$$R = y \bar{Y} \frac{(1 - m)}{(1 + m)}.$$

Hence

$$U_1^* = m^m(1 - m)^{1-m} \bar{Y}_1 + \alpha_1 \left[\bar{Y} \frac{(1 - m)}{(1 + m)} \right] \left[\frac{1 + m}{(1 - m) \bar{Y}} \right]^{\frac{1-m}{2}}$$

and

$$U_2^* = m^m(1 - m)^{1-m} \left[\bar{Y}_2 + \alpha_2 \bar{Y} \frac{(1 - m)}{(1 + m)} \right] \left[\frac{1 + m}{(1 - m) \bar{Y}} \right]^{\frac{1-m}{2}}.$$

When α_1 and α_2 vary, keeping in mind that $\alpha_1 + \alpha_2 = 1$, we have

$$U_1^* + U_2^* = B, \quad \text{with} \quad B = 2 \left(\frac{1}{1 + m} \right)^{\frac{1+m}{2}} m^m (1 - m)^{\frac{1-m}{2}} \bar{Y}^{\frac{1+m}{2}}.$$

Then B is the extreme level sought.

Problem 3

In order to compare the range of possible utilities obtained in each of the above cases, it is sufficient to compare A and B.

We have

$$\frac{B}{A} = 2^m \left(\frac{1}{1+m}\right)^{\frac{1+m}{2}}.$$

Consider B/A as a function of m:

$$\log \frac{B}{A} = m \log 2 - \frac{1+m}{2} \log (1+m).$$

Let $f(m)$ be this function:

$$\frac{df}{dm} = \log 2 - \frac{1}{2} - \frac{1}{2} \log (1+m)$$

and

$$\frac{d^2f}{dm^2} = -\frac{1}{2(1+m)}.$$

For $m \in [0,1]$ the function $f: m \to f(m)$ has a strictly negative second derivative. The first derivative is therefore always decreasing. It is positive for $m = 0$, it vanishes for $\log (1+m) = 2 \log 2 - 1$, and it is negative thereafter. For $m \in (0,1)$, f is therefore strictly positive and the ratio $B/A = e^f$ is greater than one.

In summary, for $0 < m < 1$, which is the case here, $B/A > 1$. The range of feasible utilities in problem 2 includes therefore all feasible utilities from problem 1. One should expect this result, since in problem 2 the rule of maximizing R leads enterprise E to equate the marginal rate of substitution between goods X and Y to the price ratio and therefore to the marginal rate of substitution of other agents. However, when all the convexity assumptions are combined, as is the case here for $n < 1$, equality of all the marginal rates of substitution for all the agents and for each pair of goods is a sufficient condition for the realization of a Pareto optimum. Then the operational rule recommended for an enterprise facing diminishing returns is to maximize profit, taking the prices as given.

Notice that when $n = 1$ (constant returns), the operational rules assigned to E in both problems are equivalent. We can show this in two ways. On the one hand, the marginal rate of substitution between goods X and Y for E is equal to ny/x in problem 1 and is therefore equal to the price ratio when $n = 1$. On the other hand, where there are constant returns, the maximization of profits occurs for zero profits.

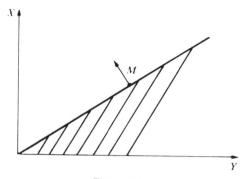

Figure 13.1

Finally, notice that the functions of supply and demand of the enterprise are always indeterminate for the equilibrium price ratio when $n = 1$. In Fig. 13.1 the production set is shaded (it forms a cone).

For the equilibrium price ratio any point on the boundary (such as M) maximizes R. It would be necessary then, for the set of equilibrium prices, to request explicitly that the enterprise adapt its supply to demand.

(b) In the case where $n > 1$ and where we assume that the enterprise balances its budget, the results in problem 1 are not affected. On the other hand, Eq. (8) in problem 2 no longer characterizes a maximum but a profit minimum taking constraint (5) into account, since for $n > 1$ the production function is convex. The only local profit maximum corresponding to a finite output of the enterprise is zero profit attained when output is zero. In this case assigning to enterprise E the behavioral rule of maximizing profit R is incompatible with the realization of an equilibrium.

As shown above, the behavioral rule of the first problem did not lead to the attainment of a Pareto optimum, except in the case $n = 1$. To determine what new rule can be defined so that its application will yield an optimum, we study the characteristics of an optimum.

An optimum corresponds to maximizing U_1 subject to the constraints

$$U_2 \geqslant \bar{U}_2 = \text{constant},$$

$$X_1 + X_2 \leqslant kY^n,$$

$$Y_1 + Y_2 + Y \leqslant \bar{Y},$$

with $\qquad X_1 \geqslant 0, X_2 \geqslant 0, Y_1 \geqslant 0, Y_2 \geqslant 0, Y \geqslant 0.$

Since U_1 and U_2 are functions that are strictly increasing in each of their arguments, all the constraints are satisfied with equality at the optimum. Let μ, β, γ be the multipliers associated with each of the constraints. Suppose that $\bar{U}_2 > 0$ and that U_1 can take strictly positive values; then all the variables considered will necessarily be strictly positive at the optimum. Consequently the following Lagrangian conditions are satisfied at the optimum:

$$\frac{\partial U_1}{\partial X_1} - \beta = 0, \qquad \frac{\partial U_1}{\partial Y_1} - \gamma = 0,$$

$$\mu \frac{\partial U}{\partial X_2} - \beta = 0, \qquad \mu \frac{\partial U_2}{\partial X_2} - \gamma = 0,$$

$$\beta nk Y^{n-1} = \gamma.$$

Elimination of the multipliers yields:

$$\frac{\partial U_1}{\partial X_1} \Big/ \frac{\partial U_1}{\partial Y_1} = \frac{\partial U_2}{\partial X_2} \Big/ \frac{\partial U_2}{\partial Y_2} = \frac{1}{nk Y^{n-1}}.$$

These equations express the equalization of the marginal rates of substitution of the agents and of the enterprise. If we interpret the common value of these rates as a price ratio, the optimum is attained if the enterprise and the agents make decisions such that their marginal rates of substitution are equal to the price ratios. The corresponding equilibrium was defined in problem 2.

As we saw in the case $n > 1$, this condition no longer corresponds to the profit maximum of enterprise E. However, it does correspond to selling at marginal cost. This classic behavioral rule therefore makes the achievement of a Pareto optimum possible even when $n > 1$. However, when $n > 1$, applying the rule of selling at marginal cost generates a deficit or loss. Therefore, we must decide how to distribute this deficit among the various agents. Such a decision, the effects of which are analogous to transfers, cannot be made without considering the concept of distributive justice.

(c) If the two enterprises both sell at marginal cost according to the rule that we have just defined, they use as an input the same amount of good $Y(Y_E = Y_{E'})$, since their production functions are identical. Such a situation cannot be optimal, because with the same total amount of good

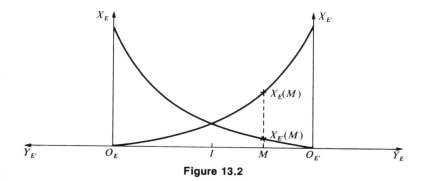

Figure 13.2

$Y: Y = Y_E + Y_{E'}$ it is possible to increase the output of good X. This can be seen in Fig. 13.2.

The curves drawn in the quadrants $Y_E O_E X_E$ and $Y_{E'} O_{E'} X_{E'}$ correspond to production functions of E and E' respectively and the segment $[O_E O_{E'}] = Y$. Therefore to any point such as M there corresponds a distribution of Y between the two enterprises and a total output of X equal to $X_E(M) + X_{E'}(M)$. Aggregate output is not maximized at point I, where the marginal rates of substitution are equal, but rather at either O_E or $O_{E'}$ when one of the two enterprises is not producing.

Another way of showing this result is to notice that the sum of the production sets of E and E' is identical to the production set of E and that an efficient point of the aggregate set, one on its frontier, can be obtained only when the output of one of the enterprises is zero (see Fig. 13.3).

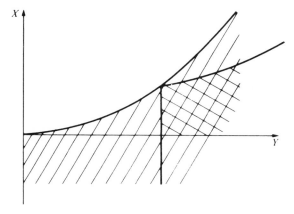

Figure 13.3

Therefore, when there are many enterprises facing increasing returns, assigning to all the enterprises the rule of selling at marginal cost is not, in general, optimal. The rule will become optimal only if, beforehand, we aggregate the various enterprises by first taking the efficient points of the aggregate set from the individual production sets. This example highlights the relationship between the aggregation of enterprises and the existence of increasing returns. In spite of its nonconvexity, the production set used is simple enough in that there is only one factor of production. The existence of many factors can lead to further difficulties in the case where the production set is not convex.

In summary, the rule of selling at marginal cost is an optimal rule in the case where the production sets are convex and can remain so in other special cases. But if the production sets are not convex, the rule in itself is not sufficient to guarantee the achievement of a Pareto optimum.

Suggested Readings

Guesnerie, Roger. 1975. "Pareto Optimality in Non-Convex Economies." *Econometrica* 43: 1–30.

Koopmans, Tjalling C. 1957. *Three Essays on the State of Economic Science,* chap. 1. New York: McGraw-Hill.

Malinvaud, Edmond. 1972. *Lectures on Microeconomic Theory,* trans. A. Silvey, chaps. 4 and 5. Amsterdam: North-Holland.

Quirk, James, and Saposnik, Rubin. 1968. *Introduction to General Equilibrium Theory and Welfare Economics.* New York: McGraw-Hill.

14 Social Welfare and the Surplus Criterion

In *Lectures on Microeconomic Theory* Malinvaud shows that "the variation in social utility for any infinitely small displacement from the optimum is equal to the variation in the value of total consumption, this value being calculated using the prices associated with the optimum" (p. 98).

The aim of this exercise is to shed more light on the way an economist determines an "infinitely small" variation of total consumption. We shall consider only the consumption sector of an economy consisting of ℓ goods ($h = 1, \ldots, \ell$) that are to be distributed among m consumers ($i = 1, \ldots, m$). For each consumer, assumptions (1), (2), and (4) listed in note 1 of exercise 2 are imposed on the consumption decision, although we shall assume that the utility functions S_i are quasi-concave and not strictly quasi-concave.

We denote as "a feasible allocation corresponding to the vector $\bar{x}$" the specification of m vectors x_i such that $\forall i$, $x_i \in X_i$ and $\sum_{i=1}^{m} x_i \leq \bar{x}$.

Given a Pareto optimal benchmark characterized by a feasible allocation corresponding to the vector $\bar{x}$, under what conditions can one say that a "small" change $\Delta \bar{x}$ in the production program of consumption goods is or is not advantageous? (The term "small" will be made precise in what follows.)

Presented in this way, the problem is still vague unless we define the word "advantageous." We must choose a definition such that it is possible to say, in a concrete situation, whether any particular transformation is or is not advantageous.

Consider the following definition which, as we shall try to show, is problematic. A change $\Delta \bar{x}$ in the production program of consumption goods is advantageous if we can find a feasible allocation associated with the vector $\bar{x} + \Delta \bar{x}$ such that, when compared to the benchmark, the utility of no one consumer is reduced and the utility of at least one consumer is increased.

Let us point out here that we do not strive to order all the consumption programs. The definition that we use puts particular emphasis on the initial situation (considered to be optimal). We limit the range of comparisons by taking once and for all as the basis for reference the given levels of utility corresponding to the Pareto optimum in the benchmark. On the other hand, as we shall show, the comparison will be valid in a measurable way only if $\Delta \bar{x}$ is not "too large"—that is, the ideas proposed here are not valid for all finite variations $\Delta \bar{x}$.

Problem 1

Show, by a direct application of Malinvaud's proposition 9 that if p^* is a price vector associated with the benchmark and if $\Delta \bar{x}$ is an advantageous transformation, then $\bar{p}^* \, \Delta \bar{x}$ is positive.[1] In order to apply proposition 9, we assume that the allocations x_i^* of the benchmark are interior to each of the sets X_i.

Problem 2

It is possible that many linearly independent price vectors are associated with the optimum benchmark. Show this by giving an example.

Problem 3

We continue to limit the analysis to an optimum benchmark such that $x_i^* \in \text{int } X_i$ for all $i = 1, \ldots, m$. We add the assumption that, for some consumer j, the function $S_j(x_j)$ is differentiable in x_j^*. Show that under these conditions the vector p^* associated with the optimum benchmark is unique to a scalar multiple.

Given a transformation $\Delta \bar{x}$ such that $p^* \Delta \bar{x}$ will be positive, show that we can find a positive constant λ_0 such that for all λ where $0 < \lambda < \lambda_0$, the change $\lambda \Delta \bar{x}$ may be considered to be advantageous, according to our definition above.

---

1. Malinvaud's proposition 9 states that if E^0 is an optimal state (that is, Pareto optimal) such that, for each of the ith consumers, x_i^0 is in the interior of X_i, if all the S_i's (individual utility functions) and all the X_i's satisfy assumptions (1), (2), and (4) and if the (production) sets Y_j are convex (not relevant in this exercise), then there exist prices p_h for all the goods, and incomes R_i for all the consumers, such that E^0 is realizable as a market equilibrium with these prices and incomes (parenthetical material added by translators).

Problem 4

We know from Malinvaud's proposition 9 that to the initial optimum we can associate an equilibrium corresponding to a distribution of income that is unique if p^* is unique and that can be defined by $R_i^* = p^*x_i^*$ $(i = 1, \ldots, m)$. Consider then the equilibrium (or equilibria) associated with the level $\bar{x} + \Delta\bar{x}$ of resources for an exchange economy where the R_i's (individual incomes) are the same as the ones in the benchmark. If $p^*\Delta\bar{x}$ is strictly positive and if, in this new situation, we allocate resources according to the "rules of the game" of a perfectly competitive equilibrium, is it true that when the incomes R_i^* are not changed, no consumer loses by the transformation? If the proposition is not true, give a counterexample. (Continue to assume that all the allocations are interior to the consumption set.)

PROPOSED SOLUTION

Problem 1

By making $\sum_{j=1}^{n} Y^j = Y = R^{\ell-}$ a set of vectors in R^ℓ whose components are all negative or zero, let us restrict the generality of proposition 9. We can say that, with the benchmark corresponding to some x_i^* $(i = 1, \ldots, m)$ such that

$$\text{for all } i, \qquad x_i^* \in \text{int } X_i; \sum_{i=1}^{m} x_i^* \leq \bar{x}, \tag{1}$$

we can associate a vector p^* such that

(a) $S_i(x_i) \leq S_i(x_i^*)$ for all x_i of X_i where $p^*x_i \leq p^*x_i^*$,

and   (b) $p^* \left(\sum_{i=1}^{m} x_i^* - \bar{x} - u \right) \geq 0$ for all u of $R^{\ell-}$.

Since 0 is an element of $R^{\ell-}$, (b) yields

$$p^* \left(\sum_{i=1}^{m} x_i^* - \bar{x} \right) \geq 0. \tag{2}$$

On the other hand, it follows from (b) that all the components of p^* are nonnegative. Suppose the contrary: that for a value of h, we have $p_h^* < 0$. Then we could find a value of u such that expression (b) is not satisfied.

Multiplying the two sides of inequality (1) by $p^* > 0$ yields

$$p^*\left(\sum_{i=1}^{m} x_i^* - \bar{x}\right) \leq 0;$$

taken together with inequality (2), this yields

$$p^*\left(\sum_{i=1}^{m} x_i^* - \bar{x}\right) = 0. \tag{3}$$

We thus arrive at a classical duality relationship from the familiar Kuhn-Tucker theorem.

From the proof of proposition 9 in Malinvaud, (a) can itself be shown to result from (a'), which is written

(a') $p^*x_i \geq p^*x_i^*$ for all x_i of X_i such that $S_1(x_1) \geq S_i(x_i^*)$.

More formally, we have:

(a) $x_i \in X_i$ and $(p^*x_i \leq p^*x_i^*) \Rightarrow S_i(x_i^*) \leq S_i(x_i^*)$,

(a') $x_i \in X_i$ and $[S_i(x_i) \geq S_i(x_i^*)] \Rightarrow p^*x_i \geq p^*x_i^*$.

But, ab absurdo, (a) is itself equivalent to

(a'') $x_i \in X_i$ and $[S_i(x_i) > S_i(x_i^*)] \Rightarrow p^*x_i > p^*x_i^*$.

To say that the transformation $\Delta\bar{x}$ is advantageous is equivalent, by definition, to the proposition $\exists x_i$, $i = 1, \ldots, m$, such that

$$x_i \in X_i, \sum_i x_i \leq \bar{x} + \Delta\bar{x}, \qquad S_i(x_i) \geq S_i(x_i^*), \tag{4}$$

and $\exists j$ such that

$$S_j(x_j) > S_j(x_j^*).$$

From (a′) it follows that

$$\forall i, \quad p^*x_i \geqslant p^*x_i^*.$$

On the other hand, from (a″)

$$p^*x_j > p^*x_j^*.$$

By summing over i, we have

$$p^* \sum_{i=1}^{m} x_i > p^* \sum_{i=1}^{m} x_i^*. \tag{5}$$

Multiplying the two sides of expression (4) by $p^* > 0$, we obtain

$$p^*(\bar{x} + \Delta\bar{x}) \geqslant p^* \sum_{i=1}^{m} x_i. \tag{6}$$

Taking (3), (5), and (6) together, we see that $p^* \Delta\bar{x} > 0$ and the problem is solved.

Problem 2

We construct an example in which an infinite number of price vectors are associated with the optimum benchmark. Figure 14.1 illustrates such a case with

$$\ell = 2, \quad m = 2, \quad X_i = \mathbb{R}^{2+}, \quad \bar{x}_1 = \bar{x}_2 = 1, \quad S_i(x_i) = \min\{x_{i1}, x_{i2}\}.$$

It is evident that all vectors p^* such that $p^* > 0$ can be associated with the optimum represented by point M.

Problem 3

Since $S_j(x_j)$ is assumed to be differentiable at the point x_j^*, we can write:

$$S_j(x_j) = S_j(x_j^*) + [\text{grad } S_j(x_j)]_{x_j = x_j^*}(x_j - x_j^*)$$
$$+ \| x_j - x_j^* \| \, \epsilon(x_j - x_j^*), \tag{7}$$

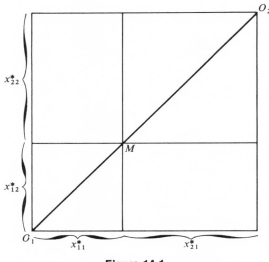

Figure 14.1

where $\epsilon(u)$ is a function that tends toward zero when $u = x_j - x_j^* \neq 0$ tends toward zero.

Since x_j^* belongs to the interior of the set X_j, if p^* is the price system associated with the optimum benchmark, and if we take supposition (a) into account, we must have

$$p^* = \mu[\text{grad } S_j(x_j)]_{x_j = x_j^*} \quad \text{(with } \mu \text{ a positive scalar)} \qquad (8)$$

Since $[\text{grad } S_j(x_j)]_{x_j = x_j^*}$ is unique, p^* is also unique to a multiplicative constant.

Now let us consider the feasible allocation corresponding to the vector

$$\bar{x} + \lambda \Delta \bar{x} \quad \text{(with } \lambda \text{ a positive scalar)}$$

satisfying the following properties: for all $i \neq j$, $x_i = x_i^*$; and for consumer j, $x_j = x_j^* + \lambda \Delta \bar{x}$.

Of course, since x_j^* is interior to X_j, we can find a $\lambda_1 > 0$ such that x_j belongs to X_j for $\lambda \leq \lambda_1$. On the other hand, we shall try to find a $\lambda_0 (0 < \lambda_0 \leq \lambda_1)$ such that

$$S_j(x_j) > S_j(x_j^*) \quad \text{for all} \quad \lambda(0 < \lambda \leq \lambda_o).$$

It is easy to show that if we can find a λ_0 such that

$$S_j(x_j^* + \lambda_0 \Delta \bar{x}) > S_j(x_j^*),$$

then for all λ such that $0 < \lambda \leq \lambda_0$ we have

$$S_j(x_j^* + \lambda \Delta \bar{x}) > S_j(x_j^*).$$

Indeed, since S_j is continuous, $x_j^* + \lambda_0 \Delta \bar{x}$ is then interior to the convex set defined by $\{x_j \mid S(x_j) \geq S(x_j^*)\}$; that is, there exists a neighborhood $V(x_j^* + \lambda_0 \Delta \bar{x})$ that is contained within the above set. If we construct a homothetic transformation of $V(x_j^* + \lambda_0 \Delta \bar{x})$ with respect to x_j^* using proportionality factor $\lambda/\lambda_0 \leq 1$, the transformed set constitutes a neighborhood of $x_j^* + \lambda \Delta \bar{x}$ and is contained in the set (see Fig. 14.2). The point $x_j^* + \lambda \Delta \bar{x}$ is then interior to the set $\{x^j \mid S(x_j) \geq S(x_j^*)\}$ so that $S(x_j) > S(x_j^*)$.

Suppose on the contrary that there exists no λ_0 such that $S_j(x_j^* + \lambda_0 \Delta \bar{x})$ will be superior to $S_j(x_j^*)$. This means that for all λ such $0 < \lambda < \lambda_1$

$$S_j(x_j^* + \lambda \Delta \bar{x}) \leq S_j(x_j^*), \tag{9}$$

with $$p^*(\lambda \Delta \bar{x}) > 0. \tag{10}$$

Taking Eq. (8) into account and returning to Eq. (7), we can rewrite the latter as

$$S_j(x_j^* + \lambda \Delta x) - S_j(x_j^*) = \lambda \mu p \Delta \bar{x} + \lambda \parallel \Delta \bar{x} \parallel \epsilon(\lambda).$$

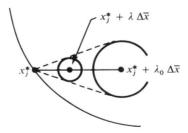

Figure 14.2

Then, dividing by λ,

$$\frac{S_j(x_j^* + \lambda\Delta\bar{x}) - S_j(x_j^*)}{\lambda} = \mu p \Delta\bar{x} + \Delta\bar{x}\epsilon(\lambda).$$

Let λ tend toward zero. Since the function S_j is differentiable up to a partial derivative in the direction $\Delta\bar{x}$, by inequality (9) this partial derivative is negative or zero. On the other hand, the term on the right-hand side tends toward $\mu p \Delta\bar{x}$, a positive quantity. Hence a contradiction occurs.

We have therefore found a feasible allocation corresponding to the vector $\bar{x} + \lambda\Delta\bar{x}(0 < \lambda < \lambda_0)$ such that the utility of all the consumers does not change except for that of the jth consumer, which increases. Therefore the proposition is proved.

Problem 4

The proposition is false. We shall give a counterexample. We specify $\ell = 2, m = 2, X_i = \mathbb{R}^{2+}$ and

$$S_1 = \alpha_1 \log x_{11} + \beta_1 \log x_{12},$$

$$S_2 = \alpha_2 \log x_{21} + \beta_2 \log x_{22},$$

with $\alpha_1 + \beta_1 = 1, \alpha_2 + \beta_2 = 1.$

As an optimum benchmark we choose the equilibrium corresponding to an exchange economy in which the incomes are R_1^* and R_2^*. This unique equilibrium is easy to calculate. The prices associated with it are

$$p_1^* = \frac{\alpha_1 R_1^* + \alpha_2 R_2^*}{\bar{x}_1}, \qquad p_2^* = \frac{\beta_1 R_1^* + \beta_2 R_2^*}{\bar{x}_2}$$

with the equilibrium allocations given by:

$$x_{11}^* = \frac{\alpha_1 R_1^* \bar{x}_1}{\alpha_1 R_1^* + \alpha_2 R_2^*}, \qquad x_{12}^* = \frac{\beta_1 R_1^* \bar{x}_2}{\beta_1 R_1^* + \beta_2 R_2^*},$$

$$x_{21}^* = \frac{\alpha_2 R_2^* \bar{x}_1}{\alpha_1 R_1^* + \alpha_2 R_2^*}, \qquad x_{22}^* = \frac{\beta_2 R_2^* \bar{x}_2}{\beta_1 R_1^* + \beta_2 R_2^*}.$$

Hence the levels of utility at the equilibrium are

$$S_1^* = \left(\frac{\alpha_1 R_1^*}{\alpha_1 R_1^* + \alpha_2 R_2^*}\right)^{\alpha_1} \left(\frac{\beta_1 R_1^*}{\beta_1 R_1^* + \beta_2 R_2^*}\right)^{\beta_1} \bar{x}_1^{\alpha_1} \bar{x}_2^{\beta_1},$$

$$S_2^* = \left(\frac{\alpha_2 R_2^*}{\alpha_1 R_1^* + \alpha_2 R_2^*}\right)^{\alpha_2} \left(\frac{\beta_2 R_2^*}{\beta_1 R_1^* + \beta_2 R_2^*}\right)^{\beta_2} \bar{x}_1^{\alpha_2} \bar{x}_2^{\beta_2}.$$

Without varying the distribution of income, we can construct in the (x_1, x_2) plane the indifference curves of each of the consumers corresponding to $S_1 = S_1^*, S_2 = S_2^*$. These curves naturally pass through the point $\bar{x}$, but as soon as $\alpha_1/\beta_1 \neq \alpha_2/\beta_2$, they have different slopes.

Along the curve $S_1 = S_1^*$ we have

$$\frac{dx_2}{dx_1} = -\frac{\bar{x}_2}{\bar{x}_1}\frac{\alpha_1}{\beta_1},$$

and along the curve $S_2 = S_2^*$,

$$\frac{dx_2}{dx_1} = -\frac{\bar{x}_2}{\bar{x}_1}\frac{\alpha_2}{\beta_2}.$$

Then it is easy to show (Fig. 14.3) that the slope

$$\pi = -\frac{\bar{x}_2}{\bar{x}_1}\frac{\alpha_1 R_1^* + \alpha_2 R_2^*}{\beta_1 R_1^* + \beta_2 R_2^*}$$

of the line orthogonal to p^* falls between the two above quantities. From

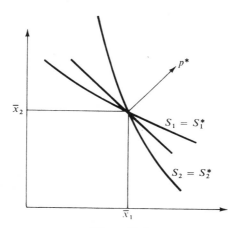

Figure 14.3

this follows the notion of a sufficiently small transformation characterized by

$$\Delta \bar{x}_1 > 0, \qquad \Delta \bar{x}_2 = -\frac{1}{2} \frac{\bar{x}_2}{\bar{x}_1} \left(\frac{\alpha_1}{\beta_1} + \frac{\alpha_1 R_1^* + \alpha_2 R_2^*}{\beta_1 R_1^* + \beta_2 R_2^*} \right) \Delta \bar{x}_1.$$

Then we show immediately that, for infinitesimal changes $d\bar{x}_1$ and $d\bar{x}_2$, we have simultaneously

$$p_1^* d\bar{x}_1 + p_2^* d\bar{x}_2 > 0, \qquad dS_1 < 0, \qquad dS_2 > 0.$$

A counterexample has thus been established.

Conclusion

The above considerations highlight the intricacy of the problem stated at the beginning. In particular, the following points emerge:

(a) When the price vector associated with the optimum benchmark is unique (and the analysis is limited to interior points of the consumption sets), the viewpoint of "social welfare" and our approach here yield equivalent conclusions; that is, the change in consumption of households measured in constant prices is a good indicator of the change in social utility.

(b) Even when we can characterize a transformation as "advantageous," an important problem of income transfer occurs. Indeed, we have seen that if we do not change the income distribution, certain individuals can be made worse off by the transformation, even though the latter is, by our definition, advantageous.

(c) Moreover, there are a few technical difficulties if we abandon the assumption that for each consumer the benchmark allocations are interior to his/her consumption set.

Suggested Readings

Arrow, Kenneth J., and Hahn, Frank H. 1971. *General Competitive Analysis*. San Francisco: Holden-Day.
Debreu, Gerard. 1959. *Theory of Value: An Axiomatic Analysis of Economic Equilibrium*. New Haven: Yale University Press.
Malinvaud, Edmond. 1972. *Lectures on Microeconomic Theory*, trans. A. Silvey, chap. 4. Amsterdam: North-Holland.

PART FIVE

Imperfect Competition and Game Theory

15

The Core:
A Nonconvex Example[1]

We consider here an exchange economy made up of two goods. The n consumers who participate in this economy are identical. Therefore they all have—

(a) the same set of consumption possibilities: $X = \{x \in \mathbb{R}^2 | x \geq 0\}$;
(b) the same vector of initial resources: $\omega = (1, 1)$;
(c) the same utility function: $U(x) = x_1^2 + x_2^2$.

Problem 1

Depending on the value of n, determine all the competitive equilibria of the economy defined above.

Problem 2

When $n = 2$, use an Edgeworth box diagram to determine the set of Pareto optima and the core. Represent these in the utility plane.

Problem 3

When $n = 3$, use the solution to the preceding problem to show that the core is empty, that is, that each allocation is blocked by at least one coalition.

Problem 4

When n is even, show that the core is not empty. Continuing with n even, show that as n increases, the core converges to the set of competitive equilibria.

---

1. The authors wish to thank C. Henry for his gracious assistance in the preparation of this exercise.

PROPOSED SOLUTION

The purpose of this exercise is to illustrate the relationships between the concepts of equilibrium and the core. We have here an example of an economy that does not have a competitive equilibrium and has an empty core because the assumption of quasi-concavity of the utility functions does not hold. The contraction of the core due to the increase in the number of agents is highlighted. Finally, we show that the set of Pareto optima is never empty even when the core is empty (because the total amounts of resources are limited and the utility functions are continuous).

Problem 1

The utility function common to all the consumers is obviously not quasi-concave. It represents preferences that are different from usual preferences for diversification, since the marginal utility from consuming a good increases as larger quantities of that good are consumed.

To maximize his utility subject to his budget constraint, the consumer always uses all of his income to buy only one of the two goods, as shown in Figure 15.1.

Let p_1 and p_2 be the prices of goods 1 and 2. If $p_1 > p_2$, all the consumers will demand only good 2, and vice versa. Consequently, in equilibrium we must have $p_1 = p_2$. Each consumer is then indifferent between spending all of his income on either good 1 or good 2; in other words, he buys either two units of good 1 or two units of good 2. Since the supply of good 1 is equal to the supply of good 2 and each is equal to n units, there can be a competitive equilibrium only if n is even. In this case $n/2$ consumers consume only good 1 and $n/2$ consumers consume only good 2. If n is odd, there is no competitive equilibrium. The reason is that, for p_2 fixed, when p_1 increases from a value less than p_2, there is a discontinuity in the consumer's demand at $p_1 = p_2$ because the utility function is not quasi-concave.

Problem 2

The Edgeworth box diagram of this exchange economy is given in Fig. 15.2. Point I corresponds to the initial situation, points E and E' to competitive equilibria. The sides of the box (that is, the segments O_1E, O_1E', O_2E, O_2E') constitute the set of Pareto optima. The curves A_1IB_1 and

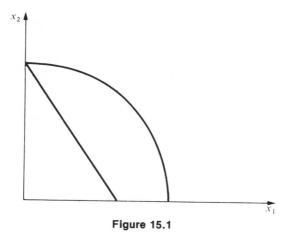

Figure 15.1

A_2IB_2 are the indifference curves of the first and second consumers respectively, passing through point I. Therefore the core is made up of the segments A_1E, B_1E', A_2E, B_2E'.

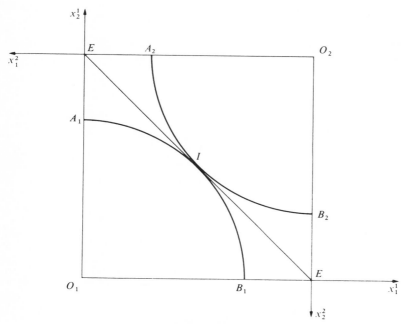

Figure 15.2

More generally, for any n, we notice that if the amounts consumed of both goods are strictly positive for at least two consumers, the situation is not Pareto optimum. Indeed, as is shown in the Edgeworth box diagram for a similar situation, it is possible to increase the utility of one of the consumers without reducing the utility of all the others.

On segments O_1E and O_1E', we have the following relationship between the utilities of the two consumers:

$$u_2 \geqslant u_1 \geqslant 0, \qquad u_2 = 8 - 4\sqrt{u_1} + u_1.$$

Similarly, on segments O_2E and O_2E', we have

$$u_1 \geqslant u_2 \geqslant 0, \qquad u_1 = 8 - 4\sqrt{u_2} + u_2.$$

The set of feasible points in the utility plane is shown in Fig. 15.3. The shaded portion $OCED$ corresponds to the set of feasible points, arc CED to the Pareto optima, and arc AEB to the core, given I.

Problem 3

Let $\{(x_1^1, x_2^1)(x_1^2, x_2^2)(x_1^3, x_2^3)\}$ be an allocation belonging to the core. This allocation also belongs to the set of Pareto optima. In view of the remark made in the preceding problem, two consumers cannot consume strictly

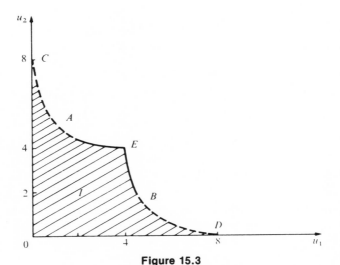

Figure 15.3

positive quantities of both goods. Since $n = 3$, we can conclude that at least two consumers consume only one good. We can always assume that these are consumers 1 and 2 and that $u_1 \geq u_2$.

From Fig. 15.3 it necessarily follows that $u_1 \geq 4$ and $u_2 \geq 2$. This implies that the two consumers consume different goods. Therefore we can write

$$x_1^1 > 0, \qquad x_2^1 = 0, \qquad x_1^2 = 0, \qquad x_2^2 > 0;$$

with
$$x_1^1 \geq x_2^2, \qquad x_1^1 \geq 2, \qquad x_2^2 \geq \sqrt{2}.$$

The consumption bundle $x_2^2 > 2$ is impossible because then $u_3 < 2$.

If $x_2^2 = 2$, u_3 can take a value equal at most to 2. But an allocation in which $u_2 = 4$ and $u_3 = 2$ would be blocked by the coalition formed by the last two consumers. Consequently $x_2^2 < 2$.

Still using Fig. 15.3, we conclude that $u_3 \geq u_2$. In order that the allocation considered not be blocked by the coalition formed by the last two consumers, it is necessary that

$$u_3 \geq 8 - 4\sqrt{u_2} + u_2^2,$$

or
$$(3 - x_1^1)^2 + (3 - x_2^2)^2 \geq 8 - 4x_2^2 + (x_2^2)^2,$$

or
$$(3 - x_1^1)^2 \geq 2x_2^2 - 1 \geq 2\sqrt{2} - 1,$$

or
$$3 - x_1^1 \geq \sqrt{(2\sqrt{2} - 1)},$$

and
$$x_1^1 \leq 3 - \sqrt{(2\sqrt{2} - 1)} < 2.$$

This contradicts the inequality already established: that $x_1^1 \geq 2$. Therefore, for $n = 3$, the core is empty.

Problem 4

The consumption sets and the utility functions satisfy assumptions 1 and 2 (see note 1 to exercise 2). Consequently, as is well known, any competitive equilibrium belongs to the core. For n even, the core is therefore not empty, since it contains the competitive equilibria. Moreover, we shall show that for $n = 2p$ and $p > 2$, the core is reduced to the set of competitive equilibria.

Taking into account our comments in the preceding problems, at least $2p - 1$ consumers consume only one good. On the other hand, of these $2p - 1$ consumers, at least $2p - 2$ have a utility level greater than or equal to 4. Therefore, we can always assume that the first k consumers each consume a quantity of good 1 greater than or equal to 2, and that they do not consume any of good 2. Also we assume that the $2p - k - 2$ following consumers each consume a quantity of good 2 greater than or equal to 2 and not any good 1. Finally, we assume that the $(2p - 1)$st consumer consumes only one good and that the last consumer eventually will consume both goods.

Because of the initial resources, we must have $p - 2 \leqslant k \leqslant p$. If $k = p$ or if $k = p - 2$, all the consumers consume only one good. Indeed, if for example $k = p$, the first p consumers each necessarily consume two units of good 1 and they all have the same utility level fixed at 4. The last p consumers can consume only good 2. On the other hand, no one of them would be willing to consume a quantity strictly less than 2, because then he could enter a coalition with one of the first p consumers to block such an allocation. In summary, if $k = p$ or if $k = p - 2$, any situation belonging to the core is a competitive equilibrium.

It remains to study the case $k = p - 1$. The last two consumers would block any allocation that gives a quantity strictly greater than 2 to at least one of the first $2p - 2$ consumers. Therefore the last two consumers have two units of good 1 and two units of good 2 to share. Neither would be willing to accept a utility level strictly less than 4, because then he would enter into a coalition with one of the first $2p - 2$ consumers. This finishes the proof.

Thus the asymptotic property of the convergence of the core toward the set of competitive equilibria is verified as soon as n is greater than 4.

Suggested Readings

Debreu, Gerard, and Scarf, Herbert E. 1972. "The Limit of the Core of an Economy." In *Decisions and Organizations,* ed. C. Bart McGuire and Roy Radner. Amsterdam: North-Holland.

Hildenbrand, Werner, and Kirman, Alan P. 1976. *Introduction to Equilibrium Analysis: Variation on Themes by Edgeworth and Walras.* Amsterdam: North-Holland.

Koopmans, Tjalling C. 1957. *Three Essays on the State of Economic Science,* chap. 1. New York: McGraw-Hill.

Malinvaud, Edmond. 1972. *Lectures on Microeconomic Theory,* trans. A. Silvey, chap. 6. Amsterdam: North-Holland.

Shapley, Lloyd S., and Shubik, Martin. 1966. "Quasi-Cores in a Monetary Economy with Non-Convex Preferences." *Econometrica* 34: 805–827.

Starr, Ross. 1969. "Quasi-Equilibria in Markets with Non-Convex Preferences." *Econometrica* 37: 25–38.

16

Imperfect Competition

The purpose of this exercise is to study the properties of the Cournot solution to an oligopolistic situation (first and second problems) and the Nash solution to a duopolistic situation (third problem).

Problem 1

Consider m enterprises indexed by j, all producing the same good. Let y_j be the output of enterprise j. Its marginal cost function $C_j(y_j)$ is linear with respect to y_j: $C_j(y_j) = a_j + b_j y_j$, with $a_j > 0$ and $b_j > 0$. The demand function for the good under consideration is characterized by

$$p = \alpha + \beta y, \quad \text{with} \quad \alpha > a_j, \forall j, \quad \beta < 0,$$

$$\text{and} \quad y = \sum_{j=1}^{m} y_j \quad \text{for} \quad y < -\frac{\alpha}{\beta},$$

and by $\quad p = 0 \quad \text{for} \quad y \geqslant -\dfrac{\alpha}{\beta}.$

Formalize a simple process (in discrete time or in continuous time) in which at each instant of time each enterprise maximizes its profit, taking as given the sum of the outputs of the other enterprises. We assume that each enterprise knows the aggregate demand function and the sum of the outputs produced by the other enterprises at the preceding instant of time.

Show that such a process converges, beginning from any initial situation, toward a Cournot equilibrium if $\forall j$, $b_j > -(m - 3)\beta$. One of the following properties should be used.

Property (1): Let M be a square, symmetric matrix ($m \times m$) in which all the nondiagonal elements are negative. If there exists a nonzero vector $x \in \mathbb{R}^m$, $x > 0$ such that the vector Mx has only strictly positive components, then M is defined to be positive.

Property (2): Let B be a square matrix $(m \times m)$ in which all the elements are negative or zero. If there exists a vector $x \in \mathbb{R}^m$ having all of its components strictly positive and if the vector $(I + B)x$ has all of its components strictly positive, then $(I - B)$ is nonsingular and the series $[I + B + B^2 + \cdots + B^n]$ converges to $(I - B)^{-1}$ when n tends toward infinity.

Problem 2

Assume that there exist m types of enterprises indexed by j. Within each type j, there are r enterprises (indexed by q) identical to enterprise j in the preceding problem. On the other hand, the demand function is characterized by

$$p = \alpha + \beta \frac{y}{r}, \quad \text{with} \quad y = \sum_{j=1}^{m} \sum_{q=1}^{r} y_{jq}.$$

When r tends to infinity, show that the Cournot equilibrium converges to the competitive equilibrium and interpret this result.

Problem 3

Consider two enterprises indexed by j ($j = 1$ or 2) in a duopolistic situation. The total cost function of the first enterprise is $C_1(y_1) = y_1^2$; the total cost function of the second is $C_2(y_2) = 2y_2$. The demand function pertaining to these enterprises is characterized by $y = 4 - p$. We assume that each enterprise has complete information on the cost functions and the demand function and that side payments are allowed.

The two enterprises agree on the following procedure to share markets and profits. Each enterprise, independently of the other, announces a level of output (y_1^* and y_2^*). Calculate the profits associated with these levels of output (which will not actually be realized):

$$B_1^* = B_1(y_1^*, y_2^*), \qquad B_2^* = B_2(y_1^*, y_2^*).$$

Then the enterprises produce quantities to maximize the sum of their profits (let B_0 be the maximum) and share equally the increment achieved by moving from the benchmark defined by B_1^* and B_2^* to the situation characterized by total profit equal to B_0. For example, enterprise 1 will receive profit equal to

$$B_1^* + \frac{B_0 - (B_1^* + B_2^*)}{2}.$$

Define the respective optimal strategies y_1^* and y_2^* for each enterprise (knowing that any given y_1^* and y_2^* determine completely the market share and profits, taking into account the initial agreement in the procedure).

Calculate the output and the profits actually realized. Then compare this solution, which is the Nash solution to a two-person cooperative game, to the perfectly competitive equilibrium and to the Cournot equilibrium.

PROPOSED SOLUTION

An oligopolistic situation can be studied in two ways: as a cooperative game or as a noncooperative game. The Cournot solution is a noncooperative equilibrium. The Nash solution is an example of a solution to a two-person cooperative game.

Treating an oligopolistic situation as a noncooperative game becomes more realistic as the possibilities of communication between the producers become more restricted and the number of producers becomes larger. This notion has been confirmed by experimental studies of simulated oligopolistic situations.

On the other hand, in a duopolistic situation with complete information, the Cournot solution seems less sensible. Actually, in the experimental studies other types of behavior arise. Either we see cooperative behavior, which leads to a solution close to the Nash solution, or we see "competitive" behavior, which undoubtedly leads the participants to execute their threats.

Problem 1

Denote $z_j = \Sigma_{i \neq j} y_i$. For a given z_j, define a level of output $y_j^*(z_j)$ for enterprise j, which maximizes its profit. Now, $y_j^*(z_j)$ is characterized by

$$y_j^* = 0 \quad \text{if} \quad \alpha + \beta z_j - a_j \le 0,$$

$$\alpha + \beta z_j + 2\beta y_j^* - a_j - b_j y_j^* = 0 \text{ otherwise.} \tag{1}$$

These equations are sufficient to assure that the profit maximum B_j of enterprise j is achieved, since the second derivative of B_j with respect to y_j is equal to $2\beta - b_j$, by assumption a strictly negative quantity.

If we divide time into equal periods indexed by t, we can define an iterative procedure by the following system of equations:

$$y_j^{t+1} = y_j^* \left(\sum_{i \ne j} y_i^t \right). \tag{2}$$

In such a procedure the only information required by each enterprise is knowledge of the demand function. In particular, communication among the enterprises is not necessary. On the other hand, if we consider time to be a continuous variable, we replace the system of equations given by (2) by a system of differential equations which expresses the property that at each instant of time each enterprise changes its output per unit of time in order to move toward y_j^*:

$$\frac{dy_j}{dt} = k_j [y_j^*(z_j) - y_j], \qquad \forall j \quad \text{with} \quad k_j > 0, \qquad \forall j. \tag{3}$$

We shall study in turn the stability of each of the procedures defined above, beginning with the one governed by the system of differential equations given by (3).

The method that we use involves defining a function that is zero at the equilibrium, strictly positive elsewhere, and has derivatives with respect to time that are strictly negative as long as the equilibrium is not achieved. It is well known that if such a function exists, then the iterative procedure studied converges to the equilibrium. (This method is known as the second method of Lyapunov.) Here the Cournot equilibrium is characterized by the system of equations:

$$y_j = y_j^* \left(\sum_{i=j} y_i \right), \qquad \forall j.$$

Therefore we can define the function V:

$$V = \frac{1}{2} \sum_{j=1}^{m} k_j \left[y_j - y_j^* \left(\sum_{i \neq j} y_i \right) \right]^2 .$$

This function is zero at the Cournot equilibrium and strictly positive elsewhere. Accordingly, we must study the sign of its derivative with respect to time, taking into account the differential equations given by (3):

$$\frac{dV}{dt} = \sum_{j=1}^{m} k_j (y_j - y_j^*(z_j)) \left(\frac{dy_j}{dt} - \frac{dy_j^*}{dt} \right)$$

$$= - \sum_{j=1}^{m} k_j^2 (y_j - y_j^*)^2 - \sum_{j=1}^{m} k_j (y_j - y_j^*) \frac{dy_j^*}{dt} .$$

From Eq. (1), we have

either

$$\frac{dy_j^*}{dt} = \frac{\beta}{b_j - 2\beta} \left(\sum_{i \neq j} \frac{dy_i}{dt} \right)$$

or

$$\frac{dy_j^*}{dt} = 0.$$

In what follows, we denote $\lambda_j = -\beta/(b_j - 2\beta)$. Since $\beta < 0$ and $b_j > -(m-3)\beta$ is assumed, we have

$$0 < \lambda_j < \frac{1}{m-1}, \qquad \forall j \in \{1, \ldots, m\}.$$

Let K be the set of enterprises for which

$$\frac{dy_j^*}{dt} = - \lambda_j \left(\sum_{i \neq j} \frac{dy_i}{dt} \right).$$

Then we have

$$\frac{dV}{dt} = - \sum_{j=1}^{m} k_j^2 (y_j - y_j^*)^2 - \sum_{j \in K} \lambda_j k_j (y_j - y_j^*) \sum_{i \neq j} k_i (y_i - y_i^*),$$

from which it follows that

$$- \frac{dV}{dt} \geq \sum_{j=1}^{m} k_j^2 (y_j - y_j^*)^2 - \sum_{j \in K} \lambda_j k_j |y_j - y_j^*| \sum_{i \neq j} k_i |y_i - y_i^*|,$$

and $-\dfrac{dV}{dt} \geqslant \displaystyle\sum_{j=1}^{m} k_j^2(y_j - y_j^*)^2 - \sum_{j=1}^{m} \lambda_j k_j |y_j - y_j^*| \sum_{i \neq j} k_i |y_i - y_i^*|.$

The differential dV/dt is therefore greater than or equal to a quadratic form $\sum_{j=1}^{m} \sum_{i=1}^{m} m_{ij} x_i x_j$, in which x_j is equal to $k_j |y_j - y_j^*|$, m_{ij} is equal to one if $i = j$ and to $-\frac{1}{2}(\lambda_i + \lambda_j)$ if $i \neq j$.

If M is a matrix of elements m_{ij}, it is easy to see that the conditions for applying property (1) are fulfilled. This allows us to assert that dV/dt is strictly negative as long as the Cournot equilibrium is not achieved. On the other hand, dV/dt is exactly zero at the Cournot equilibrium. Therefore, whatever the initial situation, we can establish the stability of the continuous procedure defined by the differential equations given by (3).

Let us now return to the iterative procedure in discrete time.

We assume that $\forall t$ and $\forall j$, $y_j^* (\Sigma_{i \neq j} y_i^t) > 0$. Taking Eq. (1) into account, we can then write Eq. (2) as

$$y_j^{t+1} = \frac{\alpha - a_j}{b_j - 2\beta} + \frac{\beta}{b_j - 2\beta} + \sum_{i \neq j} y_i^t.$$

This system of equations in matrix form is

$$y^{t+1} = \bar{y} + By^t,$$

where we denote as y^t the vector having components y_j^t, as $\bar{y}$ the vector having components $(\alpha - a_j)/(b_j - 2\beta)$, and as B the matrix whose elements are

$$b_{ij} = 0 \quad \text{if} \quad i = j, \qquad b_{ij} = \frac{\beta}{b_i - 2\beta} = -\lambda_i \quad \text{if} \quad i \neq j.$$

The vector of outputs y^* of the Cournot equilibrium is then characterized by the system of equations

$$y^* = \bar{y} + By^* \quad \text{or} \quad (I - B)y^* = \bar{y}$$

where I is the identity matrix.

On the other hand, the system of equations given by (2) yields by iteration

$$y^{t+1} = [I + B + \cdots + B^t]\bar{y} + B^{t+1}y^0,$$

where y^0 characterizes the initial situation.

Matrix B has only negative or zero elements. Let $\mathring{x}$ be the vector of $\mathbb{R}^m$ having all its components equal to one. The vector $(I + B)\mathring{x}$ has as its jth component $1 - (m - 1)\lambda_j > 0$. The conditions for applying property (2) are therefore satisfied by matrix B. We conclude that $(I - B)$ is invertible, that $y^* = (I - B)^{-1}\bar{y}$, and therefore that y^t converges to y^* when t tends toward infinity.

Problem 2

Assume that for any r there exists a unique Cournot equilibrium and that the quantities produced by each enterprise are strictly positive. We can show that two enterprises of the same type necessarily produce identical outputs in the Cournot equilibrium. Let q and q' be two enterprises of type j and denote as $z^*_{q,q'}$ the output produced by all the other enterprises in a Cournot equilibrium. The outputs y^*_{jq} and $y^*_{jq'}$ produced by enterprises q and q' for this Cournot equilibrium satisfy the equations

$$0 = \alpha + \frac{\beta}{r} z^*_{q,q'} + \frac{\beta}{r} y^*_{jq} + \frac{2\beta}{r} y^*_{jq'} - a_j - b_j y^*_{jq'}$$

and
$$0 = \alpha + \frac{\beta}{r} z^*_{q,q'} + \frac{\beta}{r} y^*_{jq'} + \frac{2\beta}{r} y^*_{jq} - a_j - b_j y^*_{jq}.$$

It is easy to show that this system of two equations in two unknowns, y^*_{jq} and $y^*_{jq'}$ has a unique solution where $y^*_{jq} = y^*_{jq'}$.

Let y^*_j be the output produced by each enterprise of type j in the Cournot equilibrium. The y^*_j's are defined by the following system of equations:

$$\alpha + \beta \left[\sum_{i \neq j} y^*_i + \frac{(r - 1)}{r} y^*_j \right] + \frac{2\beta}{r} y^*_j - a_j - b_j y^*_j = 0$$

or
$$\alpha + \beta \left(\sum_{j=1}^{m} y_j^* \right) + \frac{\beta}{r} y_j^* - a_j - b_j y_j^* = 0. \qquad (4)$$

By assumption, this system has a unique solution for any r, and this solution is a continuous function of $1/r$.

When r goes to infinity, we recognize that the unique solution of system (4) tends toward the solution of the following system:

$$\alpha + \beta \left(\sum_{j=1}^{m} y_j^* \right) - a_j - b_j y_j^* = 0. \qquad (5)$$

System (5) indicates that marginal cost $a_j + b_j y_j^*$ is equal to selling price $p = \alpha + (\beta/r)(r\Sigma y_j^*)$ for each enterprise. Therefore, it characterizes the outputs of a competitive equilibrium.

To interpret this result, consider an example in which several countries coexist with an oligopolistic situation in each country for a single good. If in each country the market equilibrium for the good considered corresponds to a Cournot equilibrium, and if all restrictions on trade between the considered countries are removed, the new equilibrium that will occur on the market for the good in question will undoubtedly approach the competitive equilibrium.

Problem 3

First, we determine B_0 by maximizing

$$B_1 + B_2 = (4 - y_1 - y_2)(y_1 + y_2) - y_1^2 - 2y_2.$$

The first-order conditions can be written

$$\frac{\partial(B_1 + B_2)}{y_1} = 4 - 2(y_1 + y_2) - 2y_1 = 0,$$

$$\frac{\partial(B_1 + B_2)}{y_2} = 4 - 2(y_1 + y_2) - 2 \quad = 0.$$

These conditions are sufficient, since the matrix of second derivatives of $(B_1 + B_2)$ is negative definite. We derive $y_1 + y_2 = 1$, $p = 3$, $y_1 = 1$, $y_2 = 0$, and $B_0 = 2$.

Then the problem is how to divide B_0 between the two enterprises. For any given y_1^* and y_2^*, enterprise 1 will receive

$$B_1^* + \frac{B_0 - (B_1^* + B_2^*)}{2},$$

which is equal to

$$\frac{B_0}{2} + \frac{B_1^* - B_2^*}{2}.$$

Similarly, enterprise 2 will receive

$$\frac{B_0}{2} + \frac{B_2^* - B_1^*}{2}.$$

Therefore, it is in the interest of enterprise 1 to find a strategy y_1^* such that $B_1^* - B_2^*$ is as large as possible, whereas enterprise 2, on the other hand, strives to maximize $B_2^* - B_1^*$.

The Nash procedure leads us to search for a solution to an entirely new game, since the sum of the functions that each enterprise strives to maximize is always zero. One such game belongs to the category of two-person zero-sum games (or "duels"), the properties of which have been studied extensively.

Let $\Psi(y_1^*, y_2^*)$ be the objective function of enterprise 1:

$$\Psi(y_1^*, y_2^*) = B_1^* - B_2^*$$

$$= (4 - y_1^* - y_2^*)(y_1^* - y_2^*) - (y_1^*)^2 + 2y_2^*.$$

Now Ψ is strictly concave in y_1^* and strictly convex in y_2^*. On the other hand, we can restrict the set of feasible strategies for each enterprise to the interval $[0,4]$, by taking into account the demand function. Then we can assert that there exists a unique solution to this game—strategy couplet $(\hat{y}_1, \hat{y}_2)$ such that

$$\Psi(\hat{y}_1, \hat{y}_2) \geq \Psi(y_1^*, \hat{y}_2), \qquad \forall y_1^*;$$

$$\Psi(\hat{y}_1, \hat{y}_2) \leq \Psi(\hat{y}_1, y_2^*), \qquad \forall y_2^*.$$

Moreover, we can show that

$$\max_{y_1^*} \min_{y_2^*} \Psi(y_1^*, y_2^*) = \Psi(\hat{y}_1, \hat{y}_2) = \min_{y_2^*} \max_{y_1^*} \Psi(y_1^*, y_2^*).$$

Thus the couplet $(\hat{y}_1, \hat{y}_2)$ corresponds to a noncooperative equilibrium on the one hand and, on the other hand, $\hat{y}_1$ is a conservative strategy for enterprise 1 in that it guarantees a minimum level for the function Ψ regardless of what enterprise 2 does. It is a conservative strategy for enterprise 2 as well, for it guarantees a maximum level for Ψ regardless of what enterprise 1 does. Strategy $\hat{y}_1$ is said to be a minimax strategy for enterprise 1, and the theorem that ensures the existence of a couplet $(\hat{y}_1, \hat{y}_2)$ having the above properties is known as the Minimax Theorem. The couplet $(\hat{y}_1, \hat{y}_2)$ is called the saddle point of the function $\Psi(y_1^*, y_2^*)$.

Thus we can calculate the strategies $\hat{y}_1$ and $\hat{y}_2$ in several ways. Take, for example, the perspective of enterprise 2. For y_2^* fixed, the worst that can happen to it is that the other enterprise chooses a strategy y_1^* that maximizes Ψ for this value of y_2^*. However, the maximum of Ψ for y_2^* fixed is

$$\max_{y_1^*} \Psi(y_1^*, y_2^*) = y_2^{*^2} - 2y_2^* + 2.$$

Then enterprise 2 will choose the strategy that minimizes this quantity; that is, a level of output $\hat{y}_2 = 1$. From this we conclude that the optimal strategy for enterprise 1 is $\hat{y}_1 = 1$. On the other hand, by taking the perspective of enterprise 1, we can easily show that the couplet $\hat{y}_1 = 1$, $\hat{y}_2 = 1$ is a noncooperative equilibrium.

Then, according to this procedure, B_0 (equal to 2) will be distributed so that one half goes to enterprise 2 and three halves go to enterprise 1. Both enterprises agree that enterprise 1 will set its level of production at one and enterprise 2 at zero.

It is interesting that the strategies $\hat{y}_1$ and $\hat{y}_2$, which are the threat strategies for this procedure even though they are not executed, correspond to the output levels of the competitive equilibrium. This is because of the particular numerical values used in this exercise. However, explicit calculation of threat strategies very often demonstrates their proximity to the output levels of the competitive equilibrium.

As far as enterprise 2 is concerned, it receives a share of B_0 equal to 0.5 unit and it produces no output. What enterprise 2 receives can therefore be interpreted as the price paid by enterprise 1 to bribe enterprise 2 not to produce anything; it may be considered a sort of takeover value of enterprise 2 by enterprise 1.

	Competitive equilibrium	Cournot equilibrium	Nash solution
Output of enterprise 1	$y_1 = 1$	$y_1 = \dfrac{6}{7} \simeq 0.86$	$y_1 = 1$
Output of enterprise 2	$y_2 = 1$	$y_2 = \dfrac{4}{7} \simeq 0.57$	$y_2 = 0$
Market price	$p = 2$	$p = \dfrac{18}{7} \simeq 2.57$	$p = 3$
Profit of enterprise 1	$B_1 = 1$	$B_1 = \dfrac{72}{49} \simeq 1.47$	$B_1 = \dfrac{3}{2} = 1.5$
Profit of enterprise 2	$B_2 = 0$	$B_2 = \dfrac{16}{49} \simeq 0.33$	$B_2 = \dfrac{1}{2} = 0.5$

Table 16.1

The Cournot equilibrium is defined by the system of equations

$$\frac{\partial B_1}{\partial y_1} = (4 - y_1 - y_2) - y_1 - 2y_1 = 0,$$

$$\frac{\partial B_2}{\partial y_2} = (4 - y_1 - y_2) - y_2 - 2 \quad = 0.$$

From these we derive the output levels of the Cournot equilibrium: $y_1 = 6/7$, $y_2 = 4/7$. Table 16.1 summarizes the various situations considered.

We conclude by mentioning that the procedure that leads to the Nash solution can be generalized to the case where side payments are not allowed.

Suggested Readings

Friedman, James. 1969. "On Experimental Research in Oligopoly." *Review of Economic Studies* 36: 399–416.

Friedman, James. 1982. "Oligopoly Theory." In *Handbook of Mathematical Eco-*

nomics, vol. 2, ed. Kenneth J. Arrow and Michael D. Intriligator. Amsterdam: North-Holland.

Karlin, Samuel. 1959. *Mathematical Methods and Theory in Games, Programming and Economics,* vol. 1, chap. 8. Reading, Mass.: Addison-Wesley.

Luce, R. Duncan, and Raiffa, Howard. 1957. *Games and Decisions.* New York: John Wiley.

Malinvaud, Edmond. 1972. *Lectures on Microeconomic Theory,* trans. A. Silvey, chaps. 5 and 6. Amsterdam: North-Holland.

Nash, John. 1953. "Two-Person Cooperative Games." *Econometrica* 21: 128–140.

Schelling, Thomas C. 1960. *The Strategy of Conflict.* Cambridge, Mass.: Harvard University Press.

Shubik, Martin. 1959. *Strategy and Market Structure.* New York: John Wiley.

Shubik, Martin, with Levitan, Richard. 1980. *Market Structure and Behavior.* Cambridge, Mass.: Harvard University Press.

Telser, Lester G. 1972. *Competition, Collusion, and Game Theory.* Chicago: Aldine-Atherton.

PART SIX

Private versus Social Costs

17 Public Goods

One of the great difficulties in studying the economic behavior of the government is the interdependence between the problems of optimal allocation of resources and those related to distributive justice (distribution of income). The object of the present exercise is to make us aware of this in a specific example involving a public good.

DESCRIPTION OF THE MODEL

The goods:

X, a private consumption good;

Y, a pure public good;

Z, labor.

The agents:

(a) *The households.* For simplification, we start by considering only two households, whose preferences are represented by a utility function:

$$U_i = \alpha_i \log X_i + \beta_i \log Y_i + \gamma_i \log (\bar{Z} - Z_i)$$

$$i = 1, 2; \qquad \alpha_i + \beta_i + \gamma_i = 1,$$

where $\bar{Z}$ is the maximum amount of labor that can be supplied by a household.

(b) *The enterprises.* We differentiate the enterprises that produce good X from those that produce good Y. Production of each is subject to constant returns: $X = aZ_x$, $Y = bZ_y$, where Z_x and Z_y are the amounts of labor allocated to the production of X and Y respectively.

(c) *The government.* The government buys the public good Y and distributes the resulting fiscal burden between the consumers.

SEVERAL IDEAS FOR CONSIDERATION

Problem 1

Define the equilibrium with subscription for this model.[1]

Problem 2

Apply the results of the previous exercises to this simple model: in particular, show that a necessary and sufficient condition for an optimum is that there must exist positive quantities x, y_i, and z, which can be interpreted as prices such that:

(a) Each consumer maximizes his utility by taking x, $y = y_1 + y_2$, and z and his nonwage income as given;

(b) The enterprises maximize their profits by taking x, $y = y_1 + y_2$, and z as given;

(c) The government has a balanced budget.

Show that with any optimum we can associate a pseudoequilibrium[2] as long as a system of income transfers between consumers is introduced into the scheme.

Problem 3

Show that there exists a unique pseudoequilibrium for the case where income transfers are zero. Determine the distribution of taxes between the consumers associated with this pseudoequilibrium. Compare this pseudoequilibrium to the equilibrium with subscription considered in problem 1.

---

1. *Translators' note:* The term *subscription* is used by the authors to indicate a situation in which each consumer decides how much individual labor to supply to the production of the public good. Although no wage is paid for such labor, the total amount of the public good is consumed in equal quantities by each consumer. The labor supplied could be considered as "volunteer" labor. An individual becomes a "free rider" when he supplies no labor to the production of the public good even though he consumes the same quantity of the good as others who have supplied their labor.

2. *Translators' note:* The authors' term *pseudoequilibrium* is used to describe a situation in which the price (tax) paid to the government for the pure public good may be different for each consumer, and income transfers among consumers may be imposed by the government.

Problem 4

Retain the assumption that the income transfers are zero, and keep the same distribution of taxes as in the preceding problem. Show that if we vary the level of production of the public good, Y, the value Y^* determined in problem 3 simultaneously maximizes the utility of each of the consumers. Explain this result.

Problem 5

In a model of ℓ goods (of which $r < \ell$ are public goods), retain the conditions on production so that there is a single primary factor (labor) and constant returns prevail. In other words, we are considering the technology introduced in exercise 12, which allows us to represent the set of feasible points by $px = R$, where $p \in \mathbb{R}^\ell$ is a row-vector (production prices) and $x \in \mathbb{R}^\ell$ is the column-vector of total consumption.

Then show that the result in problem 3 continues to hold if we constrain the utility functions to be quasi-concave and rule out corner solutions (that is, we can use the technique of Lagrangian multipliers).

PROPOSED SOLUTION

This exercise is based on the following fundamental theorem: a pseudoequilibrium can be associated with any Pareto optimum for an economy in which public goods exist. Comparison of the pseudoequilibrium without income transfers and of the equilibrium with subscription brings out the difficulty of attaining a Pareto optimum. In a model containing only private goods the noncooperative equilibrium (the competitive equilibrium) analogous to the equilibrium with subscription here is a Pareto optimum. However, if there are public goods it is not possible to reach a Pareto optimum without collaboration of the agents. It is difficult to imagine how such a collaboration could take place—especially if the number of agents is very large—without the help of an intermediary institution like the government.

In the second part of the exercise a procedure that could be used by such an institution is suggested. If each consumer knows the tax system (which has been "judiciously" chosen by the government), it is in his own self-interest that the output of the public good be set at the relatively high level necessary for an optimum; for he knows that any increase in his own contribution will be followed by an increase in the contributions of the other consumers, contrary to what happens in the case of the equilibrium with subscription.

Problem 1

Take labor as the numéraire so that the wage rate is one. Since we have constant returns, the profit maximum of each enterprise is necessarily zero in equilibrium, and the prices of goods X and Y are therefore equal to $1/a$ and $1/b$ respectively.

Let $s_i \geq 0$ be the subscription of consumer i, that is, the amount of labor voluntarily contributed by consumer i. Then the output of good Y is equal to $Y = b(s_1 + s_2)$.

Consumer i chooses jointly his subscription and his consumption taking the subscription of the other consumer as given. Thus, noncooperative behavior analogous to that which leads to a Cournot equilibrium in the theory of duopoly is assumed. Therefore consumer i maximizes his utility function

$$U_i = \alpha_i \log X_i + \beta_i \log [b(s_1 + s_2)] + \gamma_i \log (\bar{Z} - Z_i),$$

subject to the budget constraint $(1/a)X_i + s_i - Z_i = 0$.

Consider consumer 1 and eliminate the variable X_1, thanks to the budget equation. So we need to find the maximum of

$$U_1 = \alpha_1 \log a(Z_1 - s_1) + \beta_1 \log b(s_1 + s_2) + \gamma_1 \log (\bar{Z} - Z_1).$$

As long as $\bar{Z} > 0$, the maximum of U_1 necessarily occurs when $X_1 = a(Z_1 - s_1) > 0$ and therefore $Z_1 > 0$. On the other hand, as long as s_2 is large enough, the maximum of U_1 may correspond to $s_1 = 0$. There are then two cases to study:

- Case 1: $s_1 = 0$.

We must have, from the Kuhn-Tucker conditions, $\partial U_1/\partial Z_1 = 0$ and $\partial U_1/\partial s_1 \leq 0$. More explicitly:

$$\frac{\partial U_1}{\partial Z_1} = \frac{\alpha_1}{Z_1} - \frac{\gamma_1}{\bar{Z} - Z_1} = 0,$$

from which it follows that

$$Z_1 = \frac{\alpha_1 \bar{Z}}{\alpha_1 + \gamma_1} \quad \text{and} \quad \bar{Z} - Z_1 = \frac{\gamma_1 \bar{Z}}{\alpha_1 + \gamma_1}.$$

Likewise

$$\frac{\partial U_1}{\partial s_1} = -\frac{\alpha_1}{Z_1} + \frac{\beta_1}{s_2} \leqslant 0,$$

or

$$s_2 \geqslant \frac{\beta_1 \bar{Z}}{\alpha_1 + \gamma_1}.$$

If the subscription of consumer 2 is high enough, consumer 1 has no interest in subscribing (volunteering) himself and he becomes a free rider.

• Case 2: $s_1 > 0$.

We need to characterize an unconstrained maximum of U_1:

$$\frac{\partial U_1}{\partial Z_1} = \frac{\alpha_1}{Z_1 - s_1} - \frac{\gamma_1}{\bar{Z} - Z_1} = 0,$$

$$\frac{\partial U_1}{\partial s_1} = -\frac{\alpha_1}{Z_1 - s_1} + \frac{\beta_1}{s_1 + s_2} = 0.$$

This case, where $s_1 = \beta_1 \bar{Z} - (\alpha_1 + \gamma_1)s_2$ is positive, occurs when $s_2 < \beta_1 \bar{Z}/(\alpha_1 + \gamma_1)$. In particular, for $s_2 = 0$, we find

$$s_1 = \beta_1 \bar{Z}, \quad X_1 = a\alpha_1 \bar{Z}, \quad \bar{Z} - Z_1 = \gamma_1 \bar{Z}.$$

We could obtain the same results for consumer 2. In combining the two situations, the following cases arise:

(a) $s_1 > 0$ and $s_2 = 0$

In this case $s_1 = \beta_1 \bar{Z}$ and the output of the public good is equal to $Y = b(s_1 + s_2) = b\beta_1 \bar{Z}$. This is possible if

$$s_1 = \beta_1 \bar{Z} \geqslant \frac{\beta_2 \bar{Z}}{\alpha_2 + \gamma_2},$$

that is, if

$$\beta_1 \geqslant \frac{\beta_2}{1 - \beta_2}, \quad \text{or} \quad \beta_2 \leqslant \frac{\beta_1}{1 + \beta_1}.$$

(b) $s_1 > 0$ and $s_2 > 0$

Then we have

$$s_1 = \frac{(\beta_1 - \beta_2 + \beta_2\beta_1)\bar{Z}}{\beta_1 + \beta_2 - \beta_1\beta_2}, \qquad s_2 = \frac{(\beta_2 - \beta_1 + \beta_2\beta_1)\bar{Z}}{\beta_1 + \beta_2 - \beta_1\beta_2}.$$

The output of the public good is

$$Y = b(s_1 + s_2) = \frac{2b\beta_1\beta_2\bar{Z}}{\beta_1 + \beta_2 - \beta_1\beta_2}.$$

Finally we have:

$$X_1 = \frac{2a\beta_2\alpha_1\bar{Z}}{\beta_1 + \beta_2 - \beta_1\beta_2}, \qquad X_2 = \frac{2a\beta_1\alpha_2\bar{Z}}{\beta_1 + \beta_2 - \beta_1\beta_2},$$

$$\bar{Z} - Z_1 = \frac{2\beta_2\gamma_1\bar{Z}}{\beta_1 + \beta_2 - \beta_1\beta_2}, \qquad \bar{Z} - Z_2 = \frac{2\beta_1\gamma_2\bar{Z}}{\beta_1 + \beta_2 - \beta_1\beta_2}.$$

This case, with s_1 and s_2 both positive, is possible if

$$\frac{\beta_1}{1 + \beta_1} < \beta_2 < \frac{\beta_1}{1 - \beta_1};$$

in other words, if

$$\frac{\beta_2}{1 + \beta_2} < \beta_1 < \frac{\beta_2}{1 - \beta_2}.$$

(c) $s_2 > 0$ and $s_1 = 0$

We have here the case symmetrical to the one where $s_1 > 0$ and $s_2 = 0$. It occurs when

$$\beta_1 \leqslant \frac{\beta_2}{1 + \beta_2} \quad \text{or} \quad \beta_2 \geqslant \frac{\beta_1}{1 - \beta_1}.$$

Then

$$Y = b(s_1 + s_2) = b\beta_2\bar{Z}.$$

Problem 2

The search for a Pareto optimum is equivalent to the maximization of U_1 subject to the following constraints:

$$U_2 \geqslant U_2^0, \tag{1}$$

$$X_1 + X_2 \leqslant aZ_x, \tag{2}$$

$$Y_1 \leqslant bZ_y, \tag{3}$$

$$Y_2 \leqslant bZ_y, \tag{4}$$

$$Z_x + Z_y \leqslant Z_1 + Z_2. \tag{5}$$

Since U_2 is concave and the other constraints are linear, the domain over which U_1 is to be maximized is a convex set. Since U_1 is concave, the Kuhn-Tucker conditions are necessary and sufficient.

The Lagrangian L is written:

$$L = \lambda_1 U_1 + \lambda_2[U_2 - U_2^0] + x[aZ_x - X_1 - X_2]$$

$$+ y_1[bZ_y - Y_1] + y_2[bZ_y - Y_2] + z[Z_1 + Z_2 - Z_x - Z_y].$$

We assume that the given value of U_2^0 allows U_1 to attain a value $> -\infty$. This ensures that $X_1 > 0$, $Y_1 > 0$, $Z_1 < \bar{Z}$, $X_2 > 0$, $Y_2 > 0$, $Z_2 < \bar{Z}$, and $Z_x > 0$, $Z_y > 0$.

Finally, we note that all the constraints (1) through (5) are satisfied by equality at the optimum. For example, if we had $X_1 + X_2 < aZ_x$, it would be possible to increase X_1 and therefore U_1.

The Kuhn-Tucker conditions are then written as follows:

$$X_1 > 0 \Rightarrow \lambda_1 \frac{\alpha_1}{X_1} - x = 0, \tag{6}$$

$$X_2 > 0 \Rightarrow \lambda_2 \frac{\alpha_2}{X_2} - x = 0, \tag{7}$$

$$Y_1 > 0 \Rightarrow \lambda_1 \frac{\beta_1}{Y_1} - y_1 = 0, \tag{8}$$

$$Y_2 > 0 \Rightarrow \lambda_2 \frac{\beta_2}{Y_2} - y_2 = 0, \tag{9}$$

$$Z_x > 0 \Rightarrow ax - z = 0, \tag{10}$$

$$Z_y > 0 \Rightarrow b[y_1 + y_2] - z = 0, \tag{11}$$

$$-\frac{\lambda_1 \gamma_1}{\overline{Z} - Z_1} + z \leqslant 0, \quad \text{with} \quad Z_1 \left(-\frac{\lambda_1 \gamma_1}{\overline{Z} - Z_1} + z \right) = 0, \tag{12}$$

$$-\frac{\lambda_2 \gamma_2}{\overline{Z} - Z_2} + z \leqslant 0, \quad \text{with} \quad Z_2 \left(-\frac{\lambda_2 \gamma_2}{\overline{Z} - Z_2} + z \right) = 0. \tag{13}$$

We have obtained a system of thirteen equations in the following thirteen unknowns: $\lambda_2, x, y_1, y_2, z, X_1, X_2, Y_1, Y_2, Z_1, Z_2, Z_x, Z_y$ (the value of λ_1 can be set equal to one for convenience). This system has at least one solution as long as the given value of U_1^0 is feasible (which we shall assume) and the set of feasible points is compact (which could be shown).

We indicate by superscript zeros the values taken by the variables at this optimum. Let $R_i^0 = x^0 X_i^0 + y_i^0 Y_i^0 - z^0 Z_i^0$ to allow for income transfers between the consumers. Notice that

$$R_1^0 + R_2^0 = x^0(X_1^0 + X_2^0) + y_1^0 Y_1^0 + y_2^0 Y_2^0 - z^0(Z_1^0 + Z_2^0)$$

$$= x^0 a Z_x^0 + (y_1^0 + y_2^0) b Z_y^0 - z^0 (Z_x^0 + Z_y^0),$$

taking inequalities (2) through (5) into account, remembering that each is now satisfied with equality. From Eq. (10) $ax^0 = z^0$ and from Eq. (11) $b(y_1^0 + y_2^0) = z^0$. Therefore $R_1^0 + R_2^0 = 0$.

Expressions (6), (8), and (12) express the maximization of U_1 subject to the budget constraint

$$x^0 X_1 + y_1^0 Y_1 - z^0 Z_1 = R_1^0,$$

where x is interpreted as the price of good X and z as the price of good Z. Also, y_1 is interpreted as the price paid by consumer 1 to the government for the consumption of the collective good. A similar derivation holds for the maximization of U_2 with a similar interpretation of y_2. Finally, R_1^0 and

R_2^0 are interpreted as income transfers. Equation (10) expresses profit max-imization for the enterprise producing good X, and Eq. (11) expresses profit maximization for the enterprise producing good Y, inasmuch as $y_1 + y_2$ is the selling price of good Y paid by the government. The govern-ment's budget is then balanced since it collects an equivalent tax from the consumers.

Therefore, we can associate a pseudoequilibrium characterized by x^0, y_1^0, y_2^0, z^0, R_1^0, and R_2^0 with this optimum.

Problem 3

We can calculate the values taken by the variables for the case of no in-come transfers (where $R_1^0 = R_2^0 = 0$). Here we must have $Z_1 > 0$ and $Z_2 > 0$. Then, from expressions (6), (8), and (12) on the one hand and (7), (9), and (13) on the other, we derive:

$$\frac{\alpha_i}{xX_i} = \frac{\beta_i}{yY_i} = \frac{\gamma_i}{z(\bar{Z} - Z_i)} = \frac{1}{z\bar{Z}},$$

taking into account $\alpha_i + \beta_i + \gamma_i = 1$ and $xX_i + yY_i - zZ_i = 0$. It follows that

$$X_i = \frac{\alpha_i z\bar{Z}}{x}, \qquad Y_i = \frac{\beta_i z\bar{Z}}{y_i}, \qquad Z_i = (\alpha_i + \beta_i)\bar{Z}.$$

After substituting these values into expressions (2) through (5) and taking Eqs. (10) and (11) into account, we have five independent equations for the five unknowns Z_x, Z_y, $\xi = x/z$, $\eta_1 = y_1/z$, and $\eta_2 = y_2/z$:

$$(10) \Rightarrow \quad \xi = \frac{1}{a},$$

$$(3), (4), \text{ and } (11) \Rightarrow Z_Y = (\beta_1 + \beta_2)\bar{Z},$$

$$(10) \text{ and } (1) \Rightarrow Z_X = (\alpha_1 + \alpha_2)\bar{Z},$$

$$(3) \Rightarrow \eta_1 = \frac{\beta_1}{b(\beta_1 + \beta_2)},$$

$$(4) \Rightarrow \eta_2 = \frac{\beta_2}{b(\beta_1 + \beta_2)}.$$

We derive the tax paid by consumers 1 and 2:

$$t_1 = y_1 Y_1 = \beta_1 z \bar{Z}, \qquad t_2 = \beta_2 z \bar{Z}$$

with
$$Y_1 = Y_2 = Y^* = (\beta_1 + \beta_2) b \bar{Z}.$$

We can compare this output level of the public good with the one corresponding to the equilibrium with subscription.

In the case where one of the two subscriptions is zero, the output of the public good for the equilibrium with subscription is clearly inferior. In the case where the two consumers are both subscribing, the output is equal to

$$Y = \frac{2b\beta_1\beta_2\bar{Z}}{\beta_1 + \beta_2 - \beta_1\beta_2}.$$

Now, when we compare this to $Y^* = b(\beta_1 + \beta_2)\bar{Z}$,

$$\frac{Y^*}{Y} = 1 + \frac{\beta_1^2(1 - \beta_2) + \beta_2^2(1 - \beta_1)}{2\beta_1\beta_2} > 1.$$

Comparing the utility levels attained by the two agents in the pseudoequilibrium without transfers (U_1^* and U_2^*) and in the equilibrium with subscription ($\bar{U}_1$ and $\bar{U}_2$) for the case where $\beta_1 = \beta_2 = \beta$, we have:

$$U_1^* - \bar{U}_1 = U_2^* - \bar{U}_2 = \log(2 - \beta) - (1 - \beta)\log 2.$$

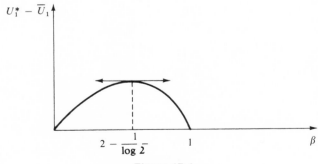

Figure 17.1

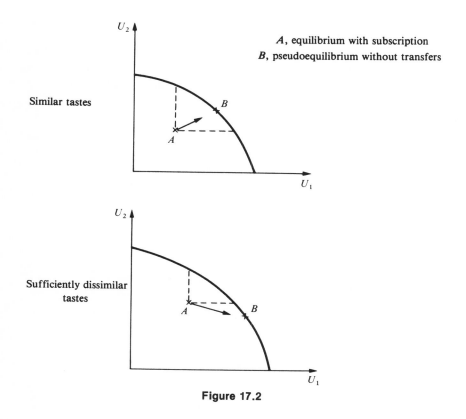

Figure 17.2

This function of β has as its derivative $-1/(2 - \beta) + \log 2$. The derivative is positive when $0 \leqslant \beta \leqslant 2 - 1/\log 2$ and negative when $2 - 1/\log 2 \leqslant \beta \leqslant 1$. This function is zero when $\beta = 0$ and $\beta = 1$; and it is strictly positive on the open interval $(0, 1)$ (see Fig. 17.1).

In summary, when their tastes are sufficiently similar, both consumers gain by moving from the equilibrium with subscription to the pseudoequilibrium without income transfers. On the other hand, if their tastes are very different, it is possible that this movement involves a decrease in the utility level for one of the two consumers. Some income transfers will be necessary if the optimum situation found as the achievement of the pseudoequilibrium is to be preferred by both consumers to the equilibrium with subscription. It is sufficient to consider the particular example $\beta_1 \leqslant \beta_2/(1 + \beta_2)$ to ascertain that here the equilibrium with subscription ($s_1 = 0$ for the first consumer) is preferred by the first consumer to the pseudoequilibrium without transfers (Fig. 17.2).

Problem 4

We shall fix the distribution of the tax burden and study the "politico-economic" equilibrium that results from determining the sole remaining collective decision parameter—the quantity of the collective good to be produced.

Let $(\beta_1 + \beta_2)b\theta$ be the quantity produced of good Y. At the same time, fix $t_1/t_2 = \beta_1/\beta_2$. Assume that the budget of the state is balanced and that the enterprise producing the collective good behaves like a perfect competitor. We derive from this

$$t_1 = \beta_1 \theta z, \qquad t_2 = \beta_2 \theta z,$$

and
$$Z_y = (\beta_1 + \beta_2)\theta.$$

Now, each consumer i maximizes U_i subject to his budget constraint $xX_i - zZ_i = -t_i$, from which it follows that

$$\frac{\alpha_i}{xX_i} = \frac{\gamma_i}{z(\bar{Z} - Z_i)} = \frac{\alpha_i + \gamma_i}{z\bar{Z} - t_i},$$

$$X_i = \frac{\alpha_i}{\alpha_i + \gamma_i} \frac{z}{x} \bar{Z} - \frac{\alpha_i}{\alpha_i + \gamma_i} \beta_i\theta \frac{z}{x},$$

and
$$Z_i = \frac{\alpha_i}{\alpha_i + \gamma_i} \bar{Z} + \frac{\gamma_i}{\alpha_i + \gamma_i} \beta_i\theta.$$

From the market equilibrium for good X we derive

$$Z_x = \frac{1}{a}(X_1 + X_2).$$

The market equilibrium of labor, $Z_1 + Z_2 = Z_x + Z_y$, then allows us to determine the ratio $\xi = x/z$, which takes the value $\xi = 1/a$. This value could have been found directly from the profit-maximizing condition of the enterprise producing good X. We then calculate U_i:

$$U_i = \alpha_i \log X_i + \beta_i \log \theta + \gamma_i \log (\bar{Z} - Z_i)$$

or
$$U_i = \text{constant} + \beta_i \log \theta + (\alpha_i + \gamma_i) \log (\bar{Z} - \beta_i\theta)$$

and
$$\frac{\partial U_i}{\partial \theta} = \frac{\beta_i}{\theta} - \frac{\beta_i(\alpha_i + \beta_i)}{\bar{Z} - \beta_i\theta},$$

from which it follows that

$$\frac{\partial U_i}{\partial \theta} = 0 \Rightarrow \theta = \frac{\bar{Z}}{\alpha_i + \beta_i + \gamma_i} = \bar{Z}.$$

The solution for Y is again found to be the value Y^* obtained at the Pareto optimum corresponding to the pseudoequilibrium without income transfers. This result parallels Malinvaud's theorem that a politicoeconomic equilibrium is an optimum.

By manipulating a single parameter, the level of production of the collective good, we have been able to achieve both an optimum and a politicoeconomic equilibrium. However, the distribution of taxes chosen to cover the cost of the collective good is significant, since it corresponds to the distribution found for the pseudoequilibrium without income transfers. Only this distribution of taxes allows us to reach an optimum. In fact, to any given distribution of income (transfers) there corresponds in general a single distribution of taxes which, by manipulation of the level of output of the public good, leads to an optimum.

Therefore, there exists an interdependence between the problem of the optimal allocation of resources (the search for a Pareto optimum) and the problems of distributive justice (the choice of a distribution of after-tax income).

Problem 5

In an effort to generalize the above approach, we shall define again the pseudoequilibrium without income transfers to which there corresponds a distribution of taxes. Following that, we shall study the equilibrium obtained by keeping the same distribution of taxes and considering arbitrary levels of output of the public goods, with these levels of output being the parameters of a collective decision. Finally, by trying to set the "best" value of these parameters, we shall retrieve the values that correspond to the initial pseudoequilibrium, which was itself a Pareto optimum.

In fact, the term *distribution of taxes* is now improper because it is necessary to maintain, for each collective good, a distribution of its cost among the various consumers which is identical to that defined for the pseudoequilibrium without transfers.

(a) Notations:

Space of goods, $\mathbb{R}^\ell$.

Space of collective goods, $\mathbb{R}^\ell = \mathbb{R}^r \times \mathbb{R}^{\ell-r} : \mathbb{R}^r$.

Space of private goods, $\mathbb{R}^{\ell-r}$. The elements of the first space are identified by an index C, those of the second by an index P.

n consumers, indexed by $i = 1, \ldots, n$.

Utility functions, $U_i[x^C, x_i^P]$.

Feasible sets, $p^C x^C + p^P x^P = R$.

Initial distribution of income, defined by R_i, $i = 1, \ldots, n$ such that $\Sigma_{i=1}^n R_i = R$. This income distribution corresponds to the distribution of the primary factor (work) among the consumers.

(b) The pseudoequilibrium associated with an initial distribution of income (no income transfers):

The equations can be written very simply as

$$\text{grad}_C \; U_i[x^C, x_i^P] = \mu_i p_i^C, \qquad i = 1, \ldots, n; \tag{14}$$

$$\text{grad}_P \; U_i[x^C, x_i^P] = \mu_i p^P, \qquad i = 1, \ldots, n; \tag{15}$$

$$p_i^C x^C + p^P x_i^P = R_i \qquad i = 1, \ldots, n; \tag{16}$$

$$\sum_{i=1}^n p_i^C = p^c, \qquad r \text{ components}; \tag{17}$$

$$\sum_{i=1}^n x_i^P = x^P, \qquad \ell - r \text{ components}. \tag{18}$$

In writing this system of equations we do not take into account the difficulties connected with nonnegativity constraints on the variables. In what follows we continue to ignore these difficulties.

The $n\ell + \ell + n$ equations are independent. By summing the constraints in Eq. (16), and taking Eqs. (17) and (18) into account, we show that the constraint which characterizes the feasible set is satisfied. In principle, Eqs. (14) through (18) allow us to determine the $n\ell + \ell + n$ unknowns x^C, p_i^C, x_i^P, x^P, and μ_i.

Let x^{C*}, p_i^{C*}, x_i^{P*}, x^{P*}, μ_i^* be a solution to the system of equations (14) through (18) (we assume that at least one solution exists).

(c) A general equilibrium of private goods where the collective consumptions x^C are taken as parameters:

Let us suppose that a vector x^C is chosen arbitrarily. This results in a charge $p^C x^C$ for the government to cover by a tax on the consumers. If we choose to calculate the tax on each consumer by imposing *for each product* a weight in the overall charge identical to that of section (b), this is equivalent to saying that the ith consumer will pay a tax of $p_{ih}^{C*} x_h^C$ toward the cost of collective good h. In other words, the ith consumer will pay an overall tax of

$$\sum_{h=1}^{r} p_{ih}^{C*} x_h^C = p_i^{C*} x^C.$$

He will be left with disposable income $R_i - p_i^{C*} x^C$ to allocate among his private consumption choices.

In summary, we are given here x^C as a parameter, an initial distribution of income characterized by the R_i's and a way of calculating the individual tax corresponding to the p_{ih}^{C*}, $i = 1, \ldots, n$; $h = 1, \ldots, r$. We are now dealing with the problem of finding an equilibrium of private goods where x^C appears as a parameter.

For a given x^C, the equations that characterize the equilibrium, if it exists, are

$$\text{grad}_P \ U_i[x^C, x_i^P] = v_i p^P, \qquad\qquad i = 1, \ldots, n; \qquad (19)$$

$$p^P x_i^P = R_i - p_i^{C*} x^C, \qquad i = 1, \ldots, n; \qquad (20)$$

$$\sum_{i=1}^{n} x_i^P = x^P. \qquad\qquad (21)$$

These $n(\ell - r) + n + (\ell - r)$ equations are independent as above and allow us in principle to determine the unknowns x_i^P, x^P, and v_i. At the equilibrium these quantities are functions of x^C, so that the utility of each consumer at the equilibrium is a function of x^C only:

$$U_i = U_i[x^C, x_i^P(x^C)]. \qquad\qquad (22)$$

(d) The program x^C:

If we consider the set of possible values for x^C, there exists a program $\hat{x}^C$ which, within the framework of the institutional hypotheses used (initial distribution of income and given distribution of taxes), wins unanimous approval. This program is nothing but x^{C^*}, the solution of the problem studied in section (b).

Limiting ourselves to first-order changes (we could be more precise), we must show that for any i, U_i characterized in Eq. (22) as a function of x^C is stationary if we set $x^C = x^{C^*}$. However, by definition we have

$$dU_i = \mathrm{grad}_c \ U_i[x^C, x_i^P]dx^C + \mathrm{grad}_P \ U_i[x^C, x_i^P]dx_i^P.$$

Equation (19) allows us to write

$$dU_1 = \mathrm{grad}_C \ U_i[x^C, x_i^P]dx^C + v_i p^P dx_i^P.$$

By differentiating Eq. (20), we obtain (since $p_i^{C^*}$ is given)

$$dU_i = \mathrm{grad}_c \ U_i[x^C, x_i^P]dx^C - v_i p_i^{C^*} dx^C.$$

If in Eqs. (19) and (20) we set $x^C = x^{C^*}$, the particular values $x_i^{P^*}$, μ_i^*, x^{P^*} will be solutions to the system of equations given by (19), (20), and (21). In other words, the solutions (which are functions of x^C) to this system are such that

$$x_i^{P^*} = x_i^P(x^{C^*}) \quad \text{and} \quad \mu_i^* = v_i(x^{C^*}).$$

Equation (14) allows us to conclude that dU_i is zero for any i.

(e) Remark:

If instead of distributing the taxes *by product*, as we have done here, we distribute the taxes in the aggregate by imposing on each consumer a fraction $t_i^* = p_i^{C^*} x^{C^*}/p^C x^{C^*}$, set once and for all, the result no longer holds. It is easy to demonstrate this by explicitly making the calculations for the following example:

$$r = 2, \ \ell = 3, \ i = 2;$$

$$U_1 = x_1 x_2 x_{13};$$

$$U_2 = x_1 x_2^2 x_{23}.$$

feasible set: $p_1 x_1 + p_2 x_2 + p_3 x_3 = R.$

initial income: R_1 and R_2, $R_1 + R_2 = R.$

THE FOLLOWING LESSONS emerge from this exercise. Even if each taxpayer knows the amount of his own taxes (when taxes are paid) and the overall structure of the government budget, taxpayers as a group do not have sufficient information to approve unanimously of the government's fiscal policy. Each taxpayer must also know how much the increase of any item in the government budget would cost him personally. This cost ideally should be tailored to the individual tastes of each taxpayer. In practice, it might be possible to imagine an individualized system that would take into account objective criteria such as age, family situation, profession, income, and the like.

***

Suggested Readings

Atkinson, Anthony B., and Stiglitz, Joseph E. 1980. *Lectures in Public Finance.* New York: McGraw-Hill.

Foley, Duncan K. 1967. "Resource Allocation and the Public Sector." *Yale Economic Essays 7.* New Haven: Yale University Press.

Green, Jerry, and Laffont, Jean-Jacques. 1979. *Incentives in Public Decision-Making.* Amsterdam: North-Holland.

Groves, Theodore, and Ledyard, John. 1977. "Optimal Allocation of Public Goods: A Solution to the Free Rider Problem." *Econometrica* 45: 783–810.

Johansen, Leif. 1965. *Public Economics.* Amsterdam: North-Holland.

Lindahl, Erik. 1958. "Just Taxation: A Positive Solution." In *Classics in the Theory of Public Finance,* ed. Richard A. Musgrave and Alan T. Peacock. London: Macmillan.

Malinvaud, Edmond. 1972. *Lectures on Microeconomic Theory,* trans. A. Silvey, chap. 9. Amsterdam: North-Holland.

Milleron, Jean-Claude. 1972. "Theory of Value with Public Goods: A Survey Article." *Journal of Economic Theory* 5: 419–477.

Roberts, Donald J. 1974. "The Lindahl Solution for Economies with Public Goods." *Journal of Public Finance* 3: 23–42.

A Case of
External Economies

Consider an economy in which there are three goods indexed by h. Good 3 is a primary factor of production (labor) available in the amount ω.

There are two enterprises. Enterprise 1 produces good 1 from labor only:

$$y_1^1 \leq (- 2y_3^1)^{1/2}, \quad \text{with } y_1^1 \geq 0, \qquad y_3^1 \leq 0.$$

Enterprise 2 can use two production techniques simultaneously. The first technique exhibits constant returns and yields one unit of good 2 from two units of good 3. The second technique yields one unit of good 2 from one unit of good 3, but the output of good 2 obtained cannot exceed the level of output of good 1 achieved by enterprise 1. In summary, we can write for enterprise 2:

$$y_2^2 \leq - y_3^2 \quad \text{if} \quad - y_3^2 \leq y_1^1;$$

$$y_2^2 \leq y_1^1 + \frac{1}{2}(- y_3^2 - y_1^1) \quad \text{if} \quad - y_3^2 > y_1^1;$$

with, of course, $y_2^2 \geq 0, \qquad y_3^2 \leq 0.$

The output of enterprise 2 depends, therefore, on the output of enterprise 1 through an external effect.

Finally, there are two consumers. Consumer 1 owns enterprise 1, consumer 2 owns enterprise 2, each has an amount $\omega/2$ of good 3, and the two utility functions are given by

$$U^1(x_1^1, x_2^1) = x_1^1 x_2^1, \qquad U^2(x_1^2, x_2^2) = x_1^2 x_2^2.$$

In what follows, we take good 3 to be the numéraire.

Problem 1

Define the competitive equilibrium for this economy. (To characterize the equilibrium, the prices will be sufficient.)

Problem 2

Show that the competitive equilibrium characterized in problem 1 is not a Pareto optimum when $\omega > 4$.

Problem 3

The government decides to grant enterprise 1 a subsidy of t per unit of output. This subsidy is financed by a direct tax, the burden of which is shared equally by the two households. If we assume that the agents continue to behave competitively, at what level(s) must the subsidy t be fixed so that the associated equilibrium will be a Pareto optimum?

Problem 4

Instead of intervening directly, the government may encourage the two enterprises to take external effects into account. One possibility is to assume that enterprise 1 produces jointly, in equal amounts, good 1 and a fictitious good denoted good 4. Good 4 is "purchased" by enterprise 2 at a price p_4 and used by this enterprise as a factor of production.

Characterize the competitive equilibrium or equilibria of this fictitious economy. Show that such an equilibrium is a Pareto optimum. What is the relationship between such an equilibrium and the equilibria characterized in the solutions to the preceding problems? Are you satisfied with this method of going from the competitive equilibrium of problem 1 to a Pareto optimum?

PROPOSED SOLUTION

The purpose of this exercise is to highlight the problems created by the existence of externalities between the outputs of various enterprises. Two possible methods to achieve a Pareto optimum are studied, but the choice of any one method can influence the resulting distribution of income.

To treat the problem more concretely, imagine that the first enterprise produces electricity from water dammed up from a river. The output of electricity during the summer months may then influence the maximum area of land irrigated downstream from the dam.

The competitive equilibrium characterized in problem 1 corresponds to the case where the enterprise producing electricity takes no account of the effect its output has on the output of agricultural enterprises situated downstream. Therefore, it is possible that this equilibrium may not be a Pareto optimum, as problem 2 requires us to verify. The government may grant a subsidy to the enterprise that generates the external effects in such a way as to encourage its output and bring about a Pareto optimum again. Still, we must determine the appropriate level of the subsidy; we grapple with this matter in problem 3. Among the various possible solutions, there is a particularly convenient one; that is, to consider the water as a joint product of the enterprise generating electricity and to charge the agricultural enterprises for it (thus water becomes the fictitious good 4 introduced in problem 4).

Problem 1

We must characterize a system of equilibrium prices for this economy. Since good 3 is the numéraire, the profit maximum for enterprise 1 when p_1 is the price of good 1, involves choosing a level of output $y_1^1 = p_1$ and realizing profit B_1 equal to $p_1^2/2$.

For enterprise 2 we distinguish three cases (see Fig. 18.1):

$y_2^2 > y_1^1$ implies $p_2 = 2$ \qquad with a profit of $B_2 = y_1^1$;

$y_2^2 = y_1^1$ implies $1 \leqslant p_2 \leqslant 2$ \quad with a profit of $B_2 = (p_2 - 1) y_1^1$;

$y_2^2 < y_1^1$ implies $p_2 = 1$ \qquad with a profit of $B_2 = 0$.

The shaded area is the production set of enterprise 2. The cases $p_2 > 2$ and $p_2 < 1$ obviously cannot arise in the equilibrium.

Each consumer allocates half his income to the purchase of each good. If R is the total income of the two consumers with $R = \omega + B_1 + B_2$, we conclude that the aggregate demand for good 1, for example, is equal to $x_1^1 + x_1^2 = R/2p_1$. In summary, there are three types of possible equilibria; we shall consider each separately.

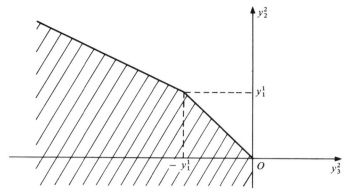

Figure 18.1

- Case 1: $y_2^2 > y_1^1$

    In this instance we have $p_2 = 2$ and $R = \omega + p_1^2/2 + p_1$. The equilibrium condition in the market for good 1 allows us to determine the value of p_1 at the equilibrium:

$$p_1 = \frac{1}{2p_1}\left(\omega + p_1 + \frac{p_1^2}{2}\right). \tag{1}$$

Since p_1 is nonnegative, this second-degree equation yields

$$p_1 = \frac{1 + \sqrt{1 + 6\omega}}{3}.$$

This solution is possible only if the demand for good 2 exceeds the demand for good 1, that is, if

$$p_1 = \frac{1 + \sqrt{1 + 6\omega}}{3} > p_2 = 2$$

and therefore if $\omega > 4$. The equilibrium condition in the market for good 2 determines the output of good 2.

- Case 2: $y_2^2 = y_1^1$

    This is possible only if the demands for each of the goods are equal, that is if $p_1 = p_2 = p$. Then we have $R = \omega + p^2/2 + p(p - 1)$, and the equilibrium condition in the market for good 1 yields

$$p = \frac{1}{2p}\left[\omega + p(p - 1) + \frac{p^2}{2}\right].$$

Then the equilibrium condition in the market for good 2 is also satisfied. Since p is nonnegative, we derive

$$p = -1 + \sqrt{1 + 2\omega}.$$

This case is possible only if $1 \leqslant p \leqslant 2$ and therefore if $3/2 \leqslant \omega \leqslant 4$.

● Case 3: $y_2^2 < y_1^1$ (the external effect is no longer relevant)
  In this case we have $R = \omega + p_1^2/2$, and the equilibrium condition in the market for good 1 yields

$$p_1 = \frac{1}{2p_1}\left(\omega + \frac{p_1^2}{2}\right) = \sqrt{\frac{2\omega}{3}}.$$

This case is possible only if the demand for good 1 exceeds the demand for good 2, that is, if $p_1 < 1$, from which it follows that $\omega < 3/2$.

Problem 2

When $\omega > 4$, we have $p_2 = 2$ and $p_1 > 2$ at the equilibrium. On the other hand, the ratio of marginal utilities of each consumer is equal to the ratio of the prices because the indifference curves do not cut the axes.

Consider a marginal variation from the equilibrium allocation of labor between the two enterprises:

$$dy_3^2 > 0 \quad \text{and} \quad dy_3^1 = -dy_3^2.$$

The negative value of inputs indicates that we have taken a small amount of the factor of production from enterprise 2 and given it to enterprise 1. Taking Eq. (1) into account, we then have

$$dy_1^1 = -\frac{1}{p_1} dy_3^1 = \frac{1}{p_1} dy_3^2$$

and
$$dy_2^2 = \frac{1}{2} dy_1^1 - \frac{1}{2} dy_3^2 = \left(\frac{1}{2p_1} - \frac{1}{2}\right) dy_3^2.$$

If the allocation of goods to consumer 2 remains constant, these variations in the outputs of goods 1 and 2 induce a variation of utility for consumer 1 proportional to

$$p_1 dy_1^1 + p_2 dy_2^2 = \frac{dy_3^2}{p_1} > 0.$$

The competitive equilibrium is therefore not Pareto optimal for $\omega > 4$.

In the case where $\omega < 3/2$, the external effect has no bearing on the equilibrium and consequently the equilibrium is Pareto optimal. In the case where $3/2 \leq \omega \leq 4$, it is easy to show that a marginal variation in the allocation of labor between the two enterprises never yields an increase in the utility of either consumer, contrary to the case where $\omega > 4$. This indicates that the Kuhn-Tucker conditions necessary to characterize a Pareto optimum are then satisfied. Moreover, these conditions are also sufficient here, since all the convexity assumptions are satisfied. In summary, for $\omega \leq 4$ the competitive equilibrium is Pareto optimal.

Problem 3

Our approach here is to arbitrarily set the level of the subsidy t and study the characteristics of the equilibrium that is established using the same method as in problem 1. There are again three types of equilibria.

- Case 1: $y_2^2 = y_1^1$

Here we necessarily have $p_1 = p_2 = p$, with $1 \leq p \leq 2$. Enterprise 1 chooses a level of output y_1^1 equal to $t + p_1$. Its profit is equal to $1/2(t + p_1)^2$. The profit of enterprise 2 is

$$(p_2 - 1)y_2^2 = (p - 1)(t + p).$$

The sum of the taxes paid is

$$ty_1^1 = t(t + p)$$

and the total income after taxes is

$$R = \omega + \frac{1}{2}(t + p)^2 + (p - 1)(t + p) - t(t + p).$$

The equilibrium condition in the market for the first good is written as follows:

$$t + p = \frac{1}{2p}\left[\omega + \frac{1}{2}(t + p)^2 + (p - 1)(t + p) - t(t + p)\right].$$

From the above we derive the equation characterizing the equilibrium value of p:

$$(t + p)^2 + 2(t + p) - 2\omega = 0,$$

from which it follows that

$$t + p = -1 + \sqrt{1 + 2\omega}.$$

Since $(p - 1)$ and t are necessarily nonnegative, this case can arise only if $\omega \geqslant 3/2$.

Is such an equilibrium Pareto optimal? If we consider a marginal variation in the allocation of labor defined by $dy_3^1 > 0$ with $dy_3^2 = -dy_3^1$, we have:

$$dy_1^1 = -\frac{1}{p + t}\, dy_3^1 < 0 \quad \text{and} \quad dy_2^2 = \frac{1}{2}\, dy_1^1 - \frac{1}{2}\, dy_3^2.$$

When we hold the allocation of goods to consumer 2 constant, the variation in the utility of consumer 1 is proportional to

$$p(dy_1^1 + dy_2^2) = p\left[-\frac{3}{2(p + t)} + \frac{1}{2}\right] dy_3^1.$$

This quantity is negative or zero as long as $p + t \leqslant 3$. In the same way, we could show that a change in the allocation of labor in the opposite direction ($dy_3^1 < 0$) would not yield an increase in the utility of the consumers.

Taking the equilibrium value determined for p into account, we find that the conditions $p + t \leqslant 3$ implies that $-1 + \sqrt{1 + 2\omega} \leqslant 3$ and therefore that $\omega \leqslant 15/2$.

In summary, for $3/2 \leqslant \omega \leqslant 15/2$ the introduction of a subsidy t satisfying

$$\max\{0, \sqrt{1 + 2\omega} - 3\} \leqslant t \leqslant \sqrt{1 + 2\omega} - 2$$

leads to the realization of an equilibrium that is a Pareto optimum as well.

The introduction of a subsidy $t > 0$, interestingly, is necessary to achieve an optimum only when $\sqrt{1 + 2\omega} - 3 > 0$, that is, when $\omega > 4$. In particular, for $\omega = 6$ it is necessary to introduce a subsidy t satisfying $\sqrt{13} - 3 \leqslant t \leqslant \sqrt{13} - 2$.

Of course, we must expect that the introduction of a subsidy $t > 0$ jeopardizes the realization of a Pareto optimum when $\omega < 3/2$.

● Case 2: $y_2^2 < y_1^1$

In this case we have $p_2 = 1$, which is possible only if $p_1 < 1$. Starting from such an equilibrium, we consider a marginal variation in the allocation of labor defined by dy_3^2 with $dy_3^1 = -dy_3^2$. Regardless of the direction of this variation, we have

$$dy_1^1 = -\frac{1}{t + p_1} dy_3^1, \qquad dy_2^2 = -dy_3^2.$$

If we hold the allocation of goods to consumer 2 constant, the variation of consumer 1's utility is proportional to

$$p_1 dy_1^1 + p_2 dy_2^2 = \left(-\frac{p_1}{t + p_1} + 1\right) dy_3^1.$$

Since dy_3^1 may take any sign, a necessary condition for optimality is that $-\dfrac{p_1}{t + p_1} + 1 = 0$, which implies that $t = 0$.

The competitive equilibrium of problem 1 recurs as long as $\omega < 3/2$, of course.

● Case 3: $y_1^2 > y_1^1$ at the equilibrium

Here we have $p_2 = 2$ and $p_1 > 2$. For a variation dy_3^1 of any sign in the allocation of labor to enterprise 1, the variation of consumer 1's utility when we hold the allocation of goods to consumer 2 constant is proportional to

$$p_1 dy_1^1 + p_2 dy_2^1 = \left(\frac{p_1}{t + p_1} + \frac{1}{t + p_1} - 1 \right) dy_3^2.$$

Such an equilibrium can be a Pareto optimum only if

$$\frac{p_1}{t + p_1} + \frac{1}{t + p_1} - 1 = 0,$$

which implies that $t = 1$.

Taking this value of t into account, we can easily calculate the equilibrium value of the price p_1 as a function of ω and show that the condition $p_1 > 2$ implies that $\omega > 15/2$. Thus when $\omega > 15/2$ it is necessary to set the level of the subsidy at $t = 1$ so that the associated equilibrium will be a Pareto optimum.

Problem 4

Maximization of profit for enterprise 1 involves choosing a level of output such that $y_1^1 = p_1 + p_4$. Enterprise 2 chooses between two techniques. We conclude that at the equilibrium we must have

$$p_2 - p_4 - 1 \leqslant 0, \qquad p_2 - 2 \leqslant 0.$$

(See, for example, exercise 6.) At the equilibrium the output of the two goods 1 and 2 is strictly positive, taking the tastes of the agents into account. The profit associated with each technique must therefore be zero for at least one of them.

On the other hand, we cannot have $p_2 - p_4 - 1 < 0$. Indeed, the demand for good 4 would then be zero, whereas the supply must be positive; this implies that $p_4 = 0$. However, $p_2 - 1 < 0$ is inconsistent with $p_2 = 2$.

All told, there are three cases to consider:

$$p_4 = 0 \text{ with } p_2 = 1;$$

$p_4 > 0$ with $p_2 - p_4 - 1 = 0$ and $p_2 < 2$;
$p_2 = p_4 + 1$ and $p_2 = 2$, which implies that $p_4 = 1$.

- Case 1: $p_4 = 0$ with $p_2 = 1$

Only the second technique is used by enterprise 2. Then we must have $y_1^1 \geq y_2^2$. On the other hand, the equations characterizing the equilibrium prices are in this case exactly the same as those that characterize the competitive equilibrium of problem 1. Therefore this equilibrium coincides with the competitive equilibrium when $\omega \leq 4$.

- Case 2: $p_4 > 0$ with $p_2 < 2$

The supply of and the demand for good 4 are necessarily equal. On the other hand, only the second technique is used by enterprise 2. Then we have $y_4^1 = y_1^1 = y_2^2$. This implies that $p_1 = p_2 = p$. On the other hand, we have $p = p_2 = 1 + p_4$.

Enterprise 1 produces an amount $y_1^1 = p + p_4$ and realizes a profit $B = \frac{1}{2}(p + p_4)^2$. The profit of enterprise 2 is always zero at the equilibrium. The total consumers' income is $R = \omega + \frac{1}{2}(p + p_4)^2$. The equilibrium condition in the market for good 1 is written

$$p + p_4 = \frac{1}{2p}\left[\omega + \frac{1}{2}(p + p_4)^2\right].$$

Since $1 + p_4 = p$, we obtain the following equilibrium value for p:

$$p = \sqrt{\frac{\omega}{2} + \frac{1}{4}}.$$

Since we must have $p_4 > 0$ and $p < 2$, we conclude that this case arises when $3/2 < \omega < 15/2$. For $3/2 < \omega \leq 4$ there are, then, two different equilibria.

- Case 3: $p_4 = 1$ with $p_2 = 2$

Enterprise 2 uses the two techniques simultaneously. The equilibrium condition in the market for good 1 is established when

$$p_1 = \frac{-1 + \sqrt{4 + 6\omega}}{3}.$$

So that the demand for good 2 will be at least equal to the demand for good 1, (which is necessary if the supply of good 4 is not to exceed its demand), we must have $p_1 \geq p_2 = 2$. This is satisfied when $\omega \geq 15/2$.

THE READER can check that for any ω the competitive equilibrium characterized in this problem and the equilibrium with a subsidy in the preceding problem yield an equivalent allocation of labor between the enterprises and identical levels of output.

On the other hand, the equilibrium value of p_4 is equal to the value of the subsidy $t (p_4 = t = 1)$ when $\omega \geq 15/2$. For $4 < \omega < 15/2$, the equilibrium value of p_4 is one-half the maximum value of the subsidy t. Finally, for $3/2 \leq \omega \leq 4$, one of the equilibrium values of p_4 always corresponds to one-half of the maximum value of the subsidy t, whereas the other value of ($p_4 = 0$) corresponds to the minimum subsidy.

At this point in the analysis it seems impossible to choose between the procedure of problem 3 and that of problem 4 to achieve a Pareto optimum. We need additional information. On the one hand, it seems that putting a procedure of the latter type into practice could lead to difficulties when we attempt to characterize the fictitious good 4, which generates the external effect (although such a characterization poses no problem in the hydroelectric example mentioned at the beginning of the exercise). On the other hand, this procedure would involve a severe redistribution of income at the expense of the owners of enterprise 2 were we to pass from a competitive equilibrium as in problem 1 to an equilibrium of the sort in problem 4. (Thus, for $\omega = 6$, the ratio of incomes R_1/R_2 goes from a value close to one to a value close to two.) Such a redistribution would be judged unacceptable by the owners of enterprise 2.

The solution that subsidizes the output of enterprise 1 allows more flexibility with respect to its consequences on the redistribution of income, inasmuch as it is possible to tinker with the distribution of the fiscal burden. However, this poses some difficulties with respect to choosing the optimal level of the subsidy t, for such a choice assumes that the government possesses sufficient information to make this calculation. Therefore this solution seems more appropriate if, for example, enterprise 1 is a public enterprise.

It is interesting to note that, starting from a competitive equilibrium as in problem 1, the two enterprises can reach an agreement such that enterprise 2 finances an increase in the output of enterprise 1. Such an agreement can bring about the realization of a Pareto optimum in which enterprise 2 pays to enterprise 1 an amount equal to the price p_4 of the problem

4 equilibrium for *every additional unit produced starting from the initial situation* (the problem 1 equilibrium). The only difference is the distribution of income: here enterprise 2 pays a smaller amount than in the problem 4 equilibrium to enterprise 1 because of the external effect. It seems much more likely that an agreement like this would be reached than that enterprise 2 would accept an equilibrium of the problem 4 type.

To CONCLUDE, let us review briefly the method that has been used systematically to check whether or not any economic situation is Pareto optimal. This method consists in analyzing the value of the variation of outputs brought about by a marginal variation in the allocation of labor, where this value is defined according to the prices associated with the initial situation: $p_1 dy_1^1 + p_2 dy_2^2$. Inasmuch as such a quantity can be made strictly positive (in which case we say that a positive surplus has been extracted), it is possible to increase the level of utility of the consumers as long as their preference functions are differentiable and each consumes strictly positive quantities of all the goods in the initial situation (which is the case here). On this subject see exercise 14.

Suggested Readings

Arrow, Kenneth J. 1970. "Political and Economic Evaluation of Social Effects and Externalities." In *The Analysis of Public Output,* ed. Julius Margolis. New York: National Bureau of Economic Research.

Baumol, William. 1972. "On Taxation and Control of Externalities." *American Economic Review* 62: 307–322.

Coase, Ronald H. 1960. "The Problem of Social Cost." *Journal of Law and Economics* 3: 1–44.

Malinvaud, Edmond. 1972. *Lectures on Microeconomic Theory,* trans. A. Silvey, chap. 9. Amsterdam: North-Holland.

Musgrave, Richard A., and Musgrave, Peggy B. 1980. *Public Finance in Theory and Practice,* ed. 3. New York: McGraw-Hill.

Negishi, Takashi. 1972. *General Equilibrium Theory and International Trade,* chap. 4. Amsterdam: North-Holland.

PART SEVEN

Time and Economic Theory

Storage and Intertemporal Arbitrage

In all the models studied so far we have assumed that the date on which a good is bought has coincided with the date on which the good is consumed. Consequently, we have excluded he possibility of the consumer's storing any of the goods. The model in this exercise will demonstrate how it is possible to formalize storage.

We consider a single consumer in a model with two goods and two periods. The goods are X and Y and the amounts *consumed* in each period are X_1, Y_1; X_2, Y_2.

To simplify the calculations, we choose an intertemporal utility function of the form

$$U = X_1^\alpha Y_1^\beta X_2^\gamma Y_2^\delta, \quad \text{with} \quad \alpha + \beta + \gamma + \delta = 1.$$

The consumer's environment is characterized by the following conditions:

The income levels R_1 and R_2 ($R_1 > 0, R_2 > 0$) in each period are known.

The prices x_1, y_1; x_2, y_2 are also known. Relative prices in period 1 and period 2 may be different.

The consumer can buy good X or good Y (or both), consume only a fraction of it (or them) in period 1, and put back on the market in period 2 the amount not consumed. We denote by M the amount of X stored and by N the amount of Y stored.

No capital market exists—that is, the only intertemporal adaptations allowed occur through the storage of goods.

Discuss the consumer's behavior as a function of the ratios x_1/x_2, y_1/y_2; specify the amounts *consumed* and the amounts *demanded* (or supplied). In particular, show that when relative prices are equal in period 1 and period 2 the demand functions can be multivalued. In what sense can we nonetheless say that demand is continuous?

PROPOSED SOLUTION

This is the first of our exercises to consider the intertemporal behavior of economic agents. Often in the literature it is assumed that the consumer determines his future consumption plan knowing the discounted present value of his income and all the discounted prices—or, what amounts to the same thing, knowing the future prices (not discounted) and the interest rate (which corresponds to the numéraire). This approach assumes that the consumer can borrow or lend as much as he wishes in any period as long as his budget is balanced over time. Analysis of consumer equilibrium is then equivalent to the analysis we have already undertaken without explicitly introducing time, the only difference being the language used.

In this exercise, on the contrary, we assume that the consumer can neither borrow nor lend. It is no longer possible to define the discounted present value of income or discounted prices. The consumer's budget must be balanced in each period. Only storage now permits the consumer to achieve any intertemporal arbitrage. In the real world the consumer's situation is undoubtedly somewhere between these two situations. Indeed, in the real world all sorts of constraints interfere with the consumer's possibilities for lending or borrowing.

THE CONSUMER maximizes his utility function U subject to the following constraints, which express the balancing of his budget in each period:

$$R_1 \geqslant x_1(X_1 + M) + y_1(Y_1 + N), \tag{1}$$

$$R_2 \geqslant x_2(X_2 - M) + y_2(Y_2 - N), \tag{2}$$

with $X_1 \geqslant 0, \quad Y_1 \geqslant 0, \quad X_2 \geqslant 0, \quad Y_2 \geqslant 0, \quad M \geqslant 0, \quad N \geqslant 0.$

The domain over which we seek to maximize U is convex, since it is the intersection of convex sets. U is concave on the consumption set. Therefore the Kuhn-Tucker conditions are necessary and sufficient. Since U is strictly increasing with respect to each of its arguments, constraints (1) and (2) must be satisfied with equality at the maximum of U. On the other hand, by designating the value of log 0 to be $-\infty$, we are able to use log U

in place of U in the calculations. Finally, since the indifference surfaces are asymptotic to the axes, at a maximum of U, we must have

$$X_1 > 0, \qquad Y_1 > 0, \qquad X_2 > 0, \qquad Y_2 > 0.$$

Let L be the Lagrangian:

$$L = \log U + \lambda_1[R_1 - x_1(X_1 + M) - y_1(Y_1 + N)]$$

$$+ \lambda_2[R_2 - x_2(X_2 - M) - y_2(Y_2 - N)].$$

The Kuhn-Tucker conditions are written:

$$\frac{\partial L}{\partial X_1} = \frac{\alpha}{X_1} - \lambda_1 x_1 = 0, \qquad X_1 > 0, \tag{3}$$

$$\frac{\partial L}{\partial Y_1} = \frac{\beta}{Y_1} - \lambda_1 y_1 = 0, \qquad Y_1 > 0, \tag{4}$$

$$\frac{\partial L}{\partial X_2} = \frac{\gamma}{X_2} - \lambda_2 x_2 = 0, \qquad X_2 > 0, \tag{5}$$

$$\frac{\partial L}{\partial Y_2} = \frac{\delta}{Y_2} - \lambda_2 y_2 = 0, \qquad Y_2 > 0, \tag{6}$$

$$\frac{\partial L}{\partial M} = - \lambda_1 x_1 + \lambda_2 x_2 \leqslant 0, \quad \text{with either } \frac{\partial L}{\partial M} = 0 \quad \text{or} \quad M = 0, \tag{7}$$

$$\frac{\partial L}{\partial N} = - \lambda_1 y_1 + \lambda_2 y_2 \leqslant 0, \quad \text{with either } \frac{\partial L}{\partial N} = 0 \quad \text{or} \quad N = 0. \tag{8}$$

There are four cases to consider:
    Case 1: $M = N = 0$.
    Case 2: $M > 0$, $\quad N > 0$.
    Case 3: $M > 0$, $\quad N = 0$.
    Case 4: $N > 0$, $\quad M = 0$.
Since U does not depend on the variables M and N, the indifference surfaces contain straight segments parallel to the plane OMN in the consumer's decision space (that is, in the space of variables X_1, Y_1, M, N, X_2, Y_2) and the solution will not necessarily be unique.

● Case 1 ($M = N = 0$)

This case corresponds to an absence of storage. Solution of the system of equations (1) through (6) with $M = N = 0$ yields:

$$X_1 = \frac{\alpha}{\alpha + \beta} \frac{R_1}{x_1}, \qquad Y_1 = \frac{\beta}{\alpha + \beta} \frac{R_1}{y_1},$$

$$X_2 = \frac{\gamma}{\gamma + \delta} \frac{R_2}{x_2}, \qquad Y_2 = \frac{\delta}{\gamma + \delta} \frac{R_2}{y_2}.$$

Everything takes place as if the decisions made in each period were totally independent. Indeed, the values obtained for X_1 and Y_1, or for X_2 and Y_2, maximize the function

$$U_1(X_1, Y_1) = X_1^\alpha Y_1^\beta \quad \text{subject to} \quad x_1 X_1 + y_2 Y_1 = R_1$$

or $\qquad U_2(X_2, Y_2) = X_2^\gamma Y_2^\delta \quad \text{subject to} \quad x_2 X_2 + y_2 Y_2 = R_2.$

A priori, in order that this solution be a proper maximum of U, there must not be any gain in satisfaction achievable by reducing consumption during period 1 and transferring some of either good to period 2. Therefore we must have:

$$\frac{\partial U}{\partial X_1} \geqslant \frac{\partial U}{\partial X_2} \tag{9}$$

and $\qquad\qquad\qquad\qquad \dfrac{\partial U}{\partial Y_1} \geqslant \dfrac{\partial U}{\partial Y_2}. \tag{10}$

Since Eqs. (3) and (5) can be written

$$\frac{\partial U}{\partial X_1} = \lambda_1 x_1 U \quad \text{and} \quad \frac{\partial U}{\partial X_2} = \lambda_2 x_2 U,$$

then inequalities (9) and (10) imply that

$$\lambda_1 x_1 \geqslant \lambda_2 x_2 \quad \text{and} \quad \lambda_1 y_1 \geqslant \lambda_2 y_2.$$

We rewrite the conditions given by expressions (7) and (8) as

$$\frac{\partial L}{\partial M} = - \lambda_1 x_1 + \lambda_2 x_2 \leqslant 0,$$

$$\frac{\partial L}{\partial N} = - \lambda_1 y_1 + \lambda_2 y_2 \leqslant 0.$$

Since $\lambda_1 = (\alpha + \beta)/R_1$ and $\lambda_2 = (\gamma + \delta)/R_2$, inequalities (9) and (10) —which determine the boundaries of the feasible domain for case 1—can be written:

$$\frac{x_1}{x_2} \geqslant \frac{R_1}{R_2} \frac{\gamma + \delta}{\alpha + \beta},$$

$$\frac{y_1}{y_2} \geqslant \frac{R_1}{R_2} \frac{\gamma + \delta}{\alpha + \beta},$$

or
$$\frac{R_1}{R_2} \leqslant \min \left\{ \frac{\alpha + \beta}{\gamma + \delta} \frac{y_1}{y_2}, \frac{\alpha + \beta}{\gamma + \delta} \frac{x_1}{x_2} \right\}.$$

If income increases sufficiently from period 1 to period 2, there will be no storage.

- Case 2 $(M > 0, N > 0)$

We have $\partial L/\partial M = \partial L/\partial N = 0$ or $\lambda_1 x_1 = \lambda_2 x_2$, $\lambda_1 y_1 = \lambda_2 y_2$. This case is possible only if $x_1/x_2 = y_1/y_2$—that is, if the relative prices do not change from one period to the next. Suppose that $t = x_1/x_2 = y_1/y_2$. Then expressions (7) and (8) combine to yield a single equation:

$$\lambda_2 = t\lambda_1. \tag{11}$$

There are only seven equations left to determine the eight unknowns λ_1, λ_2, X_1, Y_1, X_2, Y_2, M, N. In fact, by combining Eqs. (1) and (2), we can generate an equation where M and N do not appear:

$$R_1 + tR_2 = x_1(X_1 + X_2) + y_1(Y_1 + Y_2). \tag{12}$$

Then Eqs. (3) through (6), (11), and (12) allow us to calculate $\lambda_1, \lambda_2, X_1, X_2, Y_1$, and Y_2:

$$X_1 = \frac{\alpha(R_1 + tR_2)}{x_1}, \qquad Y_1 = \frac{\beta(R_1 + tR_2)}{y_1},$$

$$X_2 = \frac{\gamma(R_1 + tR_2)}{x_1}, \qquad Y_2 = \frac{\delta(R_1 + tR_2)}{y_1}.$$

Therefore M and N are indeterminate as long as they satisfy either Eq. (1) or Eq. (2), both of which are equivalent when we take the values of the other variables into account. Therefore we have:

$$R_1 = x_1 M + y_1 N + (R_1 + tR_2)(\alpha + \beta)$$

or $\qquad\qquad x_1 M + y_1 N = R_1(\gamma + \delta) - tR_2(\alpha + \beta). \qquad\qquad (13)$

This case is possible only if M and N can be strictly positive, that is, if

$$R_1(\gamma + \delta) - tR_2(\alpha + \beta) > 0,$$

or $\qquad\qquad \dfrac{R_1}{R_2} > \dfrac{\alpha + \beta}{\gamma + \delta} \dfrac{x_1}{x_2} = \dfrac{\alpha + \beta}{\gamma + \delta} \dfrac{y_1}{y_2}.$

In this situation maximizing U without storage would lead to a solution such that $\partial U/\partial X_2 > \partial U/\partial X_1$ and $\partial U/\partial Y_2 > \partial U/\partial Y_1$. This solution is obviously not optimal, since we can increase U by transferring part of the consumption of period 1 to period 2. In this case we notice that everything takes place as if, during the first period, the consumer loaned a sum equal to

$$R_1 - x_1 X_1 - y_1 Y_1 = R_1(\gamma + \delta) - tR_2(\alpha + \beta) > 0.$$

The repayment of this loan during the second period generates for the consumer an amount equal to

$$x_2 X_2 + y_2 Y_2 - R_2 = \frac{1}{t} [(\gamma + \delta)R_1 - tR_2(\alpha + \beta)] > 0.$$

The interest rate i associated with this particular loan is therefore given by $1 + i = 1/t$, or $i = (t - 1)/t$. Then $R_1 + tR_2$ is the discounted present value of income associated with this interest rate.

● Cases 3 and 4

Because these two cases are symmetric, it is sufficient to study only one—say case 3 ($M > 0, N = 0$).

In addition to Eqs. (1) through (6), we have

$$M > 0 \Rightarrow \frac{\partial L}{\partial M} = - \lambda_1 x_1 + \lambda_2 x_2 = 0 \tag{7}$$

$$N = 0, \quad \text{with} \quad \frac{\partial L}{\partial N} \leq 0. \tag{8}$$

The solution of the system of equations (1) through (8) yields:

$$X_1 = \frac{\alpha}{x_1} \left(R_1 + \frac{x_1}{x_2} R_2 \right), \qquad Y_1 = \frac{\beta}{y_1} \left(R_1 + \frac{x_1}{x_2} R_2 \right),$$

$$X_2 = \frac{\gamma}{x_1} \left(R_1 + \frac{x_1}{x_2} R_2 \right), \qquad Y_2 = \frac{\delta x_2}{x_1 y_2} \left(R_1 + \frac{x_1}{x_2} R_2 \right),$$

$$M = \frac{R_1(\gamma + \delta) - \dfrac{x_1}{x_2} R_2(\alpha + \beta)}{x_1}.$$

This case is possible only if $\partial L/\partial N \leq 0$, which, when we take expression (7) into account, implies that $x_1/y_1 \leq x_2/y_2$ or $x_1/x_2 \leq y_1/y_2$. On the other hand, $M > 0$ implies

$$\frac{R_1}{R_2} > \frac{\alpha + \beta}{\gamma + \delta} \frac{x_1}{x_2} = \min \left\{ \frac{\alpha + \beta}{\gamma + \delta} \frac{x_1}{x_2}, \frac{\alpha + \beta}{\gamma + \delta} \frac{y_1}{y_2} \right\}.$$

By storing X, the consumer acts as if he were making a loan at a rate of interest i such that $1/(1 + i) = x_1/x_2$. Depending on whether x_1/x_2 is greater or less than y_1/y_2, the consumer benefits from storing either good Y or good X in order to achieve the highest rate of return. In other words, if he stores either good, the consumer stores the one having the greater price increase (or the smaller price decrease) from period 1 to period 2.

Case 4, like cases 2 and 3, can occur only if R_1/R_2 is large enough, that is, if

$$\frac{R_1}{R_2} > \min \left\{ \frac{\alpha + \beta}{\gamma + \delta} \frac{x_1}{x_2}, \frac{\alpha + \beta}{\gamma + \delta} \frac{y_1}{y_2} \right\}$$

and if

$$\frac{x_1}{x_2} \geqslant \frac{y_1}{y_2}.$$

Case 2 emerges as the limiting case of cases 3 and 4; in other words, as the transitional case between these other two cases. One might wonder if when x_1/x_2 increases and tends toward y_1/y_2, the unique solution of case 3 tends toward a solution belonging to the set of solutions of case 2. In case 3 the values for X_1, Y_1, X_2, and Y_2 taken when $x_1/x_2 = y_1/y_2$ are identical to those of case 2. On the other hand, in case 3 we have

$$N = 0, \qquad M = \frac{R_1}{x_1}(\gamma + \delta) - \frac{R_2}{x_2}(\alpha + \beta).$$

These values of N and M satisfy Eq. (13) in the case where $x_1/x_2 = y_1/y_2 = t$. We could show a similar convergence for case 4.

For given values of R_1, R_2, y_1, y_2, and x_2, the graph of the function M is a multivalued function of the price x_1 (Fig. 19.1). The ordinate of point A is equal to

$$\frac{R_1 y_2}{x_2 y_1}(\gamma + \delta) - \frac{R_2}{x_2}(\alpha + \beta).$$

Curve $\mathscr{C}A$ corresponds to case 3, segment AB to case 2, and segment Bx_1 to case 4, if we assume that

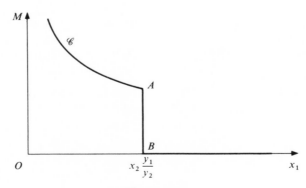

Figure 19.1

$$\frac{R_1}{R_2} > \frac{\alpha + \beta\, y_1}{\gamma + \delta\, y_2}.$$

We can say that the multivalued function M is "upper semicontinuous." (A multivalued function, or correspondence, is upper semicontinuous if its graph is closed.)

In conclusion, in the case where storage is the only possible way for the consumer to adjust his consumption between present and future bundles, the consumer acts as if he could loan—but not borrow—at a rate of interest i. This rate is determined by equating $1/(1 + i)$ to the ratio of the future price (not a discounted price, but one anticipated by the consumer) to the present price for the good that has the greater price increase (or smaller price decrease). The purchase of a good with the intent of storing it, a purchase dependent on the consumer's price expectations, can be considered a speculative purchase (an example would be a building lot).

Cases 2, 3, and 4 would also be applicable without any modification if we were to allow the consumer to borrow at a rate r and to lend at a rate r' as long as we assume, on the one hand, that $r' < i$, so that if the consumer wishes to increase his future consumption he will store goods rather than make a loan at the rate r' and, on the other hand, that $r > i$ to rule out the possibility of infinite wealth.

Suggested Readings

Malinvaud, Edmond. 1966. "Interest Rates in the Allocation of Resources." In *The Theory of Interest Rates,* ed. Frank H. Hahn and Frank P. R. Brechling. London: Macmillan.

Malinvaud, Edmond. 1972. *Lectures on Microeconomic Theory,* trans. A. Silvey, chap. 10. Amsterdam: North-Holland.

20 The Enterprise in an Imperfect Capital Market

(1) If an amount of money w obtained in period 0 is loaned at an annual interest rate r, and if the repayment schedule stipulates that the amount must be repaid in T constant annual installments denoted a (interest and principal), determine the sum of the installments over the period $1, \ldots, T$.

(2) The planning horizon of an enterprise is restricted to three periods (0 indicates the current period, 1 and 2 the future periods). The financial environment of the enterprise is characterized by the following conditions:

Its means of self-financing are zero.

As far as its financial operations are concerned, it is subject to no quantitative limitations (it has no debt ceiling).

It can lend at a rate r_0 in the form of short-term loans (a term of one period).

It can also borrow short term at a rate $r_1 > r_0$.

Finally, in period 0, it can borrow medium term (a term of two periods) at a rate $r_2 > r_0$, with repayment in constant annual installments during periods 1 and 2.

The enterprise neither lends nor goes into debt during period 2.

Characterize the set Θ of feasible budgeting programs. Show that:

If $r_2 > r_1$, efficiency precludes incurring medium-term debt. After that, considering only the case where $r_1 \geq r_2 > r_0$, establish the following properties.

If r_2 is sufficiently close to r_1, efficiency precludes the enterprise from lending, once it has used medium-term borrowing.

If r_2 is sufficiently close to r_0, efficiency precludes the enterprise from short-term borrowing.

Once it borrows short term in one period, the enterprise does not lend in the same period.

(3) Consider the following numerical values: $r_0 = 0.05$, $r_1 = 0.08$, $r_2 = 0.07$ and assume that the enterprise is obligated to borrow during the first period. Show that the set of efficient financial programs is, then, in θ_0, θ_1, θ_2 space, included in a simplex E bounded by three linear constraints that we shall determine.

(4) The enterprise chooses among four variants, corresponding to four technically feasible investment projects. The returns in each period are given in the table below.

Project:	1	2	3	4
Net returns: ρ_0	−300	−200	−400	−200
ρ_1	150	120	220	170
ρ_2	198	100	220	60

Show that two of these projects can be eliminated, since the vector $-\rho$ does not belong to the set E defined in (3).

(5) Show that because of strict set inclusion, we can choose between the two remaining projects independently of any utility function.

PROPOSED SOLUTION

It would be unusual to find an enterprise operating in a perfect capital market. Apart from the quantitative constraints on the means of financing that the enterprise has at its disposal (constraints that we have not considered here), it may happen that the market could be considered imperfect in the sense that the enterprise faces various rates of interest depending on whether it lends or borrows, depending on the term of the loan, and so forth. In such a case it seems that applying indiscriminately the criterion of maximizing the discounted present value of profit is unfounded. (What rate of interest should we consider?)

This exercise shows how an explicit description of the financial environment of the enterprise can nonetheless permit a rational choice. However, we are considering a particular case because the variant finally chosen is determined independently of intertemporal preferences, which is not true as a general rule.

Problem 1

Since w is the amount of money available to be exchanged for a flow of constant payments spread over the period $1, \ldots, T$, the present value at time 0 of this flow of payments must be equal to w. Consequently, a is determined by

$$w = \frac{a}{1+r} + \frac{a}{(1+r)^2} + \cdots + \frac{a}{(1+r)^T}$$

$$= \frac{1}{1+r} \, a \, \frac{1 - \dfrac{1}{(1+r)^T}}{1 - \dfrac{1}{1+r}}.$$

From this, we derive

$$a = \frac{rw}{1 - \dfrac{1}{(1+r)^T}}.$$

When T tends toward infinity, the amount of money w can be exchanged for an income in perpetuity corresponding to constant annual installments of $a = rw$.

Problem 2

Short-term borrowing corresponds to the sale at a price $1/(1 + r_1)$ of a bond that promises to pay one monetary unit during the following period. The enterprise sells y_0 such bonds during period 0 and y_1 bonds during period 1. Similarly, a short-term loan corresponds to the purchase at a price $1/(1 + r_0)$ of a bond yielding one monetary unit in the following period. The enterprise buys x_0 such bonds during period 0, and x_1 during period 1. Finally, medium-term borrowing corresponds to the sale at the price

$$\frac{1}{1 + r_2} + \left(\frac{1}{1 + r_2}\right)^2 = \frac{2 + r_2}{(1 + r_2)^2}$$

of a bond that promises to pay one monetary unit during each of the two following periods. The enterprise sells z such bonds during period 0. The quantities x_0, x_1, y_0, y_1, and z are naturally nonnegative. Let $\theta_t(t = 0, 1, 2)$ be the flow of money that the enterprise can obtain (or must pay) during period t when it uses the various opportunities for lending and borrowing that are open to it. We adopt the convention that if during period t the enterprise obtains funds from the capital market, θ_t is positive. In other words, the net flow of money linking the enterprise to the market is taken to be positive when it is directed from the market to the enterprise. In the opposite case, if the enterprise provides overall funds to the market, the flow θ_t is taken to be negative. Therefore we can represent θ_t as the difference between, on the one hand, the amounts borrowed in period t, net of repayments, and, on the other hand, loans in period t, net of recoupments.

Under these conditions the set Θ of feasible financial programs is defined as the set of triplets $\theta_0, \theta_1, \theta_2$ to which we can associate the nonnegative variables x_0, x_1, y_0, y_1, and z such that the conditions in the following table hold.

	Amount borrowed	Repayment	Loan	Recoupment
$\theta_0 =$	$\dfrac{y_0}{1 + r_1} + \dfrac{z(2 + r_2)}{(1 + r_2)^2}$		$- \dfrac{x_0}{1 + r_0}$	
$\theta_1 =$	$+ \dfrac{y_1}{1 + r_1}$	$- y_0 - z$	$- \dfrac{x_1}{1 + r_0}$	$+ x_0$
$\theta_2 =$		$- y_1 - z$		$+ x_1$

Since the rates r_0, r_1, and r_2 are given, Θ emerges as the image of the positive orthant of the space $\mathbb{R}^5$ of the variables x_0, x_1, y_0, y_1, and z according to the linear transformation defined above. Therefore Θ is a closed convex polyhedral cone having the origin as its vertex.

A financial program $\{\theta_0, \theta_1, \theta_2\}$ will be said to be efficient if it is not possible to increase the cash flow in one period without simultaneously decreasing the cash flow in another period. The notion is that an efficient financial program corresponds to optimal cash management by the enterprise. Since Θ is a convex polyhedral cone (Fig. 20.1)[1] we know that to any efficient element $\theta^* \in \Theta$ we can associate a strictly positive linear function such that this linear function will be maximized over Θ at θ^*. The proposition that θ^* is efficient in Θ is therefore equivalent to the following: there exist numbers $\beta_0, \beta_1, \beta_2$ all positive, such that the linear function $\beta_0\theta_0 + \beta_1\theta_1 + \beta_2\theta_2$ achieves its maximum in Θ at θ^*. To simplify what follows, we choose $\beta_0 = 1$, which is not a restrictive assumption.

Then to any efficient program θ^* we can associate nonnegative numbers $x_0^*, x_1^*, y_0^*, y_1^*$, and z^* as well as positive numbers β_1 and β_2, so that the linear function

$$\theta_0 + \beta_1\theta_1 + \beta_2\theta_2 = \left(\beta_1 - \frac{1}{1+r_0}\right) x_0 + \left(\beta_2 - \frac{\beta_1}{1+r_0}\right) x_1$$

$$+ \left(\frac{1}{1+r_1} - \beta_1\right) y_0 + \left(\frac{\beta_1}{1+r_1} - \beta_2\right) y_1$$

$$+ \left[\frac{2+r_2}{(1+r_2)^2} - \beta_1 - \beta_2\right] z$$

will achieve a maximum over the positive orthant of $\mathbb{R}^5$ at $x_0^*, x_1^*, y_0^*, y_1^*$, and z^*.

The Kuhn-Tucker conditions (necessary and sufficient in this case) imply

$$\beta_1 - \frac{1}{1+r_0} \leq 0 \quad \text{with} \qquad \beta_1 - \frac{1}{1+r_0} < 0 \Rightarrow x_0 = 0; \quad (1)$$

$$\beta_2 - \frac{\beta_1}{1+r_0} \leq 0 \quad \text{with} \qquad \beta_2 - \frac{\beta_1}{1+r_0} < 0 \Rightarrow x_1 = 0; \quad (2)$$

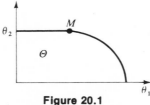

Figure 20.1

---

1. Obviously it is not true in general that given a closed convex set, we can associate a strictly positive linear function to an efficient point. To convince ourselves of this, it is sufficient to consider Fig. 20.1. However, because Θ is a polyhedral cone, the property is true.

$$\frac{1}{1 + r_1} - \beta_1 \leq 0 \quad \text{with}$$

$$\frac{1}{1 + r_1} - \beta_1 < 0 \Rightarrow y_0 = 0; \quad (3)$$

$$\frac{\beta_1}{1 + r_1} - \beta_2 \leq 0 \quad \text{with}$$

$$\frac{\beta_1}{1 + r_1} - \beta_2 < 0 \Rightarrow y_1 = 0; \quad (4)$$

$$\frac{2 + r_2}{(1 + r_2)^2} - \beta_1 - \beta_2 \leq 0 \quad \text{with} \quad \frac{2 + r_2}{(1 + r_2)^2} - \beta_1 - \beta_2 < 0 \Rightarrow z = 0. \quad (5)$$

Since $r_1 > r_0$ by assumption, we derive immediately:

$$\frac{1}{1 + r_1} < \frac{1}{1 + r_0} < 1.$$

Figure 20.2 reproduces constraints (1) through (4) in the space β_1, β_2. These constraints define a quadrilateral $ABCD$. We set

$$f(r) = \frac{1}{1 + r} + \frac{1}{(1 + r)^2} = \frac{2 + r}{(1 + r)^2}.$$

Now, $f(r)$ is a decreasing function of r. Constraint (5) can then be written

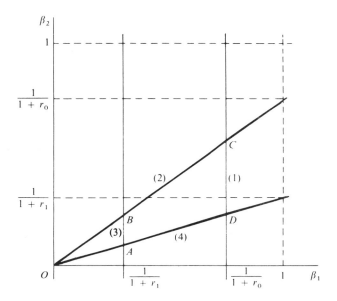

Figure 20.2

$\beta_1 + \beta_2 \geqslant f(r_2)$. We notice that the area defined by constraints (1) through (5) is never empty. Indeed, point C is always above the line that defines constraint (5), since

$$\beta_1^C + \beta_2^C = \frac{1}{1 + r_0} + \frac{1}{(1 + r_0)^2} = f(r_0) > f(r_2).$$

(Indeed, by assumption $r_2 > r_0$.)

Then it is possible to establish the following properties:

(1) if $r_2 > r_1$, we always have $z = 0$ (that is, medium-term credit is not used). We will then have

$$\beta_1^A + \beta_2^A = \frac{1}{1 + r_1} + \frac{1}{(1 + r_1)^2} = f(r_1) > f(r_2).$$

In this case constraint (5) becomes redundant with respect to the first four, so that for any efficient point $z = 0$.

(2) If r_2 is sufficiently close to r_1 (in the case where $r_1 \geqslant r_2 > 0$), the enterprise does not make a loan once it has used medium-term borrowing. If point B is above constraint (5), D will also be above (5) because

$$\frac{1}{1 + r_1} + \frac{1}{1 + r_1} \frac{1}{1 + r_0} < \frac{1}{1 + r_0} + \frac{1}{1 + r_0} \frac{1}{1 + r_1}.$$

Therefore, if

$$\frac{1}{1 + r_1} + \frac{1}{1 + r_1} \frac{1}{1 + r_0} > f(r_2),$$

that is, since f^{-1} is a decreasing function if

$$r_2 > f^{-1} \left(\frac{1}{1 + r_1} + \frac{1}{1 + r_1} \frac{1}{1 + r_0} \right),$$

constraint (5) will not cut segments BC and CD.

When we borrow on medium term ($z > 0$), constraint (5) is necessarily satisfied with equality. It follows that constraints (1) (segment CD) and (2) (segment BC) are not binding and therefore $x_0 = 0$ and $x_1 = 0$.

(3) The reasoning here is very similar to the above. Indeed, we show that if D is below constraint (5), that is, if

$$r_2 < f^{-1}\left(\frac{1}{1+r_0} + \frac{1}{1+r_0}\frac{1}{1+r_1}\right),$$

constraints (3) (segment AB) and (4) (segment AD) are not binding, so that we have $y_0 = 0$ and $y_1 = 0$.

(4) From Fig. 20.2 it is obvious that when one borrows on short term in one period, one does not lend in the same period, since the segments AB and CD on the one hand and BC and AD on the other are disjoint.

Problem 3

We introduce into the problem a new constraint—the fact that θ_0 is positive (one is obliged to borrow in period 0).

Let us begin by neglecting this additional condition and characterizing the values of β_1 and β_2 that lead to efficient programs. The numerical values imposed here imply that:

(1) D is above constraint (5). Indeed,

$$\frac{1}{1+r_0} + \frac{1}{1+r_1}\frac{1}{1+r_0} > \frac{1}{1+r_2} + \frac{1}{(1+r_2)^2},$$

or $$(2 + r_1)(1 + r_2)^2 > (2 + r_2)(1 + r_0)(1 + r_1).$$

We show that for the given values the following is true:

$$2.381392 > 2.347380.$$

(2) B is below constraint (5). We must show that

$$\frac{1}{1+r_1} + \frac{1}{1+r_0}\frac{1}{1+r_1} < \frac{1}{1+r_2} + \frac{1}{(1+r_2)^2},$$

that is, that $$(2 + r_0)(1 + r_2)^2 < (1 + r_0)(1+ r_1)(2 + r_2).$$

This inequality is consistent with the given values, since

$$2.347045 < 2.347380.$$

If we ignore the fact that θ_0 must be positive, the set of couplets $\beta_1\beta_2$ corresponding to efficient programs in Θ is therefore a quadrilateral

CDEF in Fig. 20.3. We see right away that the segment *AB* does not intersect the set of feasible values of $\beta_1\beta_2$. Consequently, the values chosen are such that constraint (3) is never fulfilled with equality and the variable y_0 is zero in an efficient solution—that is, we do not incur short-term debt during the first period.

Now let us introduce the condition that we must incur debt in the first period. Since we cannot incur short-term debt, there is only one solution remaining: to incur medium-term debt, which implies that $z > 0$ and that the corresponding values of β_1 and β_2 are characterized by points on segment *EF*.

Since, as we have seen, *D* is above constraint (5) (line *EF*), segments *EF* and *CD* do not intersect; then constraint (1) is not binding in an efficient solution in which we incur debt during the first period. Taking duality into account, we can conclude that $x_0 = 0$.

Finally, subject to the restriction that we must incur debt during the first period, the set of efficient financial programs is included in the set E of triplets $\theta_0, \theta_1, \theta_2$ to which we can associate the numbers $x_1 \geq 0, y_1 \geq 0$, and $z > 0$ such that

$$\theta_0 = \frac{2 + r_2}{(1 + r_2)^2}\, z,$$

$$\theta_1 = \frac{y_1}{1 + r_1} - z - \frac{x_1}{1 + r_0},$$

$$\theta_2 = -y_1 - z + x_1.$$

The above equations can be solved very simply for x_1, y_1, and z:

$$x_1 = \frac{1}{\dfrac{1}{1 + r_1} - \dfrac{1}{1 + r_0}} \frac{1}{(1 + r_1)(2 + r_2)}$$
$$\times\, [(1 + r_2)^2(2 + r_1)\, \theta_0 + (2 + r_2)(1 + r_1)\, \theta_1 + (2 + r_2)\, \theta_2] \geq 0,$$

$$y_1 = \frac{1}{\dfrac{1}{1 + r_1} - \dfrac{1}{1 + r_0}} \frac{1}{(1 + r_0)(2 + r_2)}$$
$$\times\, [(1 + r_2)^2(2 + r_0)\, \theta_0 + (2 + r_2)(1 + r_0)\, \theta_1 + (2 + r_2)\, \theta_2] \geq 0.$$

$$z = \frac{(1 + r_2)^2}{2 + r_2}\, \theta_0.$$

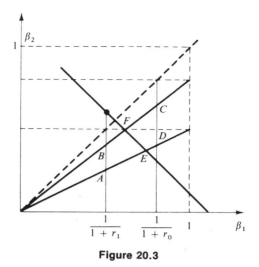

Figure 20.3

The set E can be defined, in an equivalent way, by the following three linear constraints:

$$\theta_0 > 0,$$
$$(1 + r_2)^2(2 + r_1)\,\theta_0 + (2 + r_2)(1 + r_1)\,\theta_1 + (2 + r_2)\,\theta_2 \leqslant 0,$$
$$(1 + r_2)^2(2 + r_0)\,\theta_0 + (2 + r_2)(1 + r_0)\,\theta_1 + (2 + r_2)\,\theta_2 \leqslant 0.$$

When we use our numerical values, these become

$$\theta_0 > 0,$$
$$2.381392\,\theta_0 + 2.2356\,\theta_1 + 2.07\,\theta_2 \leqslant 0, \qquad (6)$$
$$2.347045\,\theta_0 + 2.1735\,\theta_1 + 2.07\,\theta_2 \leqslant 0.$$

Naturally, under the condition that we must incur debt during the first period, the set of efficient financial programs is the set of elements of E such that while remaining in E we cannot increase θ_t in one period without simultaneously decreasing θ_t in another period.

Problem 4

In order that a technically feasible project be financially feasible as well, it is necessary that the enterprise balance its cash accounts in each of the periods, that is for $t = 0, 1, 2$ we must derive a nonnegative d_t such that $d_t = \theta_t + \rho_t$, where θ is a financially feasible program. A necessary condition for such a program (technical and financial) to lead to a menu of efficient results is that any financial program θ associated with it must itself be efficient. Therefore, for an investment project to be a candidate for efficiency, we need to find an efficient financial program such that, for any t, $\rho_t + \theta_t$ will be nonnegative.

The programs for which the conditions $\rho_t + \theta_t \geq 0$ for any t are inconsistent with conditions (6) above, which define the set E, can therefore be eliminated. When we take into account the particular structure of the inequalities considered, there will be an inconsistency if and only if, for $\theta_t = -\rho_t$ in system (6), one of the last two inequalities is not satisfied (the first one is always satisfied).

Inasmuch as the set of financial possibilities is a cone, we can simplify the calculations by replacing the values of ρ by proportionate values, so that for each project $\rho_0 = -200$. Thus we obtain for the first of the two constraints that is of interest:

Investment project:	1	2	3	4
$2.2356\ \theta_1 =$	-223.56	-268.272	-245.916	-380.05
$2.07\ \theta_2 =$	-273.24	-207	-227.7	-124.20
$2.2356\ \theta_1 + 2.07\ \theta_2 =$	-496.80	-475.272	-473.616	-504.25
$2.381392\ \theta_0 =$		476.2784		

By virtue of this table we can eliminate projects 2 and 3 as financially impossible. It remains to show that the second of the constraints—the last inequality in (6)—is not violated for projects 1 and 4.

Investment project:	1	4
$2.1735\ \theta_1 =$	-217.35	-369.49
$2.07\ \theta_2 =$	-273.24	-124.20
$2.1735\ \theta_1 + 2.07\ \theta_2 =$	-490.59	-493.69
$2.347045\ \theta_0 =$	469.4090	

Thus we are left with a choice between projects 1 and 4.

Problem 5

For each of the remaining projects the set of efficient results is made up of the set of efficient triplets d_0, d_1, and d_2 in the set defined by

$$d_0 = \rho_0 + \theta_0 \geqslant 0,$$

$$d_1 = \rho_1 + \theta_1 \geqslant 0,$$

$$d_2 = \rho_2 + \theta_2 \geqslant 0,$$

and conditions (6).

Having made all the calculations, we find the set associated with project 1 to be characterized by

$$d_0 \geqslant 0, \qquad d_1 \geqslant 0, \qquad d_2 \geqslant 0$$

$$2.381392 \, d_0 + 2.2356 \, d_1 + 2.07 \, d_2 \leqslant 30.7824$$

$$2.347045 \, d_0 + 2.1735 \, d_1 + 2.07 \, d_2 \leqslant 31.7715.$$

Similarly, the set associated with project 4 is characterized by

$$d_0 \geqslant 0, \qquad d_1 \geqslant 0, \qquad d_2 \geqslant 0$$

$$2.381392 \, d_0 + 2.2356 \, d_1 + 2.07 \, d_2 \leqslant 27.9716$$

$$2.347045 \, d_0 + 2.1735 \, d_1 + 2.07 \, d_2 \leqslant 24.2810.$$

Therefore we shall choose project 1, since it is always possible to overtake a program of efficient results corresponding to project 4 by a program corresponding to project 1.

Conclusion

This exercise shows how to make an investment choice by simultaneously considering the technical aspects (which characterize the various projects and calculate the corresponding net returns) and the financial aspects (which canvass the available means of financing and search for efficient financial programs).

Generally speaking, it seems that a rational decision requires a complete description of the set of opportunities, both technical and financial. This exercise leads one to the conclusion that at the microeconomic level the optimization procedure must be applied simultaneously to information from the technical sphere and from the financial sphere.

The simple criterion of maximizing the present value of returns is obviously insufficient here. Besides, if we calculate the present value using the medium-term interest rate (0.07) and then using the short-term interest rate (0.08), there is a difference between the rankings corresponding to each of the rates:

	Present value of returns			
Project:	1	2	3	4
Rate 0.07	13.11	−0.52	−2.26	11.27
Rate 0.08	8.63	−3.16	−7.69	8.84

In actual decisions it is therefore necessary to consider more than the present-value criterion, and to question in a systematic way the assumption of a perfect capital market to which microeconomic analysis has been limited for far too long.

Suggested Readings

Haley, Charles W., and Schall, Lawrence D. 1979. *The Theory of Financial Decisions,* ed. 2, chaps. 14 and 15. New York: McGraw-Hill.

Hirshleifer, Jack. 1970. *Investment, Interest and Capital.* Englewood Cliffs, N.J.: Prentice-Hall.

Koopmans, Tjalling C. 1951. "Analysis of Production as an Efficient Combination of Activities." In *Activity Analysis of Production and Allocation: Proceedings of a Conference,* ed. Tjalling C. Koopmans. New York: John Wiley.

Robichek, Alexander, and Myers, Stewart C. 1965. *Optimal Financing Decisions.* Englewood Cliffs, N.J.: Prentice-Hall.

Golden Rule Growth Theory

In this exercise we intend to generalize the traditional presentation of golden rule growth theory for the case in which there is strict complementarity between the factors of production.

The economy we consider here consists of the following four goods: two factors of production (manpower denoted N and capital denoted K) and two consumption goods (A and B). The production technology exhibits constant returns to scale. Three and only three techniques are assumed to be known: the first one produces good A, the second produces good B, and the third corresponds to the production of capital. The last technique restores the capital that is partially used up in the operations relating to the production of consumption goods.

The table below characterizes the technical conditions of production.

	Technique:	1	2	3
Input:	N_t	3	2	4
	K_t	2	5	3
Output:	A_t	1	0	0
	B_t	0	2	0
	K_{t+1}	1	2	5

This table should be read in the following way. For example, for technique 1, if $x_1(x_1 \geqslant 0)$ is the activity level, with $3x_1$ units of manpower used in period t and $2x_1$ units of capital used in period t, it is possible to produce x_1 units of good A in period t; furthermore x_1 units of capital are reproduced by this process. These x_1 units of capital will be available for use in period $t + 1$ (so that only x_1 units of capital are used up by this process of production).

Furthermore, we assume that the capital good is storable without cost—that is, if some capital is not used in period t, this capital is intact and available to be used in period $t + 1$.

Because we are working with stationary states, we make the following assumptions:

The technical conditions of production are independent of time (in other words, they correspond to those given above).

Manpower is constant: $N_t = \bar{N} > 0$;

The consumers' tastes are invariant. We specify simply a collective utility function, which allows us to choose between the output of A and that of B and is given by

$$U(A, B) = \alpha \log A + \beta \log B \qquad (\alpha > 0, \beta > 0)$$

(which assumes also that $A > 0$ and $B > 0$).

The capital stock must be maintained at a constant level: $K_t = \bar{K} > 0$.

Problem 1

For $\bar{N}$ and $\bar{K}$ given, find the optimal outputs. Will the factors of production always be fully employed?

Problem 2

For $\bar{N}$ given, show that there exists an infinite number of optimal stationary states. By interpreting the dual variables as prices, show that the rate of interest is then zero. In what way does the problem change if we eliminate the assumption that capital can be stored without cost?

Problem 3

Consider now balanced growth paths under the following assumptions:

(a) The technical conditions of production remain the same as before and they are identical over time.

(b) Manpower grows at rate n: $N_t = N_0(1 + n)^t$.

(c) The stock of capital is constrained to grow at rate n: $K_t = K_0(1 + n)^t$.

(d) A collective utility function for each period, which allows us to choose between the output of A and that of B, is given by

$$U_t(A_t, B_t) = U\left(\frac{A_t}{N_t}, \frac{B_t}{N_t}\right) = \alpha \log \frac{A_t}{N_t} + \beta \log \frac{B_t}{N_t}$$

For N_0 fixed, show that over the set of balanced growth paths there exists one that is optimal.

Characterize the level of capital that corresponds to this optimal growth path and show that the interest rate is then equal to the rate of growth n.

PROPOSED SOLUTION

This exercise extends the study of stationary states to a consideration of balanced growth paths.

The aim of this exercise is to compare various stationary states or various balanced growth paths. Since the quantities of the primary factor of production (labor) available in the various periods are given (these define the growth rate of the economy under consideration), a stationary state or a balanced growth path is characterized fully by the initial level of capital. On the other hand, the value attained by the utility function (which allows choice between the outputs of the two consumption goods during each period) is independent of time in the stationary state problem as well as in the balanced growth path problem.

In the absence of an intertemporal utility function, one might question the effectiveness of choice between "present" and "future" generations. Here the definition of the set of programs over which choices are made allows us to avoid this intricate problem. We are limiting ourselves to choice in the set of feasible stationary states (the case where labor is constant) or in the set of balanced growth paths (the case where labor increases at a constant rate). Under these conditions if a program is preferred by one generation it is preferred by all. On the other hand, such a procedure would no longer be satisfactory if we were looking for an optimal growth path within the set of *all* feasible paths; it would be necessary then to impose an intertemporal utility function.

As it stands, the problem is simpler: it consists in determining the value attained by the utility function when only one parameter (the initial capital stock) can vary. Thus in the stationary state case, if we maintain capital at a low level from period to period, the output of the consumption goods and therefore utility will be low (in the limiting case, it is even possible to have a zero capital stock for which output will become zero). However, when we increase the capital stock the corresponding value of utility is not always an increasing function of capital. If we find ourselves with too much capital permanently, we will use too much manpower to maintain such a substantial level of capital, obviously at the expense of the output of consumption goods. Is there an optimum between these two extremes?

Notice that it is necessary to assume constant returns in order to obtain balanced growth paths. Consequently, this exercise generalizes the classic presentation, which uses differentiable production functions, to the case where the technical possibilities are represented by a certain number of activities, as in exercise 6.

Problem 1

Let x_t be the activity level of technique 1, y_t that of technique 2, and z_t that of technique 3, all during period t. We must choose these levels to maximize $U(A_t, B_t) = \alpha \log A_t + \beta \log B_t$ subject to the following constraints, where the associated Lagrangian multipliers are given in parentheses:

$$A_t \leqslant x_t \qquad (a_t), \tag{1}$$

$$B_t \leqslant 2y_t \qquad (b_t), \tag{2}$$

$$3x_t + 2y_t + 4z_t \leqslant N_t \qquad (\sigma_t), \tag{3}$$

$$2x_t + 5y_t + 3z_t \leqslant K_t \qquad (k_t), \tag{4}$$

$$K_{t+1} = [K_t - (2x_t + 5y_t + 3z_t)] + (x_t + 2y_t + 5z_t) \qquad (h_t) \tag{5}$$

where $\qquad x_t \geqslant 0, \qquad y_t \geqslant 0, \qquad z_t \geqslant 0.$

Constraint (5), to which the multiplier h_t is associated, states that the sum of the capital stored plus the capital produced is equal to the capital stock available in the following period. If N_t is constant, $N_t = \bar{N}$; and if we impose the condition that capital be reproduced so that it remains constant from period to period (that is, $K_{t+1} = K_t = \bar{K}$), the solution of this program is independent of t and we can characterize the stationary state associated with the levels of manpower and capital given by $\bar{N}$ and $\bar{K}$ respectively.

The Kuhn-Tucker conditions are necessary and sufficient, since U is concave and the constraint set is convex.

Since U is strictly increasing with respect to each of its arguments, constraints (1) and (2) are necessarily satisfied with equality at a maximum of U. Since the indifference curves approach the coordinate axes asymptotically, $x_t > 0$ and $y_t > 0$. And since Eq. (5), for $K_{t+1} = K_t$, can be written $2z_t = 3y_t + x_t$, we have as well $z_t > 0$.

Let $\mathscr{L}$ be the Lagrangian, which can be written as

$$\mathscr{L} = \alpha \log A_t + \beta \log B_t + a_t(x_t - A_t) + b_t(2y_t - B_t)$$

$$+ \sigma_t(N_t - 3x_t - 2y_t - 4z_t) + k_t(K_t - 2x_t - 5y_t - 3z_t)$$

$$+ h_t(-2x_t - 5y_t - 3z_t + x_t + 2y_t + 5z_t).$$

Among other conditions we necessarily have the following:

$$\frac{\partial \mathscr{L}}{\partial x_t} = a_t - 3\sigma_t - 2(k_t + h_t) + h_t = 0, \tag{6}$$

$$\frac{\partial \mathscr{L}}{\partial y_t} = 2b_t - 2\sigma_t - 5(k_t + h_t) + 2h_t = 0, \tag{7}$$

$$\frac{\partial \mathscr{L}}{\partial z_t} = -4\sigma_t - 3(k_t + h_t) + 5h_t = 0. \tag{8}$$

If we interpret a_t as the price of good A and b_t as the price of good B, σ_t and $k_t + h_t$ as the nondiscounted prices of manpower and capital respectively, and h_t as the discounted price at time t of capital available at time $t + 1$, these equations demonstrate that the profit associated with each activity is zero and therefore maximal (see exercise 6). Then, we can interpret k_t/h_t as the rate of return on capital. (Indeed, by the very definition of the rate of interest associated with capital, $h_t = (k_t + h_t)/(1 + r)$, from which it follows that $r = k_t/h_t$.)

Since the solution of this program does not depend on t, from here on we shall leave out the time subscript. Furthermore, taking the previous remarks into account, we return to the following problem by eliminating variables A, B, and z:

Maximize $\alpha \log x + \beta \log 2y$ subject to

$$5x + 8y \leq \bar{N} \quad (\sigma) \tag{3'}$$

$$\frac{7x}{2} + \frac{19y}{2} \leq \bar{K} \quad (k). \tag{4'}$$

There are, then, three possible cases. In the space of outputs of consumption goods, these cases correspond to the three situations represented in Fig. 21.1. We denote by L the Lagrangian associated with the simplified form above.

● Case 1: underemployment of labor

$$5x + 8y < \bar{N} \Rightarrow \sigma = 0,$$

$$7x + 19y = 2\bar{K},$$

$$\frac{\partial L}{\partial x} = \frac{\alpha}{x} - 5\sigma - \frac{7k}{2} = 0, \tag{9}$$

$$\frac{\partial L}{\partial y} = \frac{\beta}{y} - 8\sigma - \frac{19k}{2} = 0. \tag{10}$$

The solution of this system yields

$$k = \frac{\alpha + \beta}{\bar{K}}, \qquad x = \frac{2\bar{K}\alpha}{7(\alpha + \beta)} > 0, \qquad y = \frac{2\bar{K}\beta}{19(\alpha + \beta)} > 0.$$

We must have $5x + 8y < \bar{N}$, from which it follows that

$$\frac{\bar{K}}{\bar{N}} < \frac{7 \times 19(\alpha + \beta)}{190\alpha + 7 \times 16\beta} = \tau_1.$$

● Case 2: full employment of labor and capital

$$5x + 8y = \bar{N},$$

$$7x + 19y = 2\bar{K},$$

$$\frac{\partial L}{\partial x} = 0, \qquad \frac{\partial L}{\partial y} = 0.$$

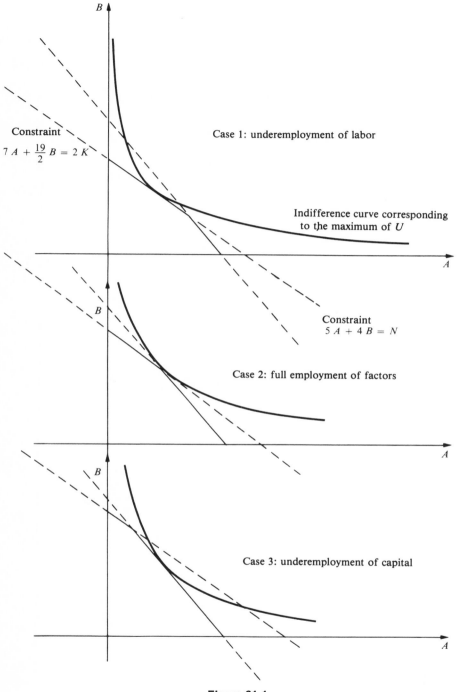

Figure 21.1

From this we derive

$$y = \frac{10\bar{K} - 7\bar{N}}{39}, \qquad x = \frac{19\bar{N} - 16\bar{K}}{39}.$$

Since k is positive, it follows that

$$\frac{\bar{K}}{\bar{N}} \leqslant \frac{190\beta + 112\alpha}{160(\alpha + \beta)} < \frac{19}{16}.$$

Since σ is positive, it follows that

$$\frac{\bar{K}}{\bar{N}} \geqslant \frac{133(\alpha + \beta)}{190\alpha + 112\beta} > \frac{7}{10}.$$

- Case 3: underemployment of capital

$$7x + 19y < 2\bar{K} \Rightarrow k = 0,$$

$$5x + 8y = \bar{N},$$

$$\frac{\partial L}{\partial x} = 0, \qquad \frac{\partial L}{\partial y} = 0.$$

It follows that

$$\sigma = \frac{\alpha + \beta}{\bar{N}}, \qquad x = \frac{\alpha\bar{N}}{5(\alpha + \beta)}, \qquad y = \frac{\beta\bar{N}}{8(\alpha + \beta)}.$$

We must have $7x + 19y < 2\bar{K}$, or

$$\frac{\bar{K}}{\bar{N}} > \frac{190\beta + 112\alpha}{160(\alpha + \beta)} = \tau_2.$$

Thus we have derived the characteristics of the stationary state as a function of the capital-labor ratio $\bar{K}/\bar{N}$.

Problem 2

We now calculate the value or values of $\bar{K}$ that maximize U for fixed $\bar{N}$. We use the results in the preceding problem to calculate U as a function of

$\bar{K}$. It is convenient to employ the following monotonically increasing transformation of U: $V = e^{\frac{U}{\alpha + \beta}}$. Clearly, V is homogeneous of degree one with respect to A and B.

For $0 < \bar{K} < \bar{N}\dfrac{133(\alpha + \beta)}{190\alpha + 112\beta}$, we have $V = V_0\bar{K}$, with

$$V_0 = \left[\frac{2}{7(\alpha + \beta)}\right]^{\frac{\alpha}{\alpha + \beta}}\left[\frac{4\beta}{19(\alpha + \beta)}\right]^{\frac{\beta}{\alpha + \beta}}$$

For $\bar{N}\dfrac{133(\alpha + \beta)}{190\alpha + 112\beta} \leqslant \bar{K} \leqslant \bar{N}\dfrac{190\beta + 112\alpha}{160(\alpha + \beta)}$, we have

$$V = \frac{1}{39}(19\,\bar{N} - 16\bar{K})^{\frac{\alpha}{\alpha + \beta}}(20\bar{K} - 14\bar{N})^{\frac{\beta}{\alpha + \beta}}.$$

Now, V is an increasing function over the interval considered and its derivative is zero when $\bar{K} = \dfrac{190\beta + 112\alpha}{160(\alpha + \beta)}$.

For $\bar{K} > \bar{N}\dfrac{190\beta + 112\alpha}{160(\alpha + \beta)}$, V is constant and

$$V = \left[\frac{\alpha}{5(\alpha + \beta)}\right]^{\frac{\alpha}{\alpha + \beta}}\left[\frac{\beta}{4(\alpha + \beta)}\right]^{\frac{\beta}{\alpha + \beta}}.$$

We can show that the function V of $\bar{K}$ defined in this way is continuous on $(0, \infty)$. Figure 21.2 shows the graph of V.

We have established the existence of an infinite number of optimal stationary states (golden rule optima), inasmuch as to any value of

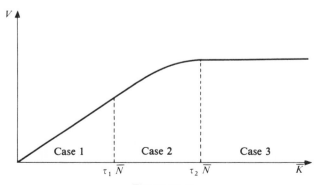

Figure 21.2

$$\bar{K} \geqslant \frac{190\beta + 112\alpha}{160(\alpha + \beta)} \bar{N}$$ there corresponds an optimal stationary state.

For $\bar{K} \geqslant \tau_2\bar{N}$, we have

$$\sigma = \frac{\alpha + \beta}{\bar{N}} > 0, \qquad k = 0.$$

Equation (8) yields $h = 2\sigma > 0$, from which we conclude that the rate of interest associated with such an optimum is zero because it is equal to k/h.

What happens if storing capital involves a cost? For $\bar{K} \leqslant \tau_2\bar{N}$ there is no change, for the corresponding stationary states do not involve the storing of capital. In particular, the stationary state corresponding to $\bar{K} = \tau_2\bar{N} = \dfrac{190\beta + 112\alpha}{160(\alpha + \beta)} \bar{N}$ is always optimal.

On the contrary, for $\bar{K} > \tau_2\bar{N}$ and with the cost of storing capital taken into account, the constraint that capital be reproduced so that the available stock remains constant from period to period implies that a portion of the available labor must be transferred from the production of consumption goods to the production of capital (regardless of whether the cost of storing capital corresponds to a direct consumption of labor or is caused by the deterioration of the capital stock at a given rate). Therefore, in this instance, the curve of V as a function of $\bar{K}$ is decreasing for $\bar{K} \geqslant \tau_2\bar{N}$. There is now a single golden rule optimum.

Problem 3

Consider the question as originally posed at the beginning of the solution to the first problem. Replace N_t and K_t by $N_0(1 + n)^t$ and by $K_0(1 + n)^t$, K_{t+1} by $(1 + n)K_t$, that is, by $K_0(1 + n)^{t+1}$. The solution of the problem in period t is then derived from the solution A_0, B_0, x_0, y_0, z_0 of the problem in the initial period in the following way:

$$A_t = A_0(1 + n)^t, \qquad B_t = B_0(1 + n)^t,$$

$$x_t = x_0(1 + n)^t, \qquad y_t = y_0(1 + n)^t, \qquad z_t = z_0(1 + n)^t.$$

Thus, we obtain a balanced growth path, characterized fully by N_0 and K_0. As we did for the stationary state case, we can attach a value of utility to each balanced growth path thus obtained, that is:

$$U_t(A_t, B_t) = U(A_0, B_0).$$

By limiting ourselves to the initial period, we can use the same reasoning as in the previous problems, so that in what follows we first maximize U for fixed N_0 and K_0 and then find the optimum level of capital.

Constraint (5) can now be written

$$2z - x - 3y = nK_0.$$

Therefore it is necessary to maximize $U = \alpha \log x + \beta \log 2y$ subject to

$$5x + 8y \leqslant N_0 - 2nK_0 \qquad (\sigma) \qquad\qquad (11)$$

$$\frac{7x}{2} + \frac{19y}{2} \leqslant K_0 \left(1 - \frac{3n}{2}\right) \qquad (k) \qquad\qquad (12)$$

where
$$x > 0, \qquad y > 0.$$

Obviously we are dealing with the same cases that we had in the second problem. In order to determine in which of the three cases we find ourselves, it is necessary to compare

$$\frac{K_0\left(1 - \dfrac{3n}{2}\right)}{N_0 - 2nK_0}$$

with the values of the limits τ_1 and τ_2.

We can show that

$$\frac{K_0\left(1 - \dfrac{3n}{2}\right)}{N_0 - 2nK_0}$$

considered as a function of K_0 is a strictly increasing function of K_0 when K_0 is between 0 and $N_0/2n$. The function takes on all the values between zero and infinity, as is shown in Fig. 21.3. Therefore, our reasoning can be applied to this function of K_0 as well as to K_0 itself.

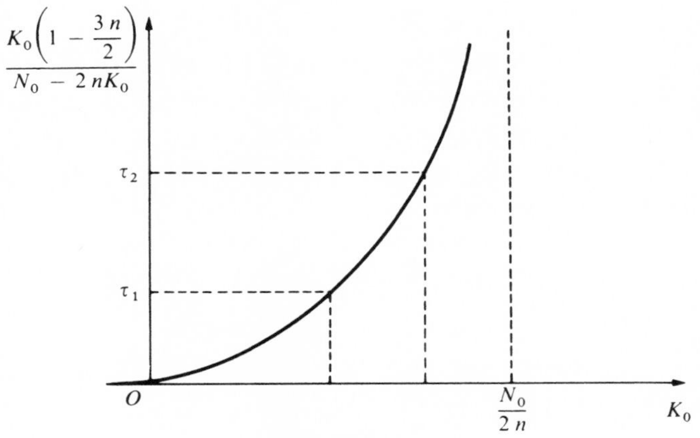

Figure 21.3

• Case 1: underemployment of labor

$$\sigma = 0 \quad k = \frac{\alpha + \beta}{K_0 \left(1 - \dfrac{3n}{2}\right)},$$

$$x = \frac{2\alpha K_0 \left(1 - \dfrac{3n}{2}\right)}{7(\alpha + \beta)},$$

$$y = \frac{2\beta K_0 \left(1 - \dfrac{3n}{2}\right)}{19(\alpha + \beta)}.$$

This case arises when

$$\frac{K_0 \left(1 - \dfrac{3n}{2}\right)}{N_0 - 2nK_0} < \tau_1$$

Then, V is both proportional to K_0 and strictly increasing.

• Case 2: full employment of labor and capital
   In this situation we have

$$x = \frac{19(N_0 - 2nK_0) - 16K_0\left(1 - \frac{3n}{2}\right)}{39},$$

$$y = \frac{10K_0\left(1 - \frac{3n}{2}\right) - 7(N_0 - 2nK_0)}{39}.$$

This case arises when

$$\tau_1 \leqslant \frac{K_0\left(1 - \frac{3n}{2}\right)}{N_0 - 2nK_0} \leqslant \tau_2.$$

Then

$$V = \frac{1}{39}\left[19N_0 - K_0(16 + 14n)\right]^{\frac{\alpha}{\alpha + \beta}}\left[K_0(10 - n) - 7N_0\right]^{\frac{\beta}{\alpha + \beta}}$$

This function of K_0 achieves its maximum when

$$\frac{K_0\left(1 - \frac{3n}{2}\right)}{N_0 - 2nK_0} = \frac{112\alpha\left(1 + \frac{7n}{8}\right) + 190\beta\left(1 - \frac{n}{10}\right)}{160\alpha\left(1 + \frac{7n}{8}\right) + 160\beta\left(1 - \frac{n}{10}\right)}, \qquad (13)$$

or

$$\frac{K_0\left(1 - \frac{3n}{2}\right)}{N_0 - 2nK_0} = \tau(n) = \frac{112\alpha' + 190\beta'}{160(\alpha' + \beta')},$$

where

$$\alpha' = \alpha\left(1 + \frac{7n}{8}\right) \quad \text{and} \quad \beta' = \beta\left(1 - \frac{n}{10}\right).$$

However, $(112\lambda + 190)/(160\lambda + 160)$, considered as a function of λ, is strictly decreasing. Since $\alpha' > \alpha$ and $\beta' < \beta$, we derive

$$\tau(n) = \frac{112\alpha\left(1 + \frac{7n}{8}\right) + 190\beta\left(1 - \frac{n}{10}\right)}{160\alpha\left(1 + \frac{7n}{8}\right) + 160\beta\left(1 - \frac{n}{10}\right)} < \tau_2.$$

Nevertheless,

$$\tau(n) > \frac{133(\alpha' + \beta')}{190\alpha' + 112\beta''},$$

and by similar reasoning,

$$\frac{133(\alpha' + \beta')}{190\alpha' + 112\beta'} > \tau_1,$$

from which it follows that $\tau_1 < \tau(n) < \tau_2$.

- Case 3: underemployment of capital
  In this instance we have

$$x = \frac{\alpha(N_0 - 2nK_0)}{5(\alpha + \beta)}, \qquad y = \frac{\beta(N_0 - 2nK_0)}{8(\alpha + \beta)}.$$

The case arises when

$$\frac{K_0\left(1 - \frac{3n}{2}\right)}{N_0 - 2nK_0} > \tau_2.$$

Then V is proportional to $(N_0 - 2nK_0)$ and is therefore a decreasing function of K_0.

As in the previous problems, we can show that there is continuity among the three cases.

The graph of V, considered as a function of K_0, is shown in Fig. 21.4. Point A, which denotes the movement from case 1 to case 2, has the following abscissa:

$$K_0 = \frac{\tau_1 N_0}{\left(1 - \frac{3n}{2}\right)\left(1 + \frac{2n\tau_1}{1 - \frac{3n}{2}}\right)}.$$

Point B, which corresponds to the optimal level of capital, has for its abscissa

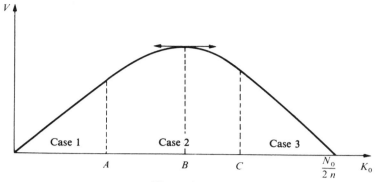

Figure 21.4

$$K_0 = \frac{\tau(n)\,N_0}{\left(1 - \dfrac{3n}{2}\right)\left(1 + \dfrac{2n\tau(n)}{1 - \dfrac{3n}{2}}\right)}.$$

Therefore, there is a unique optimal level of capital (whether or not storing capital is costless) for which there is full employment of both capital and labor.

We need now to calculate the rate of interest associated with the corresponding balanced growth path. For case 2, we can calculate σ and k from Eqs. (9) and (10):

$$\sigma = \frac{19\alpha y - 7\beta x}{39xy}, \qquad k = \frac{10\beta x - 16\alpha y}{39xy}.$$

Then Eq. (8) yields

$$h = \frac{3k + 4\sigma}{2} = \frac{14\alpha y + \beta x}{39xy}$$

and the rate of interest is equal to

$$i = \frac{k}{h} = \frac{10\beta x - 16\alpha y}{14\alpha y + \beta x}$$

$$= \frac{10\beta[19 - 16\tau(n)] - 16\alpha[10\tau(n) - 7]}{14\alpha[10\tau(n) - 7] + \beta[19 - 16\tau(n)]}$$

$$= \frac{190\beta + 112\alpha - 160(\alpha + \beta)\tau(n)}{19\beta - 98\alpha + (140\alpha - 16\beta)\tau(n)},$$

with

$$\tau(n) = \frac{112\alpha \left(1 + \frac{7n}{8}\right) + 190\beta \left(1 - \frac{n}{10}\right)}{160\alpha \left(1 + \frac{7n}{8}\right) + 160\beta \left(1 - \frac{n}{10}\right)}$$

$$= \frac{112\alpha + 190\beta + n[98\alpha - 19\beta]}{160(\alpha + \beta) + n[140\alpha - 16\beta]}.$$

From this we conclude that $i = n$.

THE ZERO interest rate associated with the optimal stationary state derived in the second problem emerges as a particular case of this result, since a stationary state is a balanced growth path with a rate of growth $n = 0$. Equality between the rate of interest and the rate of growth is an essential property of the growth path having a constant rate of growth n that overtakes all other feasible balanced growth paths having the same rate of growth. This optimal balanced growth path is called the golden rule growth path.

With a balanced growth path that corresponds to an initially given level of capital, we can associate a value for the rate of interest by using the equation $i = k/n$, which we obtained at the beginning of problem 1. This rate of interest associated with a balanced growth path is greater than, equal to, or less than the growth rate, depending on whether the corresponding initial capital stock is less than, equal to, or greater than the optimal level of initial capital.

However, the growth paths corresponding to a level of initial capital greater than the optimal level are inefficient, in the sense that they require the retention of too large a stock of capital. The natural rate of growth (which would be higher than the growth rate of population n if we took technical progress into account) emerges as a lower limit for the rate of interest below which it would be dangerous to remain for very long, as we would run the risk of useless overinvestment.

Suggested Readings

Burmeister, Edwin, and Dobell, A. Rodney. 1970. *Mathematical Theories of Economic Growth*. New York: Macmillan.

Intriligator, Michael D. 1971. *Mathematical Optimization and Economic Theory*, chap. 16. Englewood Cliffs, N.J.: Prentice-Hall.

Koopmans, Tjalling C. 1967. "Intertemporal Distribution and Optimal Aggregate Economic Growth." In *Ten Studies in the Tradition of Irving Fisher*. Contributing authors: William Fellner and others. New York: John Wiley.

Malinvaud, Edmond. 1972. *Lectures on Microeconomic Theory*, trans. A. Silvey, chap. 10. Amsterdam: North-Holland.

Phelps, Edmond S. 1961. "The Golden Rule of Capital Accumulation." *American Economic Review* 51: 638–643.

Solow, Robert. 1970. *Growth Theory: An Exposition*. New York: Oxford University Press.

PART EIGHT

Resource Allocation under Uncertainty

22 The Notion of a Contingent Commodity

Let A and B be two consumers. A owns a share, 1, that entitles him to receive payment of either one monetary unit with probability $1/2$ or zero monetary units with probability $1/2$. B owns a share, 2, that also entitles him to receive payment of either one monetary unit with probability $1/2$ or zero monetary units with probability $1/2$. The events surrounding share 1 are independent of the events surrounding share 2. A and B can exchange any portion of their respective shares.

The behavior of A is represented by a utility function, linear with respect to the probabilities; the basic utility function is given by $U^A(x) = x$, where x is earnings measured in monetary units. The same applies to B, where the basic utility function is given by $U^B(x) = \log(x + 1)$.

Problem 1

The portfolio of A is made up of x_{A1} of share 1 and x_{A2} of share 2. Similarly, B's portfolio is composed of x_{B1} of share 1 and x_{B2} of share 2. Determine the utility functions in the following form:

$$U^A(x_{A1}, x_{A2}) \quad \text{and} \quad U^B(x_{B1}, x_{B2}).$$

Problem 2

Characterize the equilibrium that will prevail in this exchange economy composed of two agents, A and B, and two goods, shares 1 and 2. In order to calculate the equilibrium composition of the portfolios for A and B, show initially that, taking the specification of U^A into account, the equilibrium price of share 2 is necessarily equal to one if we take share 1 as the numéraire.

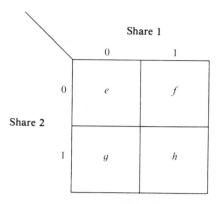

Figure 22.1

Demonstrate, further, that the levels $\bar{U}^A$ and $\bar{U}^B$ attained by the utility functions of A and B at the equilibrium are

$$\bar{U}^A = 1/2, \qquad \bar{U}^B = 1/4 \log 9/2.$$

Problem 3

When consumers A and B pool their shares and decide on an acceptable distribution of the outcome of these shares, show that it is possible for them to achieve, for example, the following levels of utility:

$$U^A = \frac{1}{2} = \bar{U}^A \quad \text{and} \quad U^B = \frac{1}{4} \log \frac{125}{27} > \bar{U}^B.$$

For this purpose maximize U^B with U^A fixed at the value $1/2$. What can you conclude about the equilibrium achieved in problem 2, and how do you explain the apparent contradiction?

PROPOSED SOLUTION

In this exercise we look for the equilibrium of an exchange economy in which the goods exchanged are uncertain. Two important aspects of the theory of uncertainty are illustrated:

(a) Even though the agents own shares that have similar characteristics, they find it beneficial to trade. This is because a risk-averse individual finds it in his best interest to "diversify his portfolio."

(b) The agents must be able to trade "contingent commodities" in order to reach a Pareto optimum.

Problem 1

There are four different events in this economy; they may be designated e, f, g, and h, with each event occurring with probability $1/4$. These events are characterized by the stochastic payments related to each share in Fig. 22.1.

We assume that the utility of each agent is linear with respect to the probabilities, that is, it is equal to the expected value of the utility function. Then $U^A(x_{A1}, x_{A2})$ is equal to the expected value of $x_{A1} + x_{A2}$, and $U^B(x_{B1}, x_{B2})$ is equal to the expected value of $\log (x_{B1} + x_{B2} + 1)$. It follows that

$$U^A(x_{A1}, x_{A2}) = 1/4 (0) + 1/4 (x_{A1}) + 1/4 (x_{A2}) + 1/4 (x_{A1} + x_{A2})$$

$$= 1/2 (x_{A1} + x_{A2})$$

and

$$U^B(x_{B1}, x_{B2}) = 1/4 \log 1 + 1/4 \log (1 + x_{B1}) + 1/4 \log (1 + x_{B2})$$

$$+ 1/4 \log (1 + x_{B1} + x_{B2})$$

$$= 1/4 [\log (1 + x_{B1}) + \log (1 + x_{B2}) + \log (1 + x_{B1} + x_{B2})].$$

Problem 2

Let p be the price of share 2 if we take share 1 as the numéraire. We begin by studying the demand of agent A. His budget constraint is given by $x_{A1} + px_{A2} = 1$. For $p < 1$, maximizing $U^A(x_{A1}, x_{A2})$ subject to the budget constraint yields

$$x_{A1} = 0, \qquad x_{A2} = \frac{1}{p} > 1.$$

Obviously, then, this case cannot represent an equilibrium, since the demand by agent A for share 2 is greater than the available supply, which is equal to one.

We notice that the utility of agent A is equal to the expected value of his earnings. Since the two actions have the same expected value of earnings, he wants a portfolio consisting solely of the share with the lower price.

For $p > 1$, we have, on the contrary,

$$x_{A1} = 1, \qquad x_{A2} = 0.$$

For this case to represent an equilibrium, it would be necessary that there exist $p > 1$ such that the demand by agent B would be

$$x_{B1} = 0, \qquad x_{B2} = 1.$$

We calculate the marginal rate of substitution of agent B in the case where he keeps his initial portfolio, that is, when $x_{B1} = 0$ and $x_{B2} = 1$:

$$\frac{\dfrac{\partial U^B}{\partial x_{B2}}}{\dfrac{\partial U^B}{\partial x_{B1}}} = \frac{\dfrac{1}{1 + x_{B2}} + \dfrac{1}{1 + x_{B1} + x_{B2}}}{\dfrac{1}{1 + x_{B1}} + \dfrac{1}{1 + x_{B1} + x_{B2}}} = \frac{\dfrac{1}{2} + \dfrac{1}{2}}{\dfrac{1}{2} + 1} = \frac{2}{3}.$$

Then, agent B wishes to trade a portion of his share 2 as soon as the price p of this share is greater than $2/3$. This indicates risk-averse behavior. In effect, agent B wishes to diversify his portfolio even if this diversification leads to a decrease in the expected value of his earnings, as it does when $2/3 < p < 1$. A fortiori, for $p > 1$ agent B wishes to sell at least some portion of his share 2; however, we know from above that agent A does not wish to buy any portion of share 2.

Therefore the only possible equilibrium corresponds to $p = 1$. Since the budget constraint $x_{A1} + x_{A2} = 1$ coincides with his indifference curve, the demand of agent A is indeterminate. The demand of agent B is characterized by the following system of equations:

$$\frac{\dfrac{\partial U_B}{\partial x_{B2}}}{\dfrac{\partial U^B}{\partial x_{B1}}} = \frac{\dfrac{1}{1 + x_{B2}} + \dfrac{1}{1 + x_{B1} + x_{B2}}}{\dfrac{1}{1 + x_{B1}} + \dfrac{1}{1 + x_{B1} + x_{B1}}} = 1,$$

$$x_{B1} + x_{B2} = 1,$$

from which we derive $x_{B1} = x_{B2} = {}^1/_2$. The equilibrium portfolio of agent A then is defined by $x_{A1} = x_{A2} = {}^1/_2$.

At the equilibrium, U^A achieves the level $\bar{U}^A = {}^1/_2$, identical to the initial level; and U^B achieves the level $\bar{U}^B = {}^1/_4 \log 9/2$, which is greater than the initial level given by ${}^1/_4 \log 4$.

Problem 3

In this economy we are interested in the distribution of certain claims to contingent commodities between the two agents. An example of a contingent commodity is the total of two units of the good "money available if event h occurs." A feasible allocation of claims to contingent commodities between the agents is characterized by the eight variables $x_A^e, x_A^f, x_A^g, x_A^h, x_B^e, x_B^f, x_B^g, x_B^h$ which are nonnegative and satisfy the following conditions:

$$x_A^e + x_B^e = 0, \tag{1}$$

$$x_A^f + x_B^f = 1, \tag{2}$$

$$x_A^g + x_B^g = 1, \tag{3}$$

$$x_A^h + x_B^h = 2. \tag{4}$$

Here x_B^g, for example, indicates the amount allocated to agent B of the contingent commodity "money available if g occurs." We have, necessarily, $x_A^e = x_B^e = 0$, so we omit these variables. The respective utility levels of the agents for such an allocation are

$$U^A = \frac{x_A^f + x_A^g + x_A^h}{4},$$

$$U^B = {}^1/_4 \left[\log (1 + x_B^f) + \log (1 + x_B^g) + \log (1 + x_B^h) \right].$$

A Pareto optimum corresponds to maximizing U^B for a fixed level of U^A, given constraints (2), (3), and (4). In particular, we look for the optimum corresponding to level $U^A = {}^1/_2$, which was attained in the equilibrium of the preceding problem. By eliminating the variables x_A^f, x_A^g, and x_A^h we must determine the maximum of U^B subject to $x_B^f + x_B^g + x_B^h = 2$. The maximum is achieved when

$$x_B^f = x_B^g = x_B^h = \frac{2}{3}.$$

This follows from the fact that agent B, who is more risk averse than A, seeks to make his earnings as independent of risky events as possible.

The allocation obtained is obviously feasible, since

$$x_A^f = 1 - x_B^f = \frac{1}{3} \geqslant 0,$$

$$x_A^g = 1 - x_B^g = \frac{1}{3} \geqslant 0,$$

$$x_A^h = 2 - x_B^h = \frac{4}{3} \geqslant 0.$$

For this optimum the utility of agent B is

$$U^B = \frac{3}{4} \log \left(1 + \frac{2}{3} \right)$$

$$= \frac{3}{4} \log \frac{5}{3}$$

$$= \frac{1}{4} \log \frac{125}{27} > \bar{U}_B = \frac{1}{4} \log \frac{9}{2}.$$

The equilibrium obtained by trading shares was not therefore a Pareto optimum, as is apparent from the calculation of the optimum. Because of the absence of markets for the various contingent commodities, it was not possible for agent B to equalize his contingent earnings as he would have liked.

Furthermore, we can establish that the allocation that characterizes the Pareto optimum above is the equilibrium allocation of the exchange economy in which the agents can trade contingent commodities. In fact, taking the form of U^A into account and following the same argument used in problem 1, we derive a system of equilibrium prices such that

$$p_f = p_g = p_h = p > 0, \qquad p_e > 3p.$$

where p_e, p_f, p_g, p_h are the prices of the various contingent commodities.

For such a system of prices agent A chooses $x_A^e = 0$ (since $p_e > p$) and is indifferent between the allocations satisfying his budget constraint, given by

$$p(x_A^f + x_A^g + x_A^h) = 2p.$$

Agent B chooses $x_B^e = 0$ (since $p_e > 3_p$) and, to be sure, an allocation such that $x_B^f = x_B^g = x_B^h$. Taking his budget constraint into account, we derive again $x_B^f = x_B^g = x_B^h = {}^2/_3$.

Suggested Readings

Arrow, Kenneth J. 1971. *Essays in the Theory of Risk Bearing.* Chicago: Markham.

Borch, Karl. 1968. "Economic Equilibrium under Uncertainty." *International Economic Review* 9: 339–347.

Debreu, Gerard. 1959. *Theory of Value: An Axiomatic Analysis of Economic Equilibrium,* chap. 7. New Haven: Yale University Press.

Malinvaud, Edmond. 1972. *Lectures on Microeconomic Theory,* trans. A. Silvey, chap. 11. Amsterdam: North-Holland.

Mossin, Jan. 1966. "Equilibrium in Capital Asset Markets." *Econometrica* 34: 768–783.

Production Uncertainty and Resource Allocation

Problem 1

Consider an economy made up of two goods: a factor of production X available in quantity $\bar{X}$ and a consumption good Y. There exist two enterprises, 1 and 2.

(a) The production function of enterprise i is given by $Y_i = X_i^{1/2}$. Determine the production optimum corresponding to full employment of the available quantity, $\bar{X}$. What should be the allocation of the factor of production between the enterprises?

(b) In reality, enterprise 1 is subject to production uncertainty, which is characterized by two equiprobable states of nature, e and f.

Denote the output of enterprise 1 as Y_1^e if the state of nature e arises, and as Y_1^f if f arises. Assume that

$$Y_1^e = {}^1\!/_2 X_1^{1/2}, \qquad Y_1^f = {}^3\!/_2 X_1^{1/2},$$

where x_1 is the specific quantity of good X used by enterprise 1. Whatever state of nature arises, we always have $Y_2 = X_2^{1/2}$. Aggregate choices can be represented by a utility function that is linear with respect to the probabilities, where the basic utility function is given by $u(Y) = \log Y$.

Determine the optimal allocation of the available quantity $\bar{X}$ between the two enterprises and compare it with the allocation found in (a). Was this result predictable?

Taking the determinate price of good X as one, calculate the contingent prices of good Y associated with this optimum and then calculate the determinate price for Y. What happens if enterprise 1 takes into account only the determinate prices in calculating the expected value of its output? How can this be remedied?

Problem 2

In addition to goods X and Y already defined, we introduce a second consumption good, Z. Enterprise 1 produces good Y and enterprise 2 produces good Z.

(a) The production function of enterprise 1 is $Y = X_1$ and the production function of enterprise 2 is $Z = X_2$. Determine the optimum corresponding to the full employment of quantity $\bar{X}$, knowing that aggregate choices can be represented by the following utility function:

$$v(Y,Z) = \log\left(Y - \frac{\bar{X}}{4}\right) + \log Z.$$

(b) In reality, enterprise 1 is subject to production uncertainty, which is characterized by two equiprobable states of nature, e and f.

Denote the output of enterprise 1 as Y^e if state of nature e arises, and as Y^f if state f arises. Assume that

$$Y^e = {}^1\!/_2 X_1, \qquad Y^f = {}^3\!/_2 X_1.$$

The output of enterprise 2 is independent of the states of nature. As in the preceding problem, assume the existence of a utility function that is linear with respect to the probabilities and assume that the function $v(Y,Z)$ defined in (a) is the basic utility function.

Determine the optimal allocation of the available quantity $\bar{X}$ between the two enterprises and compare this with the allocation found in (a). How do you interpret the apparently contradictory results in these two questions?

PROPOSED SOLUTION

This exercise has two principal aims: first, to show the necessity of using "contingent prices" in order to obtain a production optimum through price decentralization in the case where output can be affected by uncertain events; and second, to establish that taking production uncertainty into account in resource allocation (instead of using only expected value) does not always lead to a preference for the certain output, even from a risk-averse individual.

We will not recalculate the expected value of the basic utility function (a utility function that is linear with respect to the probabilities), since this has been done in the preceding exercise. All the solutions in this exercise are determined by using the Lagrangian multiplier technique. The reader can verify that the conditions obtained are sufficient as well.

Problem 1

(a) The object is to find the maximum of $Y_1 + Y_2 = X_1^{1/2} + X_2^{1/2}$, subject to the constraint $X_1 + X_2 = \bar{X}$. Obviously, we can show that $X_1 = X_2 = \bar{X}/2$.

(b) The utility function is written

$$U = \tfrac{1}{2} \log (Y_1^e + Y_2^e) + \tfrac{1}{2} \log (Y_1^f + Y_2^f).$$

The technical constraints are

$$Y_1^e = \tfrac{1}{2} X_1^{1/2}, \qquad Y_2^e = X_2^{1/2},$$

$$Y_1^f = \tfrac{3}{2} X_1^{1/2}, \quad Y_2^f = X_2^{1/2}.$$

Then it is necessary to maximize

$$U = \tfrac{1}{2} \log (\tfrac{1}{2} X_1^{1/2} + X_2^{1/2}) + \tfrac{1}{2} \log (\tfrac{3}{2} X_1^{1/2} + X_2^{1/2}),$$

subject to $X_1 + X_2 = \bar{X}$.

Setting the derivatives of the Lagrangian $L = U + \lambda(\bar{X} - X_1 - X_2)$ equal to zero, we find:

$$\frac{\partial L}{\partial X_1} = \frac{1}{4 X_1^{1/2} (X_1^{1/2} + 2 X_2^{1/2})} + \frac{3}{4 X_1^{1/2} (3 X_1^{1/2} + 2 X_2^{1/2})} - \lambda = 0$$

$$\frac{\partial L}{\partial X_2} = \frac{1}{2 X_2^{1/2} (X_1^{1/2} + 2 X_2^{1/2})} + \frac{1}{2 X_2^{1/2} (3 X_1^{1/2} + 2 X_2^{1/2})} - \lambda = 0$$

or

$$\left(\frac{X_1}{X_2}\right)^{1/2} = \frac{3 X_1^{1/2} + 4 X_2^{1/2}}{4 X_1^{1/2} + 4 X_2^{1/2}}.$$

If we set $(X_1/X_2)^{1/2} = t$, the preceding equation becomes the following equation in t:

$$4t^2 + t - 4 = 0.$$

This has a unique positive solution:

$$\hat{t} = \frac{\sqrt{65} - 1}{8}.$$

We verify that $\hat{t}$ is less than one. The appearance of production uncertainty for enterprise 1, even though the expected value of its output is the same as the determinate output of enterprise 2, leads us to allocate less of the factor of production to enterprise 1 than to enterprise 2. This result is due to the concavity of the utility function (simple risk aversion) and to the fact that the two enterprises produce the same good.

Knowing $\hat{t}$, we derive the optimal allocations:

$$\hat{X}_1 = \frac{\hat{t}^2}{1 + \hat{t}^2} \bar{X} = \frac{66 - 2\sqrt{65}}{130 - 2\sqrt{65}} \bar{X}.$$

$$\hat{X}_2 = \frac{1}{1 + \hat{t}^2} \bar{X} = \frac{64}{130 - 2\sqrt{65}} \bar{X}.$$

What contingent prices y^e and y^f should be announced to the enterprises so that they choose the appropriate output levels (with factor X taken as the numéraire)? For example, the value (using contingent prices) of the output of enterprise 1 is equal to

$$y^e \frac{X_1^{1/2}}{2} + 3y^f \frac{X_1^{1/2}}{2}$$

and the profit maximum is achieved when

$$\frac{y^e}{4X_1^{1/2}} + \frac{3y^f}{4X_1^{1/2}} = 1.$$

For given y^e and y^f, maximizing the respective profits of enterprises 1 and 2 yields the following set of equations:

$$y^e + 3y^f = 4X_1^{1/2}, \qquad y^e + y^f = 2X_2^{1/2}.$$

Conversely, these equations allow us to calculate the prices y^e and y^f that should be announced if we wish the enterprises to use quantities $\hat{X}_1$ and $\hat{X}_2$ of factor X. We can, therefore, calculate the determinate price y^* of good Y as

$$y^* = y^e + y^f = 2\hat{X}_2^{1/2} = 2\sqrt{\frac{\bar{X}}{1 + \hat{t}^2}}.$$

If enterprise 1 considers only determinant prices and the expected value of its output, it will demand the following quantity of good X:

$$X_1^* = \left(\frac{y^*}{2}\right)^2 = \frac{\bar{X}}{1 + \hat{t}^2} = \hat{X}_2,$$

that is, a quantity greater than the optimal quantity.

If enterprise 1 continues to behave this way (that is, it considers only the expected value of its output and the determinate price of good Y), in order to achieve the optimum we must tax the output of enterprise 1— either by imposing on it a determinate selling price equal to or less than

$$y = \hat{t}y^* = 2\hat{t}\left(\frac{\bar{X}}{1 + \hat{t}^2}\right)^{1/2},$$

or by charging a determinate purchase price for factor X greater than one, that is, $x = 1/\hat{t}$.

Therefore, for a factor of production to be allocated optimally in the presence of production uncertainty, the value of its marginal product must be higher than its marginal product under certainty. The difference corresponds to the notion of a risk premium.

Problem 2

(a) The objective is to find the maximum of

$$v(Y,Z) = \log\left(Y - \frac{\bar{X}}{4}\right) + \log Z,$$

subject to the constraints

$$Y \geqslant \frac{\bar{X}}{4}, \qquad Z \geqslant 0, \qquad X_1 + X_2 \leqslant \bar{X},$$

$$Y \leqslant X_1, \qquad Z \leqslant X_2.$$

The feasible set is convex and v is strictly concave over this set. The Kuhn-Tucker conditions are therefore necessary and sufficient to determine the unique solution to the problem.

Let us consider the case $Y = X_1$ and $Z = X_2$:

$$X_1 + X_2 = \bar{X}, \qquad Y > \frac{\bar{X}}{4}, \qquad Z > 0,$$

which is the most likely one.

Then the Kuhn-Tucker conditions simply express the fact that the function

$$v(X_1) = \log\left(X_1 - \frac{\bar{X}}{4}\right) + \log(\bar{X} - X_1)$$

attains an unconstrained maximum. Therefore we have

$$\frac{1}{\left(X_1 - \frac{\bar{X}}{4}\right)} - \frac{1}{(\bar{X} - X_1)} = 0,$$

from which it follows that

$$\hat{X}_1 = \frac{5\bar{X}}{8}, \qquad \hat{X}_2 = \frac{3\bar{X}}{8}.$$

This allocation is the optimal one, inasmuch as the announced constraints are satisfied:

$$\hat{X}_1 > \frac{\bar{X}}{4}, \qquad \hat{X}_2 > 0, \qquad \hat{X}_1 + \hat{X}_2 = \bar{X}.$$

(b) What effect will taking into account the production uncertainty of enterprise 1 have on the optimal allocation of good X? The utility function is written:

$$V = \frac{1}{2}\left[\log\left(Y^e - \frac{\bar{X}}{4}\right) + \log Z^e\right] + \frac{1}{2}\left[\log\left(Y^f - \frac{\bar{X}}{4}\right) + \log Z^f\right].$$

We must maximize V subject to the constraints

$$Z^e \geqslant 0, \quad Z^f \geqslant 0, \quad Y^e \geqslant \frac{\bar{X}}{4}, \quad Y^f \geqslant \frac{\bar{X}}{4},$$

$$Z^e \leqslant X_2, \quad Z^f \leqslant X_2, \quad Y^e \leqslant \frac{X_1}{2}, \quad Y^f \leqslant \frac{3X_1}{2}.$$

As before, the Kuhn-Tucker conditions are necessary and sufficient. Consider now the appropriate maximum for the case when

$$Z^e > 0, \quad Z^f > 0, \quad Y^e > \frac{\bar{X}}{4}, \quad Y^f > \frac{\bar{X}}{4},$$

$$Z^e = X_2, \quad Z^f = X_2, \quad Y^e = \frac{X_1}{2}, \quad Y^f = \frac{3X_1}{2}.$$

An unconstrained maximum is achieved by the following function of X:

$$\frac{1}{2}\log\left(\frac{X_1}{2} - \frac{\bar{X}}{4}\right) + \frac{1}{2}\log(\bar{X} - X_1) + \frac{1}{2}\log\left(\frac{3X_1}{2} - \frac{\bar{X}}{4}\right) + \frac{1}{2}\log(\bar{X} - X_1).$$

Hence

$$\frac{1}{\bar{X} - X_1} = \frac{1}{4\left(\frac{X_1}{2} - \frac{\bar{X}}{4}\right)} + \frac{3}{4\left(\frac{3X_1}{2} - \frac{\bar{X}}{4}\right)}$$

and
$$6X_1^2 - 6X_1\bar{X} + \frac{5\bar{X}^2}{4} = 0, \quad X_1 = \bar{X}\left(\frac{1 \pm \sqrt{\frac{1}{6}}}{2}\right).$$

Only the solution $\hat{X}_1 = (\bar{X}/2)(1 + \sqrt{1/6})$ allows $Y^e > \bar{X}/4$ and our other conditions to be satisfied. This is the solution sought.

The optimal allocation is then

$$\hat{X}_1 = \frac{\bar{X}}{2}\left(1 + \sqrt{\frac{1}{6}}\right) > \frac{5\bar{X}}{8},$$

$$\hat{X}_2 = \frac{\bar{X}}{2}\left(1 - \sqrt{\frac{1}{6}}\right) < \frac{3\bar{X}}{8}.$$

Contrary to the result of problem 1, there is an increase in the allocation of factor X to enterprise 1 even though the utility function exhibits risk aversion. However, the two enterprises no longer produce the same good: enterprise 1 produces a good considered more important than the good produced by enterprise 2. In addition, the existence of production uncertainty for enterprise 1 leads to an increased allocation of factor X, so that in case of an unfavorable outcome (here outcome e), its output will not fall too much and will be prevented from reaching the lower bound $\bar{X}/4$, which could be interpreted in this instance as an essential minimum level.

Suggested Readings

Malinvaud, Edmond. 1972. *Lectures on Microeconomic Theory,* trans. A. Silvey, chap. 11. Amsterdam: North-Holland.
Tobin, James. 1958. "Liquidity Preference as Behavior Towards Risk." *Review of Economic Studies* 25: 65–86.

Index